BLACK STAR, CRESCENT MOON

BLACK STAR, CRESCENT MOON

The Muslim International and
Black Freedom beyond America

Sohail Daulatzai

UNIVERSITY OF MINNESOTA PRESS
MINNEAPOLIS | LONDON

The University of Minnesota Press gratefully acknowledges financial assistance provided for the publication of this book from the University of California, Irvine.

Every effort was made to obtain permission to reproduce material used in this book. If any proper acknowledgment has not been made, we encourage copyright holders to notify us.

Published by the University of Minnesota Press
111 Third Avenue South, Suite 290
Minneapolis, MN 55401-2520
http://www.upress.umn.edu

Library of Congress Cataloging-in-Publication Data

Daulatzai, Sohail.
  Black Star, Crescent Moon : The Muslim International and Black Freedom beyond America / Sohail Daulatzai.
  Includes bibliographical references and index.
  ISBN 978-0-8166-7585-2 (hc : alk. paper)
  ISBN 978-0-8166-7586-9 (pb : alk. paper)
1. Blacks—Politics and government. 2. Muslims—Political activity.
3. Civil rights movements—History. 4. Blacks—Intellectual life. 5. Muslims—Intellectual life. 6. Malcolm X, 1925–1965—Influence. I. Title.
  DT16.5.D38 2012
  323.1196—dc23
                        2012007594

Printed in the United States of America on acid-free paper

The University of Minnesota is an equal-opportunity educator and employer.

19 18 17 16 15 14 13   10 9 8 7 6 5 4 3 2

This thought keeps consoling me:
though tyrants may command that lamps
    be smashed
in rooms where lovers are destined to meet,
they cannot snuff out the moon, so today,
nor tomorrow, no tyranny will succeed,
no poison of torture make me bitter,
if just one evening in prison
can be so strangely sweet,
if just one moment anywhere on this earth.

FAIZ AHMED FAIZ, "A PRISON EVENING"

CONTENTS

Introduction

AN EMPIRE STATE OF MIND

On January 20, 2009, Barack Hussein Obama was inaugurated as the forty-fourth president of the United States. On that day, perfectly planned to coincide with the national celebration of the Martin Luther King Jr. holiday, more people gathered in Washington, D.C., than for any other event or protest in the nation's history, eclipsing even the original March on Washington, which Dr. King made as the highpoint of American political theater. As hundreds of thousands of people gathered, tens of millions more watched on television to witness the inauguration of the first admittedly Black president in the nation's history.

Also present that day were other forces that were visible but unseen, felt but not heard. For the ghosts of America's past and present hovered all over the nation. The ghosts of Frederick Douglass and Ida B. Wells, of lynching and of slavery. There were also the ghosts of the silent wars of mass incarceration and the living dead in poverty, the ghosts of the nameless war dead in Iraq, Af–Pak, and other unnamed places, as well as the looming specter and the phantom figure of the Muslim. For many, Obama's election was a national exorcism, a purging of the past and a reckoning with the present, as the empire was reeling from massive discontent, economic anxieties, and the perpetual wars fought in its name.

While the spirit of Dr. King was already present, the figure of Malcolm X was also conjured, if only to try to exorcize him from the national past and the nation's future. A key and telling moment occurred when Senator Dianne Feinstein, of California, gave the introductory remarks at the inauguration, saying, "Those who doubt the supremacy of the ballot over the bullet can never diminish the power engendered by nonviolent struggles for justice and equality—like the one that made this day possible." Feinstein continued, saying that future generations would "look back and remember that this was the moment that the dream that once echoed across history from the steps of the Lincoln Memorial finally reached the walls of the White House."[1]

Feinstein's roughly two-and-a-half-minute speech was emblematic of the larger frame through which the country and the world were now to view Obama and, by extension, the United States. With the ghost of King hovering, Feinstein celebrated King by mentioning the "non-violent struggles" that had made the day possible and declared that the "dream" King had expressed in his 1963 March on Washington speech had now come true and reached the walls of the White House through the election of Obama. But as the nation sought to commemorate and frame the election of a Black president through Dr. King and the Civil Rights movement, Feinstein also conjured Malcolm X in her reference to "the ballot or the bullet." Using the phrase that is the title of one of his most iconic speeches, Malcolm argued in it that Black electoral participation was futile, that the United States posed "itself as the leader of the free world," and that this contradiction led him to conclude that Black freedom would come only by using what he called "new methods," one of which was internationalizing the problems of Black peoples in the United States by moving from a civil rights framework to a human rights one and getting out of "the jurisdiction of Uncle Sam" and into the Third World, "where our African brothers can throw their weight on our side, where our Asian brothers can throw their weight on our side, where our Latin American brothers can throw their weight on our side."[2]

Not surprisingly, on the inauguration day of a Black president, both King and Malcolm X—the twin poles of Black redemptive possibility—were conjured and invoked. And the stark choices they purported to represent no longer seemed relevant with the election of Obama. For the choices between integration and separation, dream and nightmare, Civil Rights and Black Power, patriot and internationalist were now seemingly irrelevant, for as Feinstein suggested, King's and Civil Rights' emphasis on the ballot and nonviolence in contrast with what was assumed about Malcolm and the bullet was vindicated by history through the election of Obama to the White House.

But in celebrating King and Civil Rights that day, Feinstein not surprisingly viewed King through a narrow interpretive lens, invoking a frozen and ossified memory of him—one in which he is remembered as the "I Have a Dream" American, not the insurgent anti-imperialist who changed his views in 1967 and linked racism and U.S. militarism, vehemently protesting the Vietnam War and calling the United States "the biggest purveyor of violence in the world," only to be assassinated in 1968.[3] While King's internationalism and criticism of U.S. society were ignored in favor of a more accommodating image of him, Feinstein invoked Malcolm in order to dismiss him not only because of his call for a Black internationalism that tied the fates of Black peoples with decolonization in the Third World but also because of his penetrating critiques of U.S. foreign policy. In celebrating that pacifist memory of King and ignoring and dismissing the penetrating depth of his and Malcolm's thought, not only did Feinstein and the political establishment frame Obama's victory with the triumphalist narrative of Civil Rights, but more important, Obama's victory also served as a vehicle to co-opt, contain, and strip away any of the remaining vestiges of internationalist impulses emanating from Black political culture.

But in the logic of Civil Rights, Feinstein was suggesting and reaffirming that, yes, Black peoples do have a stake in this country and that the feeling is mutual—that not only does their vote count, but it also matters. The narrative of Civil Rights has tremendous purchase and traction in the United States, because it has been used to rewrite the 1960s, underwrite the white backlash and the "culture wars" of the 1980s and '90s, and cement the politics of the New Right, which assumes that race has been transcended and that the United States has fulfilled its national destiny. Most important, the Civil Rights narrative has assumed that Black freedom could be achieved within the legal frameworks and political institutions of the United States.[4]

As scholars and historians have shown, Civil Rights has also had a flip side to it that has had to do with its assumptions about U.S. foreign policy and Black peoples' relationship to the rest of the world. When it emerged from the Cold War and the Red Scare of communism in the aftermath of World War II, Civil Rights assumed that the United States' moral standing in winning the hearts and minds of the decolonizing nations of Africa and Asia (which includes what is now the "Middle East") was linked to its treatment of Black peoples in the United States. In exchange for legislation on education, interstate transportation, voting rights, and other measures, the Civil Rights establishment supported an aggressive U.S. foreign policy in the name of anticommunism, including U.S. covert interventions and wars in Africa and Asia to prevent Soviet influence from spreading there, because communism was viewed by the United States as a bigger threat to the Third World than colonialism.[5]

But while Civil Rights has assumed that Black freedom is attainable within U.S. legal frameworks and political institutions, critical Black internationalists have historically questioned that assumption, seeing white supremacy as a global phenomenon and looking to international struggles in the Third World as lenses for their own battles with white power, exploring the tactics and strategies of those struggles, and also seeking solace and solidarity by expanding their racial community of belonging. And while Civil Rights has assumed that the United States has been a force for good in the world, whether it be through fighting and eradicating communism or any other perceived threats to U.S. national security, Black internationalists have been skeptical and have even outright challenged U.S. foreign policy, viewing it as similar to European colonialism, as an extension of Manifest Destiny and a racist logic that it practices at home.[6]

The election of Obama only served to further intensify the euphoria around the narrative of Civil Rights, as his election suggested to many that white supremacy no longer exists in a "postracial" America and that Black freedom not only *can* be realized in the United States but already *has* been. In affirming the triumphalist narrative of Civil Rights and seeking to create domestic consensus of racial harmony, Obama's election also sought to project the United States as a force for good in the world, making Black internationalism irrelevant or, through the Kenyan-descended Obama, as now being embodied in the larger narrative of American universalism. In contrast to what many perceived to be a reckless and rogue unilateralism of President Bush in the post-9/11 era, the election of Obama was seen as a calming balm, a kind of national healing, as the United States could now be presented as a moral beacon to the world that spreads democracy and freedom while restoring faith to those at home.

The containment of Black internationalism and the attempt to erase the possibility of it are recurrent features within U.S. political culture. In the post-9/11 climate, this containment has had to do with the current moment of U.S. empire, which views "Islam" and "the Muslim" as the defining threats to U.S. interests and to the global order that the United States has assumed to defend. With Blackness now the face of a U.S. empire in a state of permanent war with the Muslim Third World through occupation, overt war, drone attacks, the gulag at Guantánamo, and other covert means, Obama's presidency raises compelling questions about not only the relationship of Blackness to U.S. imperial power, but also of the relationship of Blackness to Islam and the Muslim Third World. Not surprisingly, it was Malcolm X who Feinstein conjured, only to dismiss. Why? Because not only is Malcolm's "Ballot or the Bullet" speech his most well-known meditation on the futility of Black electoral participation and the urgent need to internationalize Black freedom dreams, but also because it is Malcolm X whose legacy reveals a rich and compelling history between Blackness, Islam, and the Muslim Third World, a history and legacy that has not only profoundly shaped Black radical thought, but a history and legacy that provides a powerful challenge to the post-9/11 era and the election of Obama.[7]

Through Malcolm's conversion to Islam and his critical Black internationalism, he has become a historical lens and a contemporary frame for understanding U.S. power, the global dimensions of white supremacy, and the relationships between Black freedom struggles in the United States and those in Africa and elsewhere in the Muslim Third World. *Black Star, Crescent Moon* explores this political and cultural history of Black Islam, Black radicalism, and the Muslim Third World in the post–World War II era, when Black freedom struggles in the United States and decolonization in the Third World were taking place.[8] In probing ideas about Black identity, tactics and strategies of liberation, art and aesthetics, questions around national belonging and citizenship, and the global nature of white supremacy, *Black Star, Crescent Moon* examines the history of Black Islam, Black radicalism, and the Muslim Third World within the context of the Civil Rights and Black Power eras, the post–Civil Rights era of mass incarceration, and the post–Cold War and post-9/11 eras.

Largely due to Malcolm, but also because it is deeply rooted in Black resistance to New World slavery, the relationship between Blackness and Islam has raised a tremendous amount of anxiety within the larger U.S. national imagination, as it continues to circle and even haunt contemporary ideas and debates around U.S. political culture.[9] In the post-9/11 climate, in which some are seemingly Muslim simply by association, Obama himself has been "smeared" with the "slur" of being Muslim. Throughout his campaign and even as president, the rumor and innuendo around Obama have created a climate in which 61 percent of Americans believe either that he is a Muslim or that he might be, according to an August 2010 PEW poll.[10] And there is so-called evidence to back it up, whether it is the focus on his middle name (Hussein), his father's identity as a Muslim, the short time he lived in Indonesia during his childhood and attended a madrassa (school) there, the famous *60 Minutes* episode during the 2008 primary in which Ohio voters expressed fear that he might be a "Muzz-lum," and the infamous *New Yorker* cover, the specter of Islam in the post-9/11 climate haunts not only U.S. national identity and the larger West but also that it has been projected onto Obama in interesting ways that reveal an even deeper anxiety about the history of the relationship between Blackness and Islam. For to be Black is one thing in America that marks you as *un*-American, but to be Black *and* Muslim is quite another, as it marks you as *anti*-American, suggesting that potentially Obama is not the Manchurian candidate of the twentieth century but an Arabian candidate in the twenty-first, an executive fifth column poised to overthrow the United States.

Black, Red, and Green Scares

Just as previous Black figures, political orientations, and intellectual traditions sought to challenge European and white supremacist authority on knowledge, truth, and history, Malcolm himself was deeply engaged with the historical record. Not only did he recount the history of European and U.S. atrocities against Black and Third World peoples, but also as his Pan-Africanist perspectives developed, he diligently cited the denial and theft of Black history and identity, the loss of language and name, and the vulgarization of Africa as "savage," as he implored Black peoples in the United States to reconnect with the African continent. As he said, "You left your mind in Africa!"[11] For Malcolm and for Black Islam more generally, a central part of this historical recovery had to do with conversion to Islam, which has reclaimed the power to redefine oneself, to change from a "slave name" to the "X" (the unknown), and then to the "original" Muslim name. In this way, Islam became a vehicle for Malcolm and other Black converts to reject the master narrative of slavery—and by extension America—and to redefine themselves from property to person, and from slave to human. For these converts, Islam has become a vehicle for a kind of return to a preslavery past, a reclamation project that has sought to connect Black peoples in the United States to those on the African continent and beyond, restoring a sense of history and the past that was violently stolen.

When Black Islam emerged as a powerful force within Black radical circles and struggles in the post–World War II era, it challenged the dominant Cold War liberalism of the time through its critique of a domesticated framework for Black freedom, its aggressive anticommunist foreign policy, and its formation of the Christian-dominated Civil Rights movement. For many, Islam was seen as "the Black Man's religion," an alternative form of a radical Black consciousness that was fundamentally at odds with what was perceived to be the integrationist goals of Black Christianity, a consciousness that was internationalist in nature and aligned itself with the national liberation movements of the Third World.

Black Star, Crescent Moon explores the profound circulation of ideas that emerged between Black radical thought and the Muslim Third World in the post–World War II period, ideas that were inspired by the politics of decolonization and antiracism. From Harlem to Cairo, Mecca to Bandung, Algiers to Baghdad, and in places in between, it was through the Nation of Islam, Malcolm X, Muhammad Ali, and others that the Muslim Third World has come to occupy a central place within the Black radical imagination. For Malcolm X and others, not only did Islam tie Africa to Asia, but it would also become the bridge between Black peoples in the United States and those on the African continent. As Malcolm X said, "Islam is the greatest unifying force in the Dark World today. . . . We here in America were of the Moslem world before being brought into slavery, and today with the entire dark world awakening, our Moslem brothers in the East have a great interest in our welfare."[12]

Whether it be through the interactions and alliances of Malcolm X, Muhammad Ali, and others with the Muslim Third World in the 1950s and 1960s, or the ways in which Black Power politics, cinema, and literature have been influenced and inspired by the politics and culture of the Muslim Third World of Algeria and Iraq, or the ways in which Muslim artists such as Rakim, Mos Def, and Public Enemy have used hip-hop culture as a platform from which to speak truth to power against the violent forces of the post–Civil Rights era, in *Black Star, Crescent Moon* I explore the ways in which these interactions and imaginings have helped to map out and shape the contours of the Muslim International, which reveals the rich and shared histories among Black Muslims, Black radicals, and the politics of anticolonialism in the Muslim Third World. In mapping these intertwined histories and overlapping diasporas, I hope to reveal the ways in which these activists and artists have envisioned themselves not as national minorities but as global majorities, as they have poetically linked themselves with larger communities of resistance that transcend the limiting structures of the modern nation-state.

Part of my interest has to do with exploring the ideological similarities between the current "War on Terror" and the emergence of the Cold War in the late 1940s, both of which have radically altered domestic and international politics. Henry Luce's seminal 1941 essay "The American Century" and the more recent ideological manifesto known as the Project for a New American Century, put forth by the New Right in the post–Cold War era, have in some ways become the unofficial philosophical blueprints for U.S. empire.[13] And so in exploring the relationships between the Cold War era and the "War on Terror," I am interested in the kinds of alliances, imaginings, and possibilities that have been thought of, forged, and animated through politics and art (literature, cinema, hip-hop) by the relationship of Blackness to Islam and the Muslim Third World and what these might suggest about race and nationhood, being and belonging. In exploring these histories, I am interested in how they might reveal the logics between the Cold War and the "War on Terror" and how they expose the ideological rationales for the emergence and continuation of U.S. power in the post–World War II era and into the twenty-first century.

For in many ways, American imperial culture is really a struggle to define how race is going to operate in any given historical period, whether as in the anticolonialism and national liberation movements that defined much of the twentieth century or in the neoliberalism that has come to define the twenty-first. So when the United States, a country so ambivalent and unresolved regarding its own troubled past around Native genocide and African enslavement, became the new superpower, supplanting Europe in the post–World War II era, the unaddressed questions around race and the fissures and fractures that had been created domestically played themselves out within an international context as America had to contend with the racial realities abroad—a complex dynamic in which the sins committed at home sought redemption globally.

In the current global order, which has long been structured along the lines of race, the "War on Terror" continues to replay the unresolved racial dramas of U.S. power, as a Black president and an imperial multiculturalism project U.S. power as a benevolent force, simultaneously silencing antiracist movements domestically. But this is not the first time this tension has occurred. In fact, with the end of World War II and the dawning of the Cold War, the United States used the threat of communism as a proxy for race when it sought to replace Europe as a global power in the era of decolonization and national liberation movements. Using "anticommunism" (via the Truman Doctrine) to fulfill American imperial desire through interventions in the Third World, the United States destabilized the burgeoning anticolonial and anti-imperialist movements taking place in Asia and Africa. The "communist threat" also achieved its domestic goals around race by fracturing very powerful alliances being forged by U.S.-based Blacks who sought to tie their claims for racial justice to those within the Third World. As a result, the rhetoric of "anticommunism" birthed a heightened American nationalism, as influential Black liberals who sought to gain concessions on domestic civil rights supported violent American foreign policy throughout Africa and Asia. This fractured an emergent Black internationalism by containing antiracism within a national framework, and it created new kinds of imperial citizens during a new period of empire building. But it also isolated and increased the domestic repression of Black activists such as W. E. B. Du Bois and Paul Robeson, among others, who linked the legacies of slavery to colonialism in the Third World as a means for systemic change rather than reform against Jim Crow segregation, disenfranchisement, and civil death.[14]

Similarly, in the current "War on Terror," the rhetoric of "terrorism" has also become a proxy for race, generating tremendous political and ideological capital. As the embodiment of the "terrorist," the Muslim haunts the geographic and imaginative spaces of U.S. empire, a specter and menace not only to U.S. national identity but also to the global community the United States claims to defend. The tortured figure of the Muslim mobilizes a variety of constituencies both nationally and internationally in the service of American imperial designs. Whether the United States is sanctioning perpetual war, subverting any remaining due process, legalizing torture, "freeing Muslim women," or mobilizing Christian evangelicals, liberal multiculturalists, right-wing extremists, New Right culture warriors, and anti-immigrant xenophobes, the figure of the Muslim has been used to cultivate tremendous ideological ground by containing and limiting the scope of dissent, forging an imperial citizenry, masking structural inequalities and massive economic instability through the creation of a global security state, and reinforcing the philosophical basis of "color blindness" by promoting an American triumphalism in which a pan-racial enemy (the Muslim) threatens a multicultural America.

In many ways, as Anouar Majid, Gil Anidjar, Talal Asad, and Junaid Rana write, the very idea of the West emerges from and through the figure of the Muslim, which was Europe's archetypal Other before 1492, the year of Spain's expulsion of the Moors. For it was through the Muslim that the modern concept of race and its structuring of national identity was born. As Europe and the idea of "the West" began to cohere around concepts of whiteness and Christianity, race and religion deeply informed each other, so as European expansion led to colonialism and slavery, "the world's non-European natives or religions were stamped with the taint of Muslim impurity."[15] As a result, the idea of Islam and Muslims has represented a perpetual strangeness to the West and to whiteness, occupying a set of meanings that has continued until today. Although 9/11 is what seems to have raised the specter of Islam in relation to the West, a genealogy of the idea of race reveals that the Muslim—as the Other to a normative whiteness—has not only haunted the very the foundation of the West since its inception but has also given the West (now Europe and the United States) meaning, defining who is civilized and who is savage, who is democratic and who is autocratic, who is peaceful and who is violent, who is human and who is not.[16]

Lending truth to Fanon's claim that "Europe is literally the creation of the third world,"[17] one could argue that in the current moment, Europe and the United States are creations of the Muslim Third World. Whether we consider the centuries-long project of Western modernity and conquest, or the current wars in Iraq, Afghanistan, Pakistan, and elsewhere, or the "culture wars" and rampant Islamophobia in Europe and the United States around immigration, the banning of the veil, the controversy over the building of mosques (including the "Ground Zero" mosque), the hysteria over and fear of "terrorism," or congressional and parliamentary hearings and investigations on "radicalization," Islam and the Muslim Third World clearly provide tremendous political, ideological, and material capital for Europe and the United States.

Be that as it may, in *Black Star, Crescent Moon* I am interested in a very different history of ideological and political influence, one in which the Muslim Third World framed and inspired a radical anti-imperialist *challenge* to American and European power and the ways that this has shaped other histories and narratives and constructed other worlds and worldviews, particularly within the Black radical imagination. But Black engagement with the politics of the Muslim Third World carries with it both potential pitfalls and possibilities, in particular because of the specter of Orientalism. In his magisterial tome *Orientalism*, Edward Said argued that Europe and the West have constructed ideas about "the Muslim East" as irrational, savage, uncivilized, and despotic, not only to justify Western control over these regions and their resources, but also to define the West as rational, civilized, and democratic. As a racial discourse that has defined the white Westerner as superior to the nonwhite Muslim Other, Orientalism carries with it a will to power that was closely and intimately tied to continued Western colonial control and imperial domination over the Muslim Third World.

But as Black writers, artists, activists, and others have connected themselves in various ways to "the Orient" of the Muslim Third World, they have not had the same relationship to imperial power and, in fact, have been victims themselves of European racial discourses and New World slavery. This relationship of Blackness to white power, however, has not meant that Black artists and activists have not participated in the logic of Orientalism and have not employed Orientalist rhetoric in their travel diaries, slave narratives, political writings, and art. In fact, as numerous scholars have shown, what might be called Black Orientalism and the embrace of the tropes of "savage" and "irrational" Muslims have occurred over centuries in a broad range of the writings and ideas of Pan-Africanists, Black Christian evangelicals, the Civil Rights establishment, the Black Left, and into the present-day imperial multiculturalism where the Black political establishment has embraced the rhetoric of the "War on Terror."[18]

Though Black writers, artists, scholars, and activists have mobilized and invoked Orientalist tropes and ideals, unlike the white West, they clearly have not had the will to power over the Muslim Third World or the brutal means to achieve it. And though Black Orientalist discourse clearly does not have the same intention or impact as classical Orientalism, it does in some ways serve to legitimize the Orientalist project more broadly. For just as a Black president is thought to be "proof" of a "postracial" United States, which erases the stigma of whiteness from U.S. empire, Black participation in Orientalist tropes can suggest the erasure of white supremacy as well, while also suggesting that these racist ideas about the Muslim Other contain some "truth" that justifies the West's violent control of the Muslim Third World.

Black Star, Crescent Moon explores an alternative cultural and political history of Blackness, Islam, and the Muslim Third World that complicates any simplistic view of these histories, narratives, and ideas. For in these pages are found redemptive visions in which Black radicals—both Muslims and not—have linked themselves, their art, and their activism politically and symbolically with the decolonization taking place in the Muslim Third World. Unlike the white West, which has used the Muslim Third World as an exotic locale or a timeless place serving as a backdrop to resolving white anxieties, the histories of resistance in *Black Star, Crescent Moon* reveal powerful forms of Black agency that have not legitimized Orientalism or concealed its racist origins. Instead these Black thinkers, activists, and communities have sought to *reveal* white supremacy as a global phenomenon that not only has subjugated the Muslim Third World but has also perpetuated the continuing legacies of slavery and genocide in the Americas.

Numerous scholars have written about the deep and enduring history of internationalism and solidarity between Black activists and organizations in the United States and those in the broader Third World of Africa, Asia, and Latin America.[19] Nineteenth- and early twentieth-century internationalists such as Martin Delany, Frederick Douglass, Edward Wilmot Blyden, Marcus Garvey, the African Blood Brotherhood, and the first Pan-African Congresses expressed what could be viewed as early Black Nationalist sentiments and Pan-Africanist hopes that imagined Africa as a promised land of redemption for the diaspora. And as the twentieth century witnessed a rising U.S. expansionism and deepening engagement in Africa, Asia, and Latin America, U.S.-based Black activists, such as W. E. B. Du Bois, Paul Robeson, Claudia Jones, Robert Williams, Malcolm X, and Angela Davis, and organizations such as the Council on African Affairs, the Revolutionary Action Movement, and the Black Panther Party continued to wave the banner of internationalism with the Third World, viewing their own plight of Jim and Jane Crow segregation and racial violence as part of a global struggle against white supremacy.

In linking the struggle for Black freedom in the United States with the anticolonial struggles of the Third World, Black political culture has situated this solidarity within the crucible of the centuries-long colonial violence and racial slavery of the West. As Nikhil Singh suggests, it's important to see Black liberation struggles in the United States, particularly after World War II, as part and parcel of the broader global struggle for decolonization that consumed Africa, Asia, and Latin America. For to see the Black Left during the 1950s or the freedom struggles in the early 1960s and on into Black Power as distinct from Third World decolonization and a global struggle of antiracism is to replicate the very idea that these movements sought to challenge and tear down: the mythic idea of American exceptionalism that presents the United States' position of global supremacy as distinct and separate from European expansion and colonialism. Instead, what radical Black political thought in the post–World War II moment sought to claim was a terrain that laid bare connections between the United States and Europe to a history of racist domination, colonialism, and control throughout the world. For as Singh argues, the failure to recognize this link "further prevents us from recognizing that perhaps the most consistent and enduring strand of modern black activism has been the opposition to imperialism and colonialism."[20] In tying Black freedom to a global struggle against white power and capitalist control, *Black Star, Crescent Moon* situates

U.S. imperial culture not simply as tangential to the rise of European colonialism but vehemently and violently complicit with it.

Between Enemy Lines: The Muslim International

In *Black Star, Crescent Moon* I examine power and resistance through a broad range of lenses and an eclectic set of practices, from social movement history and the prison to cinema, documentary culture, literature, and hip-hop, revealing what I am calling the Muslim International. Having shaped and been shaped by U.S.-based Black liberation struggles and Third World decolonization in the post–World War II era, the Muslim International is measured by what Aimé Césaire has called "the compass of suffering,"[21] connecting geographies of violence and shared territories of struggle against racial terror, global capital, and war.

In mapping a terrain in which the "First World" and the "Third World" have intersected, overlapped, and bled into each other through slavery, colonialism, migration, and war, *Black Star, Crescent Moon* reveals the beautiful struggles and poignant narratives of rebellion that have shaped the shared histories of Black Islam, Black radicalism, and the Muslim Third World through the Cold War and decolonization, the Civil Rights and Black Power eras, the post–Civil Rights era and mass incarceration, the post–Cold War 1990s and the "Clash of Civilizations," and into the post-9/11 era of the perpetual "War on Terror." As such, *Black Star, Crescent Moon* explores the Muslim International through artists, activists, movements, and popular culture, including Malcolm X, Frantz Fanon, Third Cinema, Sam Greenlee, Black Power, Gang Starr, Public Enemy, the Black Arts Movement, the film *The Battle of Algiers*, and Muhammad Ali, to name a few.

In exploring and revealing the histories and narratives of resistance that have shaped and are shaped by the Muslim International, *Black Star, Crescent Moon* challenges Paul Gilroy's conception of internationalism and the Black Atlantic by viewing the histories between Black Islam, Black radicalism, and the Muslim Third World as part of the broader history of the Afro-diasporic imagination.[22] While Gilroy understandably examines the histories of slavery and Jewish persecution as central threads within the unfolding narrative of modernity and its attendant racial violence, he ignores the ways in which Black activists, writers, and artists have sought alliance with, allegiance to, and affirmation from the anticolonial politics of the broader Muslim Third World. By exploring these narratives and legacies, *Black Star, Crescent Moon* reveals a fuller and more robust history of the Afro-diasporic imagination and the histories of Black internationalism.

For it is more than ironic that diasporas have been imagined as spaces that house and absorb those peoples who are what Partha Chatterjee has called the fragments of the nation—those who, along with their histories, are silenced by and excluded from the national community. But just as nations have their fragments and exclusions, so too do diasporas and imagined communities—silences that are revealed when we understand history through what Earl Lewis has called "overlapping diasporas."[23] In this way in *Black Star, Crescent Moon*, the political and cultural histories told of Malcolm X in Egypt, Mecca, and Bandung, of Black Power politics and culture in Algeria, Palestine, and Iraq, and of the poet–rapper Rakim Allah in Iraq, Mecca, and Medina, which, while silenced within the histories of U.S. nationalism and the Black Atlantic, are made legible through the Muslim International.

In this way, the Muslim International acts as a permeable contact zone, sharing territories of struggle with the larger Afro-diasporic imagination, in which ideas about community, resistance, and belonging can be engaged. And unlike Gilroy's conception of Black internationalism, which ironically replicated the very problem it sought to challenge by replacing one geographic entity (the nation-state) with another (the Black Atlantic), the Muslim International is not geographically located. Instead it is composed of not only multiple and overlapping diasporas that have resulted from slavery, colonialism, and migration, but also by communities and collectives that have been shaped by uneven and disparate relationships to nation-states, capitalism, and imperial power, a zone of struggles and solidarity in which new kinds of politics emerge.

Similar to how the Muslim Third World is composed of non-Muslims and nonbelievers, Black Islam in the United States—primarily through Malcolm X—has influenced and shaped non-Muslim Black radical politics in groups such as the Revolutionary Action Movement (RAM), the Student Nonviolent Coordinating Committee (SNCC), and the Black Panther Party, as well as artists, writers, and activists within Black freedom struggles and beyond. The Muslim International, then, shapes and is shaped by the convergent histories and narratives that are central to the shared struggles of these overlapping diasporas. For these diverse histories and narratives are what influence the various modes of resistance and forms of political mobilization that have continued to challenge power in enduring ways. It is here that the politics of the Muslim International is revealed and elaborated, a site of contact and difference, within and across territories, a perpetual border zone where ideas about justice, agency, and self-determination take root and are given shape.

As such, the Muslim International is not monolithic; it even resists homogeneity and encourages radical difference, for it is difference that not only reflects positions and subjectivities but also reveals the structures and forces that seek to define and delimit resistance and opposition, oftentimes along the lines of nationhood, gender, race, class, and language. As such, the Muslim International is not universalist, nor is it cosmopolitan in the European humanist tradition. Embodying and carrying with it a multiplicity of ideas and actors, the Muslim International is not an ontological given, nor is it some transcendent, timeless ideal. Because it is produced by national boundaries, racial categories, class dynamics, gendered forms of control, legal constructions, imperial wars, and neoliberal contexts, the Muslim International does not ignore these powerful forces. Instead it represents a shape-shifting and fluid demand for subjectivity in the face of modernity's horror. Forged, created, and re-created by political activists, nonstate actors, artists, writers, the working poor, women, exiles, refugees, and others, the Muslim International is a dissident and exilic space that encourages transgression, applauds border crossing, and foments forms of sabotage and resistance not possible within European and U.S. discourses about individualism, the nation-state, "democracy," and the broader philosophical and juridical frameworks of the Enlightenment, modernity, and Western liberalism.

Because a central part of the Muslim International is the formal political activities and state-driven initiatives of labor unions, student and worker strikes, women's rights movements, peasant revolts, rebel activity, armed struggle, and other forms of sabotage, the Muslim International recognizes that there is no space outside of domination and that power is omnipresent. And because universalizing and grand claims of liberation and freedom have the potential to warp our sense of how power works and operates, the Muslim International also sees the local and the everyday as potential sites for movement, activity, and subversion. Indebted to the work of James Scott, Robin Kelley, and Asef Bayat, the Muslim International also includes informal and nontraditional spaces and forms of resistance, such as art and the unorganized forms of everyday agency. In what Scott refers to as "infrapolitics" and what Bayat calls the "quiet encroachment" of everyday practices in the informal economy, the Muslim International includes those who struggle for dignity by other means after being left at the margins by the violence of neoliberalism.[24]

Scott, Kelley, and Bayat present compelling portraits of these struggles, and I am deeply intrigued by what Bayat calls the "epidemic potential" of these actors to spread through communities and of collectives that operate in the shadows of the state. But these activities, instead of being viewed as a choice between reform and radical change, suggest that power, far from being static and top-down, is a process that is activated and actualized everywhere. If we are truly to understand power in order to defeat it, we must not stop at how it silences, contains, and destroys formal political and social movements and organizations. We also have to be attuned to how power contends with other forms of resistance that are outside its traditional orbit, because it is there where power is forced to extend and even overextend itself, giving us a more nuanced and sophisticated lens through which to see how it unfolds. Rather than seeing alternative forms of resistance, such as art and the everyday, as apolitical or even antipolitical, we should see them as powerful and productive sites toward power's undoing.

Because neoliberalism is rampant and has usurped the postindependence period of the Third World through global racial capital, the shift from welfare states to warfare states in the West and in the Third World has witnessed the emergence of new forms of resistance in which the state is viewed as, if not corrupt, then corruptible. For while the Muslim International doesn't privilege movement leaders, organizations, and cooperatives as the sole site of "true" politics, it does value them and see them as central to the constitution and creation of ideas about justice and equality. But by including both formal and informal modes of resistance that include art and the everyday, the Muslim International seeks to be a space where ideas about the state can be reconstituted and alternative forms of governance and existence can be negotiated. Far from being a perfect equilibrium, the Muslim International is a space where the very idea of the "political" can come under scrutiny, revealing that there need not be a belief in politics per se but rather a recognition that all activity is *political*. In that way, at the very least, the Muslim International can be a shadow or parallel space to the state, a space that harnesses and seeks to transform discontent, agency, and resistance into new social movements dedicated to subverting power in enduring ways.

Though vital, for some the state is not the only site of struggle. And when formal political channels are shut off or seen as limiting, the realms of art and culture become vehicles to express what the official language of politics is incapable of translating. It is crucial then that we see activism and agency not only in social movements, labor unions, and other radical activity but also in song and cinema, vital that we see "politics" occurring not only in organizations and political gatherings but also in performance, on-screen, and on the page. Art and expressive culture can become sites for expressing ideas about identity, possibility, and even power itself. In this way, art and aesthetics, narrative and representation, are important means through which to explore ideas about resistance, helping us to imagine what is possible or, even sometimes more important, what is not.

History is replete with how the state and the powerful deploy popular culture as a means of generating and reproducing dominant ideas about race, gender, imperialism, and other forms of social inequality. But the socially excluded, the poor, and the oppressed are the ones who reclaim the power of art to truth-tell and bear witness. Borrowing from the traditions of the Birmingham School and cultural studies, in *Black Star, Crescent Moon* I explore popular culture as a powerful site for revealing the struggles over ideology and power, race and nationhood, and the politics of identity.

Although art and expressive culture have complemented, inspired, and given momentum to social movements in the past, I explore the role of expressive culture and art within the Muslim International as a site of struggle itself, a fruitful place to challenge and resist dominant ideas about race, class, gender inequality, and imperial forms of power. The cultural histories contained here reveal how, in the cinema from the

Muslim Third World, the camera became a weapon, how Black literature and film became spaces where the anticolonial struggles in the Muslim Third World were used to probe ideas about Black internationalism, and how Muslim hip-hop artists in the Reagan–Bush age of mass incarceration turned the possibility of prison bars into musical bars of rebellion and hope. This is a dimension of the Muslim International, a cultural and artistic space in which Black artists, writers, and poets have waged battles over aesthetics, narrative, and ideology as they challenge state repression and the containment of Black freedom within the confines of America.

Black Star, Crescent Moon

In examining the terrain of the Muslim International through political and cultural histories, chapter 1, "You Remember Dien Bien Phu," explores the history of Black Islam in the post–World War II era through the figure of Malcolm X and the ways in which the Muslim Third World became both a literal and an ideological backdrop to his unfolding narrative of resistance and internationalism. From Cairo to Harlem, Mecca to Bandung, Algiers to Palestine, and beyond, the Muslim Third World played a central role in shaping Malcolm's political vocabulary and grammar of resistance as he crafted an imaginative geography that connected Black liberation struggles in the United States to decolonization in Africa and the Muslim Third World.

Chapter 2, "To the East, Blackwards," explores how the Muslim Third World influenced and informed Black radical politics and culture within the Muslim International. This chapter examines how the anticolonial struggles in the Muslim Third World of Algeria and Iraq in the 1950s and '60s, not only shaped ideas about tactics and strategy, solidarity and political possibility, but they also informed ideas about film, literature, and cultural criticism within the Black Power imagination. By examining the influence of Frantz Fanon and *The Battle of Algiers*, Sam Greenlee and *The Spook Who Sat by the Door*, this chapter explores how the national liberation struggles in Algeria and Iraq became the literal and ideological backdrop for the redefinition of Black cultural practice, aesthetic developments, thematic concerns, and political orientations during the Black Power era.

Chapter 3, "Return of the Mecca," explores the aesthetic and political dimensions of the Muslim International through hip-hop culture during the hypernationalism of the post–Civil Rights backlash, when the "Black criminal" and the "Muslim terrorist" were viewed as the fundamental threats to U.S. national identity. Through the resurgence of Malcolm X and the embrace of Black Islam, hip-hop culture in the 1980s and 1990s tapped into a deep vein of Black internationalism to challenge racial domination, militarism, and mass incarceration, imagining Black freedom beyond the United States and into Africa and the Muslim Third World. As an embodiment of what Amiri Baraka called the "changing same,"[25] hip-hop culture—like jazz and the Black Arts Movement before it—became a space in which Black radicalism, Islam, and the politics of the Muslim Third World have had a powerful impact on the lyrical imaginations, sonic landscapes, and political visions that have been expressed by artists such as Rakim, Public Enemy, Mos Def, Ice Cube, Gang Starr, and Lupe Fiasco, to name a few.

Chapter 4, "Ghost in the House," explores the political and cultural history of Muhammad Ali and his embrace as a national hero in the post–Cold War 1990s, when the legacy of Black Islam and its relationship to the Muslim International that hip-hop culture had struggled so hard to rekindle and reinvigorate. The post–Civil Rights fear of the "Muslim terrorist" gave way to a full-blown ideological paradigm of the "Green Menace" of Islam, replacing the "Red Scare" of communism through Samuel Huntington's "Clash of Civilizations" thesis in the 1990s,[26] which forms the basis of chapter 4's examination of how Muhammad Ali's recuperation became a symbol for the fear and containment of Black Islam within a narrative of American universalism, stripping Black Islam of its internationalist impulses.

Because the "Black criminal" and the "Muslim terrorist" formed the twin pillars of U.S. statecraft in the post–Civil Rights era, chapter 5, "Protect Ya Neck," explores how, in the post-9/11 moment, the U.S. security state has collapsed these two figures into the Black Muslim. Combining the rhetoric and logic of the "War on Crime" and the "War on Terror" to assault and erase the history of Black Islam, this chapter explores the collapse of the domestic and foreign realms of U.S. power and views the prison as a site of violent containment for the Muslim International, revealing the intimacies between domestic U.S. prison regimes and the emergence of imperial imprisonment in Iraq, Afghan-istan, Guantánamo, and other so-called Black sites.

Because the new "peculiar institution" of the prison has become the literal and even the metaphoric home for Blackness and Muslims on a global scale in the post-9/11 era, *Black Star, Crescent Moon* is not only where this "compass of suffering" gets mapped, but it is also where the prequel to the current "War on Terror" gets revealed—a set of stories and histories showing that this "war" did not begin on September 11, 2001, but well before. With Blackness, Islam, and the Muslim Third World front and center in the current political and popular debate within the United States and the West, U.S. power continues to silence and even erase the histories and voices of those who radically resist. The legacy and history of Black artists and activists who appear in these pages bear witness to a collective war against oblivion, a rebellion that has raged from Harlem to Mecca, L.A. to Cairo, Chicago to Baghdad, Detroit to Bandung, Oakland to Algiers, and beyond. Through radical activity, rhetorical rebellion, and insurgent ideas, these Black activists and artists sought to create a more just world for themselves and for others, as they hoped to alleviate injustice at all cost and by any means. That there exists a racial reality to their secular suffering still holds true today. But the question remains: how will artists, activists, and thinkers respond? Through these stories and histories, we get a glimpse of what that might look and sound like.

1

"YOU REMEMBER DIEN BIEN PHU!"
Malcolm X and the Third World Rising

> A racist society can't but fight a racist war—this is the bitter
> truth. The assumptions acted on at home are the assumptions
> acted on abroad, and every American Negro knows this, for he,
> after the American Indian, was the first "Viet Cong" victim. We
> were bombed first. How, then, can I believe a word you say, and
> what gives you the right to ask me to die for you?
>
> —James Baldwin, *The Cross of Redemption:*
> *Uncollected Writings*

"I AM A CITIZEN OF ASIA." So read the draft card for Malcolm X upon his induction into the Korean War. Malcolm didn't burn his draft card, as many would later. Instead, he used it as his declaration of independence. And when asked if he had filed a declaration to become a citizen of the United States, he replied, "No." Hip-hop's natural mystic Rakim Allah, decades later, in his prophetic song "Casualties of War," would defy America's first Gulf War invasion by saying about Iraq, "This is Asia from where I came." As the Cold War hysteria raged throughout the United States, Malcolm declared his allegiance. This wasn't the Asia of Mao and Ho. Though it was. And it wasn't the Asia of Cairo or Karachi. But it was that, too. This was the Nation of Islam's radical geographic remix of Black origins, a compass of resistance that imagined Black peoples as "Black Asiatics" from the "holy city of Mecca, Saudi Arabia."[1] This was the "X" marking the spot, what the poet–philosopher Nas would later say on his masterpiece *Illmatic* is the "Afro-centric Asian, half man, half amazing."

In the post–World War II era, the struggle over the meaning and significance of race was a critical component of U.S. imperial desire for global control and the domestic consensus needed in order to gain that control. On the one hand, how was the United States going to contend with emerging African and Asian nations who were seeking independence after centuries of European colonial racism? And on the other hand, how was the United States going to deal with Black activists who were making the connections between those liberation movements in Africa and Asia and their own demands for racial justice and equality?

Malcolm X's imaginative geography of resistance coincided with the anticolonial struggles then taking place throughout the Third World. And his conversion to Islam, his embrace of Third World internationalism, and his remapping of Black struggle in the crucible of the Cold War have had an enduring effect on Black political culture. Through the prisms of his shifting Muslim identities, from Nation of Islam firebrand to Sunni Pan-Africanist and Muslim Internationalist, Malcolm X challenged the very foundational assumptions that undergirded the logic of the post–World War II U.S. ascension to global power, the fulfillment of Henry Luce's manifesto "the American Century," and the Cold War liberal orthodoxy that would so limit and contain the possibilities of not only Black liberation but also the national liberation movements taking place in Africa and Asia.

As such, this chapter explores how, for Malcolm X, the Muslim Third World became both a literal and an ideological backdrop to his unfolding narrative of resistance and internationalism. From Mecca to Bandung, Cairo to Algiers, Harlem to Palestine, and beyond, the Muslim Third World held a central and iconic place within his worldview. Whether influenced by the political compass and radical redefinition of the self that Mecca offered, to the historical significance of the Bandung Conference in Indonesia, to the linking of ancient Black greatness with Islam that Egypt embodied, to Algiers, Palestine, Harlem, and every place in between, Malcolm's travels, speeches, and political activity forged an imaginative geography of the Muslim International that envisioned Black peoples not as national minorities but as global majorities.

As Black activists increasingly tied their demands for equality to the national liberation struggles of the Third World, the Truman Doctrine, McCarthyism, and the Red Scare sought to erase the insurgent ideas of U.S.-based Black anticolonialists who critiqued U.S. foreign intervention in Africa and Asia, a Cold War policy that sought to destroy those very same movements that Black freedom was connected to. As the political establishment targeted the Black Left, in particular W. E. B. Du Bois, Shirley Graham, Paul Robeson, Claudia Jones, Benjamin Davis, the Council on African Affairs, and numerous others, Malcolm X continued to cultivate this ideological ground of deeply left critique, shining light on a landscape of rebellion and a geography of power that would indelibly influence Black radical thought.

While the U.S. security state interpreted international, national, and even local concerns through the lens of the Cold War, Black and Third World peoples sought to seize the terrain and argue for colonial and working peoples' control of their resources and rights, their land and their labor, and ultimately their destinies. As the U.S. Cold War logic assumed that communism would replace colonialism as the biggest threat to the Third World, Malcolm X seized the interpretive authority over the politics of liberation and inverted this Cold War assumption by using the national liberation movements in the Muslim Third World as critical lenses that served to define the contours of Black identities, liberation struggles, and their solidarities with the broader Third World.

By exploring the Muslim Internationalism of Malcolm X and by understanding him in relation to broader Black anticolonial histories that linked imperialism to the domestic struggles over race, this chapter reveals some of the central debates and conflicts over the role and place of the United States in the post–World War II global landscape. It was a rough and rugged terrain in which America sought and seized superpower status, a position that in many ways determined and dominated not only U.S. relationships with the continents of Africa and Asia but also U.S. responses to Black liberation struggles domestically.

As such, this chapter will place Malcolm firmly within these Cold War times in order to demonstrate that he was a direct product of the post–World War II Black radical tradition, the Black anticolonial Left, the rise of the Muslim International, and a counterweight to the rise of the liberal wing of Black political culture. In addition, I want to place Malcolm in the context of the anticolonialism of the Muslim Third World, the decolonization in Africa and Asia, and a heightened Black internationalism at a time when political voices were being silenced and redemptive visions were being blinded by American nationalism and a Cold War liberal orthodoxy.

While consensus history views Malcolm as the complement to King and Civil Rights, it is important to put into context the ideological crucible of Cold War liberalism that Civil Rights emerged from. Malcolm criticized more than just the agenda of the Civil Rights movement and its methods, means, and assumptions about the place of Black peoples in America. He simultaneously critiqued the Cold War liberalism that had come to define and determine the ideological contours of the Civil Rights movement: domesticated rights, an embrace of anticommunist foreign policy, aggressive intervention abroad, and the presumption that American power has been a force of good in the world. By situating Malcolm within this crucible of Cold War liberalism, anticolonial insurgency, and Black liberation struggles and by situating his political thought and trenchant critiques of race and imperialism within the context of Cold War struggles over Blackness, we gain a broader and more robust understanding of the implications that Malcolm's visions had on the burgeoning and even defiant radicalism emerging from the Muslim Third World of Africa and Asia. Malcolm must be understood within this Cold War context of Black radicalism and decolonization, because it situates him within a broader tradition that includes Du Bois, Robeson, Claudia Jones, George Padmore, Frantz Fanon, Aimé Césaire, Kwame Nkrumah, Gamal Abdel Nasser, Jomo Kenyatta, and Patrice Lumumba.

For just as Aimé Césaire did in his monumental and damning *Discourse on Colonialism*, where he poignantly revealed the similarity between Nazism and European colonialism of the Third World,[2] Malcolm exposed the lie of American exceptionalism and saw the relationship between Jim Crow segregation and racial terror in the United States and American empire building abroad. And like Césaire's *Discourse*, which revealed the relationship between Nazism and colonialism as a means of pointing out the hypocrisy of the West in using World War II to reassert control over the Third World, Malcolm's "discourse on empire" revealed that the Cold War was really a project of empire building for the new Leviathan and that, under the guise of "democracy" and "anticommunism," America was going to replace Europe as an imperial power in what he referred to as "benevolent colonialism" or "philanthropic imperialism."[3]

Malcolm's "discourse on empire" may be understood by asking, how did his shifting and transforming political vision, while in the Nation of

Islam and then after his departure from it, inform, influence, and give contour to the Muslim International? One narrative of Malcolm's paints a picture of him in which his internationalism and political solidarities with the Third World occurred after leaving the Nation of Islam and making his pilgrimage to Mecca—a portrayal that assumes as much as it ignores. With Malcolm's history written in this way, this logic assumes that it was the "orthodox" Sunni Islam that awakened and redirected him away from a supposedly narrow, parochial, and even heretical Nation of Islam and toward a broader and more expansive religious and political vision. This portrayal also assumes that after Hajj and Malcolm's embrace of "orthodox" Islam, he refrained from talking about race and became a color-blind universalist in the tradition of a supposed "true" Islam.

Both of these assumptions ignore the fact that prior to making his pilgrimage to Mecca and while with the Nation of Islam, Malcolm was deeply engaged in global affairs and the decolonizing Third World. In fact, Malcolm made his first trip to the African and Arab world in 1959, was deeply affected by the assassination of Patrice Lumumba, met with Fidel Castro in Harlem, supported Gamal Abdel Nasser of Egypt and his defiant stand against the colonial powers, was vocal about the Mau Mau rebellion in Kenya and the Vietnamese victory at Dien Bien Phu, and made numerous references not only to Third World national liberation struggles but also to the historic Bandung Conference in 1955, all while he was still *in* the Nation of Islam.

This narrative also ignores the profound and powerful ways that Malcolm, after leaving the Nation of Islam, continued to center race and white supremacy as the dominant lenses through which he understood power to unleash itself in the modern world. This often met with the consternation of some Muslim leaders and organizations in the Muslim Third World of Egypt, Saudi Arabia, and elsewhere, many of whom assumed a universalist posture and discouraged Malcolm from talking about race, for they interpreted it as un-Islamic. In his travels Malcolm challenged this kind of thinking by arguing, "Being one of 22 million oppressed Afro-Americans I can never overlook the miserable plight of my people in America. . . . I will never hesitate to let the entire world know the hell my people suffer from America's deceit, and her hypocrisy, as well as her oppression."[4] Malcolm did not see religious belief and anti-racism as mutually exclusive; instead, he saw them as deeply enmeshed, for he saw the struggle of Black peoples in the United States as a responsibility not just for the continent of Africa but claimed that it "must also be the concern and the moral responsibility of the entire Muslim world—if you hope to make the principles of the Quran a living reality."[5]

In his political vision, Malcolm situated and highlighted the racial context in which Black peoples existed in the United States as well as the racial context in which those very universalist Muslims also existed, because they, too, were victims and subjects of white supremacy, European colonial power, and the oncoming U.S. imperialism. In framing white supremacy as a global phenomenon that structured daily life, Malcolm was suggesting to universalist Muslims that justice and equality are determined by who is white and who is not and that if Islam's prophetic ideals are about fighting injustice and inequality, then it is the duty of all Muslims to join in the struggle of antiracism on a global scale.

For Malcolm then, Islam was not only the link between Africa and Asia but also what connected Black Muslims in the United States to the broader Muslim Third World, linking their struggles through the Muslim International and revealing it to be a space of overlapping diasporas and shared histories of struggle. For through his own personal conversion to Islam, his wide-ranging travels, speeches, and political activities, and his formation of Muslim Mosque Inc. and the Organization of Afro-American Unity, Malcolm also brought into the Muslim International the future and the destinies of non-Muslim Africans throughout the diaspora, including non-Muslim Black peoples in the United States. In doing so, Malcolm forced and compelled the Muslim International to be a broad and inclusive space that understands the overlapping histories and interconnected struggles that not only shaped the modern world but that also shaped the conscience of the Muslim International as a site for radical justice and equality.

Because of Malcolm X's wide recognition as the architect of Black radical thought since the 1960s, this chapter explores his speeches, interviews, and travels throughout the Muslim Third World, through Africa and Asia, as he sought to link Black liberation struggles in the United States with the worldwide rebellions taking place against European colonialism. As an alternative racial compass that gave a new political direction to Black quests for freedom, Islam provided a pathway and a road map for Black political culture that led to the Muslim Third World of

Africa and Asia during the anticolonial struggles of the Cold War, helping Malcolm to craft an imaginative political geography and a versatile
and fluid political vocabulary that shook the foundations of the white
world.

Dark World Rising

Revolutionary redemption and anticolonialism were central to what
Malcolm X called the "tidal wave of color" and the "worldwide revolution" taking place in the post–World War II moment and on through
the 1960s, as countries throughout Africa, Asia, and Latin America were
in outright rebellion against European colonialism and white supremacy.
In the United States, Black movement leaders, grassroots activists, organizations, and others viewed what was happening throughout the Third
World with great interest. So from the early twentieth century through
the post–World War II moment, they crafted new languages and vocab-
ularies for freedom in voices that had a distinctly international tongue
and that were locally situated but globally aware. According to Brenda
Plummer, "Serious and intense debate had begun among Afro-Americans
about the meaning of the civil rights struggle on a strategic level" as core
questions "arose about the nature of black Americans as people, their
relationship to the mainstream and to liberationist movements in other
parts of the world," movements that "formed the backdrop for the air-
ing of disputes about religion, race, tactics, authenticity, and legitimacy"
as "decolonization provided a channel for these issues to emerge."[6]

In fact, throughout the twentieth century but particularly up to,
during, and in the aftermath of World War II, Black political culture
framed Black struggles for freedom through the lens of anticolonialism,
using a racial rhetoric that expanded the notion of a racial community
to include nonwhites the world over. Arguing that the fate and freedom of Black peoples in the United States were inextricably linked to
nonwhite peoples throughout the world, Black leadership, newspapers,
grassroots activists, and other organic intellectuals "raised a vigorous
protest against European colonialism and against the American foreign
policy which they found in support of that colonialism."[7] During this
period, the five major Civil Rights organizations—the National Association for the Advancement of Colored People, the National Council

of Negro Women, the March on Washington Movement, the National Urban League, and the National Negro Congress—all spoke out vociferously against colonialism and for internationalizing the question of race. A. Philip Randolph, the leader of the March on Washington Movement, declared that his organization intended to link "the interest of the Negro people in America to the interest of Negroes all over the world," and he went on to demand a free Africa, Asia, and the Americas while asking, "Are we fighting this global war to restore Singapore, Malaya, and Burma to Great Britain?"[8] In addition, the National Urban League declared, "This global struggle represents the gigantic effort of men everywhere to be free," and the National Negro Congress argued that the struggles of Black peoples in America were linked to the success of "people's revolutions" throughout the world.[9] The congress declared that Black peoples in America shared a responsibility to fight against imperialism and colonialism and vigorously oppose any policies that the United States would undertake that might prolong colonialism. Mary McLeod Bethune, the founder and president of the National Council of Negro Women, warned American leaders that they would be mistaken if they thought the new militancy among Black peoples in America was only a domestic phenomenon, arguing that it was an integral part of a larger and broader unrest among the oppressed peoples of the world.[10]

The largest and most powerful organization, the NAACP, which had just brought the defiant W. E. B. Du Bois on as adviser on colonial affairs, also expressed strident positions on the nature of racism and colonialism. In his book *Rising Wind*, Walter White, the executive secretary of the NAACP, issued a warning to the Western powers: "Allied nations must choose without delay one of two courses—to revolutionize their racial concepts and practices, to abolish imperialism and grant full equality to all of its people, or else prepare for World War III."[11] Roy Wilkins, the editor of the NAACP's magazine, *Crisis*, made anticolonial issues of central concern to the journal, of which the vast majority of issues featured articles that condemned the racism of the European colonial empires. Wilkins as well as Du Bois questioned the Atlantic Charter and openly critiqued it for being limited to only white nations. At the NAACP's annual convention in 1946, White said that nonwhite peoples around the world were "determined once and for all time to end white exploitation and imperialism." White went on to say that Black peoples in the United States were "part and parcel of the problems of other colored peoples in the West Indies, South America, Africa, the Pacific and Asia." The convention went on to condemn the "slaughter of Indonesian and Palestinian youths" by British troops and questioned an impending U.S. loan to Britain, asking rhetorically how much of it would "be used to perpetuate empire and to suppress by force of arms or otherwise the legitimate demands of colonial peoples?"[12]

In addition to these major organizations, many other prominent Black organizations and leaders joined the chorus of racial internationalism, including Paul Robeson, whose Council on African Affairs (CAA) sought to influence and advocate U.S. government policy toward Africa. As Penny Von Eschen and others have brilliantly shown, the voices of numerous major Black newspapers also joined in, including the *Pittsburgh Courier*'s George Schuyler, who wrote that all nonwhite peoples around the world are victims of "aggression and occupation by Caucasian powers," and the *Chicago Defender*'s editorial argued, "If the war is for democracy and freedom, imperialism must end."[13]

In fact, with very few exceptions, prominent Black leaders and organizations of the time engaged and participated in the panracial and anticolonial movements taking place then. According to Von Eschen, these Black anticolonialists "insisted that African Americans not only shared an oppression with colonized peoples but that their fate in the United States was intertwined with the struggles of those peoples" in the Third World.[14] The struggles for freedom taking place internationally sensitized Black peoples in the United States to issues of repression and racism, creating a lens with which to not only interpret their own experiences but also understand the global nature of white supremacy. The global resistance that was taking place had also revealed to Black peoples that despite the uniqueness of their history of slavery, they were not isolated in their struggles against white power, apartheid, and brutal racism—a powerful sentiment that no doubt carried tremendous moral weight.

But despite this racial internationalism and enlarged racial community that was emerging among these Black anticolonialists in the United States, the ground beneath their collective feet began to shift as the Cold War consensus was coming to the surface in a series of diplomatic maneuvers, policy pronouncements, and rhetorical gestures that were most clearly embodied in the Truman Doctrine in 1947. With Truman's declaration that worldwide communism was the biggest threat to post-war security, democracy, and freedom, American Cold War statecraft determined that communism, not Western colonialism, was the biggest threat to the Third World. With the Atlantic Charter already assumed, the Marshall Plan in full effect, and Winston Churchill's "Iron Curtain" speech, which sought to cement an Anglo-American alliance against an emerging Soviet Union, the Cold War calculus saw the United States interested in maintaining and supporting Cold War alliances, establishing and strengthening NATO, and supporting regional alliances such as the Baghdad Pact, among other measures—all at the expense of a fully realized decolonization of the Third World.

George Kennan, known as the "father of containment" and one of the main architects of America's Cold War policy, issued his "Long Telegram" from Moscow in March 1946, warning Truman that decolonization would create a vacuum of power that would make the nations within Africa and Asia vulnerable to "Communist–Soviet penetration."[15] As a result, American policy makers ultimately supported, through either silence or sanction, the ability of western European powers to maintain control of their colonies, and they also demanded that the United States aggressively expand its political, diplomatic, and military presence within the Third World through arming opposition groups, destabilizing governments, supporting dictators, and even assassinations as a bulwark against the spread of communism. The United States' continued support of the old colonial empires, as well as its own aggressive engagement with countries in Africa, Asia, and Latin America, was not lost on Black activists, who viewed the United States in these developments as not only underwriting and strengthening British and European control of African, Asian, and Latin American countries during their anticolonial struggles but also extending and intensifying its own political and military involvement throughout Africa, Asia, and the Americas under the banner of anticommunism.

The effects of the Cold War on Black anticolonialism and anti-racism were profound, because "after 1947 [Black activists'] protest on behalf of colonial peoples, expressions of international racial solidarity, and references to universal white oppression fell off sharply."[16] The formerly broad Black anticolonial coalition split and gave shape to the emerging Civil Rights movement, as liberals such as Walter White and the NAACP abandoned their previous positions of support for colonial peoples and supported an American foreign policy in Asia, Africa, and the "Middle East" that oftentimes subverted legitimate nationalist democratic movements around the world, supported dictatorial regimes, and even assassinated democratically elected leaders, all in the name of anticommunism.

In anticipation of Black liberals' demands for antidiscrimination legislation in exchange for support of Cold War foreign policy, Truman formed the President's Committee on Civil Rights in 1946, which called for an end to segregation in education, a fair employment act that prohibited discrimination, the prohibition of state voting-rights restrictions based upon race, and other measures.[17] In addition, Truman appeared at the NAACP convention in 1948, calling for a strengthening of the Civil Rights arm of the Justice Department, the passage of antilynching legislation, the end of Jim Crow in interstate travel, the end of inequality throughout the federal government and the armed forces, and the abolition of the poll tax, arguing that the United States could "no longer afford the luxury of a leisurely attack upon prejudice and discrimination."[18]

As a result, White and the NAACP began to shape an anticommunist Civil Rights agenda that embraced Truman's foreign policy by placing Civil Rights for Black peoples at the center of it, arguing that America's Achilles' heel in fighting communism abroad was its record of racial subordination at home. For White and the Cold War liberals who came to dominate, the United States would seem hypocritical to the rest of the world—but particularly to Africa, Asia, and Latin America—if it were to wave the banner of democracy and equal rights abroad while maintaining segregationist and racist politics at home. As a result, they made demands about domestic Civil Rights and Jim Crow by arguing that the only way America could win a war against communism was to be a moral beacon by eradicating racism at home.[19]

Walter White and the NAACP also embraced an anticolonialism that was anticommunist, arguing that the continued abuse and abject racism of the colonial powers would only open the door to communist sympathy among African and Asian nations. But their position assumed that the countries of the Third World were there to be exploited for the benefit of the West, and better by the United States and its allies than by the Soviet Union. According to the NAACP and White, a rejection of the West by the countries of the Third World "could mean the loss of man power, raw materials, and markets, without which the industrial West could not survive."[20] Though there was some resistance from the local chapters of the NAACP as well as from other supporters, the NAACP and numerous Civil Rights organizations muted their criticisms of the failure of America to support decolonization, and instead they expressed support for American foreign policy, including the Marshall Plan, the Korean War, and other Cold War policies meant to bolster American empire.

In light of the Truman Doctrine and the intensifying political repression that ensued under the Red Scare, the passage of the Smith Act, McCarthyism, and the House on Un-American Activities Committee, "the embrace of Cold War American foreign policy by many African American liberals, as well as U.S. government prosecution of activists such as Robeson and the CAA, fundamentally altered the terms of anti-colonialism and effectively severed the black American struggle for civil rights from the issues of anti-colonialism and racism abroad . . . as questions concerning political, economic, and social rights in an international context were neglected in favor of an exclusive emphasis on domestic political and civil rights."[21] As Von Eschen reveals, some Black activists abandoned their support of colonial peoples as well as their critiques of American foreign policy in favor of the argument that racism in the United States should be opposed because it "undermined the legitimate global goals of the United States,"[22] namely, anticommunism and control in the Third World.

When Cold War liberals such as White argued that Jim Crow, segregation, and racial violence were America's Achilles' heel in the war for the hearts and minds of the Third World, they tapped into a deep vein of American anxiety, because incidents of racial violence had been and would continue to be seized on by the international press as a way of pointing out American hypocrisy in world affairs. As A. Philip Randolph argued, "The American race problem represents the proving ground to the colored peoples of the world as to the sincerity of the United States in the democratic cause. Jim Crow is America's national disgrace. Its existence confuses and embarrasses our foreign policy."[23] The attention of global opinion on the United States' treatment of Black peoples was a powerful factor in the Cold War calculus that the United States carefully and cunningly attempted to balance, for at the core of Cold War liberalism's narrative of race was the idea of Black integration and equality in society, a narrative that would project an inclusive American nationalism, which would then cement the moral legitimacy of the United States as a global power and world leader. According to the President's Committee on Civil Rights, formed by Truman in 1946, "Throughout the Pacific, Latin America, Africa, the Near, Middle and Far East, the treatment which our Negroes receive is taken as a reflection of our attitudes towards all dark-skinned peoples," which plays "into the hands of Communist propagandists." The report went on to say that the United States cannot "ignore what the world thinks about our record."[24]

But as Black blood continued to flow and state violence against Black peoples persisted, newspapers from all over the world ran stories of American racism and hypocrisy, whether it was the treatment of Black peoples in the United States or the treatment of foreign diplomats traveling to the United States. From Soviet and Indian papers to the Italian newspaper *Unita;* Mexico's *El Universal, La Prensa,* and *El Nacional;* China's *Ta Kung Pao;* Haiti's *La Nation* and *La Phalange;* and Iraq's *Al Yaqdha,* America's status as a superpower commanded that light be shed on its domestic policies and practices for a very interested global audience.[25]

Black leadership weighed in heavily on the topic as well, putting pressure on the State Department, Congress, and the Oval Office to increase the visibility of Black officials in the diplomatic corps abroad to signal U.S. racial progress to the Third World in order to further Cold War aims in Africa and Asia. Adam Clayton Powell underscored this posture by claiming, "One dark face from the US is of as much value as millions of dollars in economic aid" to the Third World,[26] and Ralph Bunche argued that in order to win over Africa and Asia, the "legend of America as a liberalizing force in world affairs" would and could be established, because "carefully chosen Negroes could prove more effective than whites owing to their unique ability to gain more readily the confidence of the Native."[27] Years later, in a similar vein, the secretary of state Dean Rusk said, "The biggest single burden that we carry on our back in our foreign relations in the 1960's is the problem of racial discrimination."[28]

But rather than try to protect Black peoples and provide the legal, economic, and political redress for racism, the United States instead sought to manage the global *perception* of race in America through a variety of propaganda campaigns. In its attempt to seduce the national liberation movements of Africa and Asia, "the State Department was increasingly energetic in efforts to shape perceptions of race relations globally," so "by 1950, the Voice of America and State Department film, radio, and publication series had been set up in several parts of Africa" under the name Cultural Affairs, Psychological Warfare, and Propaganda, producing programs that "attempted to defend American foreign policy and manipulate African perceptions of Black American life and U.S. 'race relations,' and sometimes included direct attempts to discredit African American anti-colonial and civil rights activists."[29]

Whether it was through the appointment of Black embassy staff throughout the world, the State Department's sponsorship of jazz tours around the world, the speaking tours of prominent Black figures such as Edith Sampson, Carl Rowan, and J. Saunders Redding throughout Africa and Asia, or Adam Clayton Powell's presence at Bandung, the State Department constantly attempted to project America as a race-free utopia that could not only serve as a model for "enlightened leadership" in the emerging Cold War but could also dismiss the claims of African and Asian nations that U.S. foreign policy was an extension of European colonialism and based in racism.[30]

But the Third World, particularly because of its experience with racist colonialism, was not so gullible. For instance, Prime Minister Nehru of India, who had become an icon not only in the Third World, when a prepartitioned India was breaking free of British rule, but also among U.S.-based Blacks, said, "I am answered quite often by questions about America's attitudes towards dark skinned people. The people of Asia don't like colonialism or racial prejudices. They resent condescension. When American talk to them about equality and freedom, they remember stories about lynchings."[31]

On the domestic front Truman's overtures toward Civil Rights generated a great deal of hopefulness among Black liberals, a tack that no doubt helped in narrowing their attention solely to domestic gains and not to global racial equality. But while White and the NAACP abandoned critiques of American foreign policy, they also failed to obtain the

Civil Rights initiatives they were not only seeking but had also been promised, for both Truman and then Eisenhower turned their backs on them to focus on the Korean War and a refusal to challenge the southern wing of the Democratic Party. In addition, Black protest and not Jim Crow violence came to be seen as the biggest threat to the security of the United States. Despite embracing Cold War policy and immersing themselves within the reddened waters of anticommunism in order to achieve Civil Rights legislation, White and the NAACP were themselves seen, in tragic irony, as "communist inspired" in demanding Civil Rights, a stigma that came back to haunt them and thwart their attempts at attaining those rights.

The split of the Black anticolonial Left from mainstream Black liberals and the resulting domestic repression of activists such as Robeson and Du Bois due to Cold War paranoia profoundly affected diasporic and internationalist politics. According to Von Eschen, "As the Cold War escalated, the affirmation by many black American leaders that 'Negroes are Americans' left no room for the claim of commonality with Africans and others oppressed peoples."[32] This process of Americanizing Blackness forced the anticolonialists into a political and rhetorical corner that marginalized them not only from Beltway politics and the levers of power but also from mainstream Black activists who now supported a Cold War liberalism that dictated that race and the legacies of slavery in the United States were to be separated from the histories of colonialism in the Third World. By policing Blackness and containing it within a nationalist framework, the new Cold War calculus fractured the potential for diasporic solidarities and an anti-imperialist critique, in turn bolstering empire and creating a new kind of imperial citizen as the United States became a global superpower to fulfill what Henry Luce had termed "the American Century."

The centerpiece of American Cold War policy continued to view communism as not only the biggest threat to the "free world" of the West but also as a bigger threat to the Third World than European colonialism. For if Europe were to be defeated and decolonization were to succeed anywhere in Africa, Asia, or Latin America, then the "void" that was assumed to be left would be filled by "the Reds." This logic gave sanction to America's underwriting of European control over its colonies, and it also legitimized American involvement and intervention in the Third World as a bulwark against this "communist menace"—a position that Black liberals supported. While the embrace of this framework oftentimes assumed that American intervention around the world was benevolent, many on the Black Left were skeptical and even outright critical of American interests and intentions, as Black critiques of American foreign policy continued to redefine Black peoples' relationship with the Third World.

In fact, when the Cold War was in full swing and the repression of the Black Left and anticolonialists was on the rise, it was through the Nation of Islam that Malcolm X carried the torch and illuminated a path of Black liberation that traveled the road alongside the national liberation movements of Africa, Asia, and Latin America. For it was Malcolm X whom Max Stanford, Stokely Carmichael, Huey Newton, Bobby Seale, and Eldridge Cleaver all claimed to be the singular ideological architect and intellectual force behind the Black radicalism of the Revolutionary Action Movement, the Student Nonviolent Coordinating Committee, and the Black Panther Party, which so forcefully and heroically challenged the brutality of America's imperial police state in the late 1960s and early 1970s. Through an examination of the domestic and global political forces that gave rise to Malcolm X and Black Islam, a fuller and richer account of the tones and textures of the Muslim International emerges. For it is at this moment that the Muslim Third World came to play a central role in a narrative of Black political resistance. Whether it was Mecca and its importance as a spiritual center and compass of origins for remapping Black identity, to Egypt, Bandung, Algeria, Palestine, or elsewhere, the Muslim Third World had a profound effect in shaping the political vision of Malcolm X, Black radicalism, and the Muslim International.

The Detroit Red Scare

Although Malcolm X and the Nation of Islam were arguably the most visible and vocal cadre of anticolonialists from the mid-1950s and into the 1960s, writers and activists such as Lorraine Hansberry, Robert Williams, Harold Cruse, and Max Stanford also sought to link Black and Third World peoples as a means to better understand and challenge racial inequality, white supremacy, and economic injustice. As a result,

China, Cuba, India, and numerous other places throughout the Third World played important roles in defining and redefining Black political and cultural identities.[33] As Cynthia Young astutely notes, Black identity at this time "was not forged in isolation; it did not emerge solely from within the U.S. political context. Rather, it resulted from a transnational consciousness, one that drew on anticolonial critiques for its political analysis and international legitimacy."[34]

The Third World in general began to play a more prominent role in Black radical thought, but the Muslim Third World also played a central role in shaping Blackness. In fact, as the Middle East, the Arab–Israeli conflict, and the politics of the Muslim Third World began to play a more prominent role within the geopolitical interests of the United States, Black leaders, intellectuals, and activists who were being influenced by the anticolonial movements taking place in Africa and Asia began to look at the Muslim Third World as an emerging battleground upon which to negotiate their own political identities, affiliations, and agendas. In fact, as historians have noted, although the tendency has been to understand "the transnational elements of black culture in the United States as focused exclusively on Africa," there has also been an enduring impulse by Black leaders, intellectuals, and artists to not only look to Africa "but also to other areas, and particularly to the Middle East, as site and source for explorations of blackness and the recovery and reconstruction of black history."[35]

For Black Christians, the religious narratives of Exodus, slavery, and suffering have been powerful tropes for analogizing biblical histories to contemporary struggles around racism, all of which have served to create ties to the Middle East through religious narratives of liberation and redemption. But while it was important to understand the emotional and spiritual power of the Middle East to Black Christianity and the burgeoning Civil Rights movement, Black Islam also laid claim to the region and its histories, including but not limited to Islam's holiest sites, Mecca and Medina. When the Nation of Islam began to emerge as a powerful force within Black radical circles and struggles and when it complemented or oftentimes countered the rhetoric of the Cold War liberalism of the Christian-dominated Civil Rights movement, there was a concomitant rise in the role and place of ancient Egypt, Arab nationalism, and Islamic history within the discourses of Black political culture after 1955. As the struggles around racism and the politics of race began to escalate during this period, Islam came to be seen as an alternative form of radical Black consciousness quite distinct from what was perceived to be the integrationist goals of Black Christianity—a consciousness that was internationalist in nature and more clearly reflected and aligned with the political currents of anticolonialism and revolutionary nationalism that were overtaking the Third World.[36]

Because of the continued massive and violent resistance to desegregation by white America, the persistence of Jim Crow, and the growing dissatisfaction with establishment Civil Rights leaders in the face of apartheid terror, entrenched racism, and the failure of moral appeals to white supremacy, Christianity increasingly came to be seen as inadequate to the political aspirations and spiritual needs of Black peoples in America. In an essay titled "Down at the Cross," published in 1963 in *The Fire Next Time*, James Baldwin openly questioned the role and place of Christianity within Black public life and the increasing popularity of Islam as a force within Black liberationist thought and struggle. According to Baldwin,

> The Christian church itself—again, as distinguished from some if its ministers—sanctified and rejoiced in the conquests of the flag, and encouraged, if it did not formulate, the belief that conquest, and the resulting relative well-being of the Western population, was proof of the favor of God. God had come a long way from the desert—but then so had Allah, though in a very different direction. God, going north, and rising on the wings of power, had become white, and Allah, out of power, and on the dark side of Heaven, had become—for all practical purposes anyway—black.[37]

In Baldwin's analysis and echoed throughout Black communities, God—via Christianity—came to be associated not only with whiteness but also with the powerful imperialist aggressors of the Western world, including the United States. Allah—via Islam—however, was "out of power" and understood as Black. In this way, Baldwin openly questioned the efficacy of Christianity for Black liberation, a critique that also challenged Black identifications with and allegiances to the United States. According to McAlister, although Black Christians continued to seek brotherhood and solidarity with whites despite the continued violence by white Christians against nonviolent Civil Rights activists, "Islam offered an alternative, a basis for a black nationalist consciousness that was separate from the civil rights goals of integration into a white dominated and oppressive nation."[38] Central to the Nation of Islam's appeal was its emphasis on redefining Blackness in the face of continued white violence and racist terror throughout the country. In weaving together redemptive longings, religious sentiment, Black internationalist undertones, and a symbolic return-to-origins narrative, Islam came to be viewed as "the Black man's religion."

For Black peoples in the United States, conversion to Islam suggested a radical redefinition of the self, which began with the name change from one's "slave name" to the moniker "X" (which signified the unknown) and then to an Islamic name (i.e., one's "original name"). A rejection of the name that was imposed by the white slave master who had owned that person's ancestors signified a meaningful attempt to resist the legacy of chattel slavery and the racist history of modernity that gave it birth. By reclaiming agency and self-determination, Black peoples, through their conversion, subtly but poignantly sought to redefine themselves not as property but as person, not as slave but as human.[39]

For Malcolm X and the Nation of Islam, as a result of the violent erasure of Black history through slavery, a narrative of redemption that took on both prophetic and political overtones was closely tied to a newfound self-determination, what the Nation of Islam called "knowledge of self." So with the embrace of a Muslim name and the rejection of the name and identity imposed by whiteness, this newly empowered Black identity also suggested a kind of return to origins and an embrace of a lost past that had been destroyed by the violence of slavery and reinforced by continued white supremacy. This act of renaming, then, challenged the racist logic that came to define America and Black peoples' relationship to it. By claiming authority over historical truth and a preslavery glory, conversion to Islam also meant an embrace of a Black identity that symbolically predated America and challenged American authority over not only the Black past but also a Black future. Conversion then imagined Blackness outside and beyond America, making a Muslim identity, in the words of Amiri Baraka, "post-American."[40]

This remapping of Black identity forged a sense of collective autonomy and symbolic sovereignty from America. And when put in contemporary terms, in an era of decolonization and Third World rebellion, the Nation of Islam's project of redefinition placed Black political identities and possibilities in international terms, creating a sense of community and racial internationalism with the Third World that was part and parcel of the era.

These struggles over race and Black identity during the early years of the Cold War coincided with the broader currents of anticolonial struggles against racism and colonialism. As the national liberation movements were gaining momentum throughout the world, leaders such as Kwame Nkrumah of Ghana, Fidel Castro of Cuba, Ahmed Ben Bella of Algeria, and Gamal Abdel Nasser of Egypt came into global consciousness as a result of their strident critiques of colonialism and its cancerous corollary: white supremacy. This kind of global racial consciousness led to the 1955 Asian–African Conference in Bandung, Indonesia, where twenty-nine countries from Africa and Asia converged to renounce both white supremacy and the false choice—between the United States and the Soviet Union—being offered to newly liberated countries throughout the world. As a clear challenge to white world supremacy and American–Soviet dominance, these countries participating at Bandung created a defiant platform of resistance that resonated throughout the Third World. For Black anticolonialists, particularly with the emergence of the Nation of Islam, this was the beginning of a transformative period in Black political culture, one that would literally and metaphorically remap Black identity and struggle and fundamentally challenge the Cold War liberalism of the time.

In fact, just as the Nation of Islam sought to redefine Black identities through a redemptive past and the creation of an independent future, Third World peoples summoned similar desires for collective renewal by trying to create what Fanon called the "new man" in relation to Europe, new identities that the national liberation movements sought to bring into existence from the ashes of European colonialism. Just as occurred within the Nation of Islam, these attempts at redefinition also included name changes, such as when the Belgian Congo became the Republic of the Congo upon independence in 1960, the British colony of the Gold Coast became Ghana, and the Kingdom of Iraq became the Republic of Iraq in 1958. By attempting to unburden themselves of the weight of whiteness and the catastrophe of colonialism, which had imposed European languages, ideas, and institutions, Third World peoples sought to transform themselves from protectorates and colonies into sovereign nations and from colonial subjects into political agents controlling their own destinies. Like Black Muslims, the peoples of Africa and Asia sought to make themselves agents of history instead of passive victims of it.

In imagining Black liberation beyond the United States, the Nation of Islam internationalized the fate of Black peoples, placing their struggles firmly within the massive global resistance to white supremacy that was taking place. In fact, as countries throughout the Third World struggled for national liberation, the language of nationhood became a powerful trope in the era of decolonization, serving as a potent organizing principle for resistance and a platform for self-determination. The Nation of Islam also tapped into this vein of nationalist sentiment, using the language of "the nation" to harness and provide a vehicle for centuries of Black longing for freedom. For the Nation of Islam, the "nation" it sought to create was a separate one from the United States, a distinct entity from the wilderness of whiteness that would claim a distinct history and destiny and tap into a deep reservoir of worldwide rebellion that would serve as a symbolic ideal, if not one that would inspire hope. And in doing so, the organization's call for nationhood also linked Black peoples' battles against white supremacy in the United States with the battles of those in the Third World, globally enlarging Black peoples' sense of racial community so that not only was the scale of Black struggle expanded but so was the scope of Black peoples' allies.

This grammar of resistance centered on Islam as the focal point for refashioning a new Black identity that had built upon earlier periods of Black anticolonial sensibilities, one that sought to forge transnational links with the larger Muslim Third World, affiliations that traded upon the global scope of Islam as a major world religion. In doing so, the Nation of Islam sought to expand the geographic referents of Black identity beyond the exclusivity of the continent of Africa to include much of the nonwhite world, making Blacks "aware of their cultural and historical connections to Africa and the effects of Western imperialism and colonialism on all the areas of the world where people of color lived."[41] As part of this imaginative geography, the NOI employed numerous rhetorical strategies to define Black identity within and against the United States, as well as in relation to the expanded definitions of

Blackness central to the Nation of Islam. Terms such as *Asiatic, Asian Black nation, Afro-Asiatic Black man,* and *Asiatic Black man* were constantly and consistently deployed to provide an alternative genealogy for Black peoples in America, one that respatialized Black identity without exclusively looking at Africa as the site for the recuperation, recovery, and reconstitution of Black history. Central to this vision of Blackness was the role of the Muslim Third World, whose broader geography, which included the Middle East, was also employed by the NOI within its construction of Black identity. As Elijah Muhammad says of Black peoples in America in his seminal text *Message to the Black Man,* "We are descendants of the Asian black nation . . . the rich Nile Valley of Egypt and the present seat of the Holy City, Mecca, Arabia."[42]

Through the significance and influence of Malcolm X and the Nation of Islam, Mecca, as well as the larger Muslim Third World, became a symbolic center for reorienting Black identities in the era of decolonization. Through conversion and a reclamation of history and destiny, Black Muslims built upon the rich resource of anticolonial defiance that was part and parcel of the era, a fabric of resistance that brought Black Islam, the Muslim Third World, and Afro-diasporic radicalism together to challenge white world supremacy. By expanding the geographic referents of Blackness, Black Islam did not map the potential for Black liberation onto the domestic space of U.S. nationalism. Instead, Black Muslims imagined a very different kind of community that was not national in character but rather was diasporic in its consciousness, as "the community it envisioned provided an alternative to— and in some sense a fundamental critique of—the nation-state. [For] African-American Muslims could claim a symbolic counter-citizenship, an identity that challenged black incorporation into the dominant discourse of Judeo-Christian Americanness."[43] In challenging the bounds of U.S. nationalism and in imagining U.S.-based Muslims as part of the larger Muslim Third World, Black Islam challenged the hypernationalism of Cold War America—a project of empire building that assumed an aggressive U.S. foreign policy in the Third World and a liberal narrative of race that envisioned Black equality within a domesticated Civil Rights framework. But this countercitizenship for Black Muslims instead found a larger community of belonging that could be called the Muslim International, a space in which, in his political vision, Malcolm X was deeply invested as he connected Harlem to Mecca, Cairo to Bandung, Algiers to Palestine, and every place in between.

Respect the Architect

For Malcolm, Islam would become the link not only between Africa and Asia but also between Black Muslims in the United States and the broader Muslim International. As an alternative racial compass that gave a new political direction to Black quests for freedom, Islam provided a pathway and a road map that led to the Muslim Third World of Africa and Asia during the anticolonial struggles of the Cold War. As Malcolm said in his opening remarks at a New York gathering of international dignitaries from Syria, Egypt, and the United Nations, "Islam is the greatest unifying force in the Dark World today. The unity of 600 million Moslems from the China Sea to the shores of West Africa, is a force and a factor that has long been recognized by the major powers of the world."[44]

As U.S. involvement in Africa and Asia increased throughout the Cold War, the anticolonial politics of the Muslim Third World became a more prominent part of Black radical political culture. Gamal Abdel Nasser, of Egypt, was one of the key figures during this period, for not only did he attend the 1955 Bandung Conference, but he was also instrumental in hosting the follow-up event in Cairo in 1957, the Afro-Asian People's Solidarity Conference. By weathering the Suez Crisis of 1956, in which he defiantly stood up to France, England, and Israel, Nasser solidified his place as an anticolonial hero among Black radicals in the United States, the Muslim Third World, and throughout Africa and Asia. Having influenced a broader Pan-Arab anticolonial movement in the 1950s, the "Nasserian Revolution" spread to surrounding countries, such as Iraq, Syria, and elsewhere, overthrowing European and U.S. client states in the process and sending shock waves throughout the capitals of the colonial powers. In addition, his visit to Harlem along with Fidel Castro, who met Malcolm X there, captured the imagination of Black activists in the United States. As one observer noted, "We have a unique and rare personality in the person of Gamal Abdul Nasser. This man's ancestry is African and Arabic, but he refuses to follow the classic road of championing white supremacy and exploiting black people. . . .

[Nasser] made it scientifically clear that Africans, the Arabs and the Muslims have one common enemy, European imperialism. He made the freedom of Africa a major priority along with Arab unity and Muslim cooperation."[45]

Soon after the Suez Crisis, which had galvanized Black Muslims and non-Muslims in the United States, Malcolm organized a meeting on colonial and neocolonial issues, bringing together government representatives from Iraq, Morocco, Egypt, Ghana, and Sudan, all of whom sent greetings to Nasser at Cairo's 1957 Afro-Asian follow-up meeting to Bandung.[46] In addition, Elijah Muhammad also sent a letter addressed to Nasser, writing, "Freedom, justice and equality is of far-reaching importance, not only to you in the East, but also to 17,000,000 of your long-lost brothers of African-Asian descent here in the West."[47] Malcolm was also a huge admirer of Nasser, and he said that when Nasser nationalized the Suez Canal, Europe was beside itself: "It scared them to death—why? Because Egypt is in Africa. In fact, Egypt is in both Africa and Asia."[48] For Black Muslims in the United States, not only was Egypt the center of African civilization and proof of Black historical greatness, but it was also now a Muslim country. In linking Black greatness and Islam, Nasser and Egypt came to represent a powerful symbol that connected Africa and Asia, a space in which the Muslim Third World and Black Islam forged a defiant anticolonial posture against white supremacy.

As the Cold War continued and as Black demands for equality intensified, so too did the presence of the Muslim Third World within the political imaginations of Malcolm X and other Black activists in the United States. For although Egypt would reappear as a stage for Malcolm's enduring political vision in his address to the Organization of African Unity there in 1964, other sites in the Muslim Third World, such as Bandung, Indonesia, would more immediately capture the zeitgeist of Third World radicalism that was overtaking the globe. As a result of the 1955 Asian–African Conference in Bandung, Malcolm spoke with an Indonesian delegation in Harlem in 1957, saying, "The 90 million Moslems in Indonesia are only a small part of the 600 million more in other parts of the Dark World, Asia and Africa. We here in America were of the Moslem world before being brought into slavery, and today with the entire dark world awakening, our Moslem brothers in the East have a great interest in our welfare."[49] Malcolm reiterated the links between Black Muslims in the United States and those in the broader Muslim Third World as part of a strategy to gain allies and internationalize the plight of Black peoples during the height of Cold War repression and Third World decolonization. And like Egypt, Indonesia became an iconic site for Malcolm X and his relationship to the Muslim Third World, as the landmark Bandung Conference left an indelible imprint on his deepening political vision.

"I Say You're Afraid to Bleed!" Bandung Dreaming

The 1955 Afro–Asian Conference in Bandung, Indonesia, was arguably the most important international gathering of the century, one with incredible implications not only for the Third World, Europe, and the Cold War but also for Black peoples in the United States. Occurring just ten years after the end of World War II and amid tremendous political upheaval, the twenty-nine countries that Bandung brought together represented half of the world's population at the time. Held in the Muslim country of Indonesia, in the city of Bandung, almost half of the countries that attended were from the Muslim Third World, which was part of the reason the conference appealed so much to Malcolm X and became the source of much of his racial internationalism and desire to connect Black peoples in the United States with those in the Third World. The Bandung Conference, then, becomes a powerful and enduring moment in which to explore the politics of the Muslim International, its possibilities, and its pitfalls in the era of decolonization, Cold War rivalry, and the emergence of Malcolm X and Black Islam in the United States.

As decolonization continued to spread throughout the Third World, new vistas and possibilities for newly independent countries began to take shape. With the Cold War presenting only two seemingly different possibilities and with the Third World as the literal battleground on which this Cold War was fought, leaders of newly independent countries sought to imagine alternatives to the bipolar world they had been thrust into. In the shadows of U.S.–Soviet interference in the affairs of newly independent countries, the stated position of Bandung was a call to end colonialism and neocolonialism from European powers, the

United States, and the Soviet Union and a vow to support the anticolonial struggles of countries still under the boot of colonialism and the eventual creation of what was called the Non-Aligned Movement, a third path that refused both U.S. and Soviet dogma.[50]

At the opening address of the conference, Indonesian president Ahmed Sukarno captured the hopeful tone in his speech, "Let a New Asia and a New Africa Be Born," when he declared that "the nations of Asia and Africa are no longer the tools and playthings" of Europe, the United States, or the Soviets.[51] Bandung was more than a shot across the bow at the powerful; it was a gathering that held the promise of a radically different world order from the centuries of white power, colonialism, and capitalist control of almost the entire globe. And so it's no surprise that the conference and the implications it held became a battleground upon which questions of sovereignty, white supremacy, and nationalism would unfold. In fact, Bandung challenged the white world, foregrounding the role of race in both international and domestic affairs. For the United States, which was not invited and did not formally recognize the conference, Bandung posed considerable challenges to its dominion. Not only did Bandung present the possibility of alliances between African and Asian countries, which deeply troubled the State Department, but it also shed light on the United States' strengthening of European control over the Third World, its imperial designs under the guise of anticommunism, and its treatment of racial minorities within its borders, especially Black peoples.

As a result, the United States carefully sought to manage the racial implications of the conference. Secretary of State Dulles feared the effects of Bandung, going so far as to circulate a telegram stating, "If without strong-arm methods Conference could be prevented or considerable number significant countries influenced decline attend US would welcome such outcome."[52] But Bandung did happen, though the United States sought to disrupt the conference "unofficially" by parlaying Cold War alliances and pressuring sympathetic allies at the conference to undercut anti-U.S. sentiment among the delegates. Even shrewder was the means by which the United States sought to contain and even undermine Bandung's emphasis on race, as the State Department used Blackness as a tool to present an image of the United States as racially progressing. In fact, the State Department sent Black journalist Carl

Rowan to offset and even challenge the critiques of the United States and its foreign and domestic policies. In addition, Congressman Adam Clayton Powell also attended, despite initially being discouraged by the State Department and the CIA because of his maverick liberalism, but his participation there was somewhat ambiguous. For while Powell and Malcolm X considered each other friends and often spoke at rallies together, Powell was a shrewd and intelligent negotiator of political fault lines. His comments at Bandung were ultimately a defense of the United States and "racial progress," suggesting an evolving and re-formist posture on the part of Eisenhower and U.S. foreign policy. Years later, Powell would write, "Bandung was a pilgrimage to a new Mecca. I was one of the pilgrims and I went because I had to. . . . I had no idea that I would be more than an interested bystander rubbing elbows with history and breathing in the ferment of a new world. I went to Bandung knowing it could be one of the most important events of the twentieth century. I left Bandung knowing that it had been."[53]

Expatriate novelist Richard Wright also attended Bandung, and in *The Color Curtain*, his book-length exploration of his time at the conference, Wright wrote that Bandung was a "judgment on the Western world." He went on to say, "I'm an American Negro; as such, I've had a burden of race consciousness. So have these people," adding that as a Black person, he could further identify with "the despised, the insulted, the hurt, the dispossessed—in short, the underdogs of the human race who were meeting."[54]

Although Rowan, Powell, and Wright attended Bandung, many prominent Black activists could not go, primarily because of the Cold War repression of the Black Left. Both Paul Robeson and W. E. B. Du Bois were not allowed to attend, because their passports had been revoked by the U.S. government. But this could not prevent them from participating in the spirit of Bandung, as they still sent telegrams of solidarity to its delegates. As the spirit of Third World liberation suffused radical Black political culture in the United States, enlarging the scale, scope, and stakes of Black struggle, the Muslim Third World continued to influence Black political culture through the Nation of Islam and Malcolm X. And Bandung was no exception, as it would become a rallying cry for Black activists, including the Revolutionary Action Movement and others who saw themselves as part of the Bandung world.[55]

Malcolm X invoked Bandung often, most notably in his famous "Message to the Grassroots" speech in Detroit in 1963.[56] For Malcolm, the Bandung Conference of Afro-Asian unity was a lens not only for understanding the fractures that exist within Black communities in the United States but also for placing the struggles of Black peoples within a global context. In "Message to the Grassroots," Malcolm used the Bandung Conference as the dominant frame for his wide-ranging and penetrating critique of U.S. nationalism, Black radicalism, and decolonization in the Third World. Using the framework of the conference and the links he saw between Black and Third World peoples and a history of global white supremacy, Malcolm discussed revolutionary violence and mobilized tropes such as "Black revolution versus the Negro Revolution" and "the House Negro/Field Negro" as a means to critically engage ideas about race and national belonging, armed struggle versus nonviolence, American nationalism and racial internationalism, anticolonialism versus anticommunism, and imagining Black peoples as national minorities or as global majorities.

In the "Message to the Grassroots" speech, Malcolm said that Bandung was the "first unity meeting in centuries of black people" in which "all the nations came together. There were dark nations from Africa and Asia. . . . All of them were black, brown, red, or yellow." By deploying the Nation of Islam's expanded definition of "Black" to include all nonwhites, Malcolm asserted, "The number one thing that was not allowed to attend the Bandung conference was the white man," framing Bandung as an antiracist and anticolonial gathering that was a symbol of defiance against the colonial and imperial powers. At Bandung, Malcolm said, these countries "began to recognize who their enemy was. The same man that was colonizing our people in Kenya was colonizing our people in the Congo. The same one in the Congo was colonizing our people in South Africa, and in Southern Rhodesia, and in Burma, and in India, and in Afghanistan, and in Pakistan. They realized all over the world where the dark man was being oppressed, he was being oppressed by the white man."[57]

By clearly defining Bandung as an antiracist and anticolonial gathering, Malcolm used the conference as a lens to define Black liberation struggles in the United States, saying, "When you and I here in Detroit and in Michigan and in America who have been awakened today look around us, we too realize here in America we all have a common enemy, whether he's in Georgia or Michigan, whether he's in California or New York. He's *the same man* . . . so what we have to do is what they did."[58] In analogizing Black peoples' struggles in the United States to those of the Third World, Malcolm used the Bandung Conference not only as a metaphor for understanding Black disunity and the tensions between the Civil Rights establishment and the Black anticolonial Left but also as a possible model of organizing the disparate and diverse threads of Black resistance to white racism.

In mapping Third World solidarity against white supremacy onto the racial terrain of the United States and arguing that the man who colonized Pakistan, Afghanistan, the Congo, and Kenya is the "same man" who is in Georgia, Michigan, California, and New York, Malcolm radically challenged the sacred narrative of American exceptionalism. As an idea that intimately defines the nation, American exceptionalism continues to reproduce the idea of a benevolent United States rooted in the principles of freedom and democracy. These principles distinguish the history of the United States from European empire building and cast the United States as democratic and distinct from European colonialism, even going so far as to position the United States in opposition to the idea of colonial power itself. As a result, American exceptionalism generates tremendous ideological capital for the United States, and it became a central part of Cold War policy when the United States sought to woo the Third World away from Soviet influence with claims of democracy and freedom. Malcolm's insight in linking European colonial power and America's history of racial violence and segregation was brilliant in that it revealed the racial matrix that was determining the postwar landscape. But beyond that, Malcolm laid bare to both U.S.-based Blacks and those in the Third World, that white supremacy is a global phenomenon endemic to the very fabric of European and American identity.

In using Bandung to set up an analogy between Black peoples in the United States and peoples of the Third World, Malcolm explored the role of armed struggle throughout history and particularly in the Third World as a means to challenge the dominant ethos of U.S. Civil Rights, which subjected Black life to white violence under a mantra of nonviolence. Malcolm said, "You haven't got a revolution that doesn't involve bloodshed. And you're afraid to bleed. I said, you're afraid to bleed,"[59] chastising and challenging his audience at the same time. But Malcolm brilliantly followed this with a critique of Black soldiers who fight in America's wars abroad: "How are you going to be nonviolent in Mississippi, as violent as you were in Korea? How can you justify being nonviolent in Mississippi and Alabama, when your churches are being bombed, and your little girls are being murdered, and at the same time you're going to get violent with Hitler, and Tojo, and somebody else that you don't even know?"[60] Malcolm raised the question of Black participation in American wars as a means to interrogate the very rationales given to fight those wars. That is, if America fights wars for democracy and freedom, then why are Black peoples excluded from the benefits of that very "freedom"? Malcolm answered his own rhetorical question by saying, "If violence is wrong in America, violence is wrong abroad. If it's wrong to be violent defending black women and black children and black babies and black men, then it's wrong for America to draft us and make us violent abroad in defense of her."[61]

Made famous within hip-hop culture over three decades later as the sampled introduction to Gang Starr's classic song "Tonz O' Gunz," Malcolm's quote exposed the Cold War Civil Rights maxim that "Negroes are Americans" and challenged the Cold War liberalism of Blacks who were fighting communism abroad, spilling and shedding their blood for America but not for Black freedom. In doing so, Malcolm poignantly implicated and indicted the very basis of Cold War liberalism when he critiqued the role and place of violence and nonviolence within Black liberation movements and in Cold War discourse. Malcolm's poignant assertion that Black peoples are "afraid to bleed" when it comes to revolution is underscored by the occasions when they do in fact fight, bleed, and likely die—at the hands and at the request of white America in her imperial adventures abroad and against the very people in the Third World who would likely be allies of Blacks seeking freedom in the United States. Malcolm brilliantly underscores the role of violence within American society and the contradictory roles that Black peoples play within it, striking at the heart of the liberal logic of the warfare state: that to murder for the state is legal and worthy of medals and commendations, but when the state and its racist and brutal authority are challenged, then nonviolence is the sanctioned and privileged means to achieve it.

In the speech, Malcolm invoked defiant self-defense, guerrilla wars such as the Mau Mau against the British in Kenya, the Algerian struggle against the French, and other armed struggles as a central part of his liberation theology. And like Frantz Fanon, Malcolm clearly understood armed struggle's parameters. In fact, Fanon claimed that decolonization was a violent phenomenon, giving theoretical, ideological, and even ethical support to armed struggle against racist power. Despite popular opinion, Malcolm's rhetoric of armed struggle and self-defense wasn't misplaced or even romantic. Instead, he expressed an acute and perceptive understanding of the role of violence in American history. For violence, through Manifest Destiny, established "civilization" and "democracy" in the United States, and it revealed the central place of violence within the formation, perpetuation, and legitimation of the American state. Malcolm's embrace of armed struggle, then—like the Black Panthers' years later—was a way of seizing the interpretive authority over democracy in America, for violence is the mechanism through which American democracy has been established and maintained, both domestically and abroad. And if violence is the necessary path toward democracy, as only America's past and present has proven, then in America, democracy, to paraphrase Fanon, is always a violent phenomenon.

In "Message to the Grassroots," Malcolm also examined the difference between the "Black Revolution" and the "Negro Revolution." More than focusing on a distinction between armed struggle and nonviolence or between Black radicalism and Civil Rights, Malcolm struck at the heart of the politics of the Cold War era. In asserting that the Black revolution is "worldwide in scope" and is "sweeping Asia, sweeping Africa, is rearing its head in Latin America," Malcolm underscored the racial alchemy that undergirded his political perspectives, using a racial logic in which "Black" had a broad meaning. As he explained in another speech, "The Black revolution has been taking place in Africa and Asia and Latin America. When I say Black, I mean non-white, black, brown, red or yellow."[62] As a result, when Malcolm delineated between the "Black Revolution" and the "Negro Revolution," he was expanding the geographic and ideological reference points for Black liberation. But he was also ultimately commenting on the differences between "Black" and "Negro," for as Malcolm would say, "Negro" had little to no coherence outside the United States; so when Black peoples referred to themselves as "Negroes," their history went only as far back as the word *Negro* goes, and they had no historical legibility outside the United States. "Black," however, stretched beyond the borders of America and tapped into a longer and deeper history that gave Black peoples a legibility outside the American nation-state. For Malcolm, then, "Black" becomes a political identity that is rooted in the antiracist struggle against white supremacy and is not nationally bounded, whereas the "Negro Revolution" is a central part of the Cold War liberalism that is contained within a national framework, the liberal narrative of rights that the Cold War ushered in. The "Negro Revolution" is domestic and national; the "Black Revolution" is global and international.

Malcolm's internationalization of the political struggle against white supremacy was underscored when he used the history of the "House Negro/Field Negro" dichotomy in the "Message to the Grassroots" speech. Of the many brilliant axioms that Malcolm invoked throughout his writings, speeches, and interviews, the House Negro/Field Negro trope was arguably the most compelling, bringing together various strands of Malcolm's thought around class, resistance, authenticity, and Black belonging in America, while also challenging Cold War liberalism and Black peoples' relationship to the anticolonial impulses in the Third World. In the "Message to the Grassroots," Malcolm invoked the House Negro versus the Field Negro in order to comment on contemporary Black political culture during the Cold War, Black liberation struggles, and Third World anticolonialism. According to Malcolm, during slavery there were two types of Black people: "The house Negroes—they lived in the house with master, they dressed pretty good, they ate good 'cause they ate his food . . . and they loved their master more than the master loved himself. They would give their life to save the master's house quicker than the master would. The house Negro, if the master said, 'We got a good house here,' the house Negro would say, 'Yeah, we got a good house here.' Whenever the master said 'we,' he said 'we.'"[63]

Malcolm continued by describing the ideological implications of the House Negro, saying, "If the master's house caught on fire, the house Negro would fight harder to put the blaze out than the master would. If the master got sick, the house Negro would say, 'What's the matter, boss, we sick?' We sick! He identified himself with his master more than his master identified with himself." Malcolm drove his point home saying, "And if you came to the house Negro and said, 'Let's run away, let's escape, let's separate,' the house Negro would look at you and say, 'Man, you crazy. What you mean, separate? Where is there a better house than this? Where can I wear better clothes than this? Where can I eat better food than this?'"[64]

For Malcolm this was in stark contrast to the Field Negro. "Those were the masses. . . . The Negro in the field caught hell. He ate left-overs. . . . The field Negro was beaten from morning to night. He lived in a shack, in a hut. He wore old, castoff clothes. He hated his master. . . . He was intelligent. That house Negro loved his master." Malcolm continued, "When the house caught on fire, he didn't try and put it out; that field Negro prayed for a wind. . . . When the master got sick, the field Negro prayed that he'd die. If someone come to the field Negro and said, 'Let's separate, let's run,' he didn't say, 'Where we going?' He'd say, 'Any place is better than here.' You've got field Negroes in America today. I'm a field Negro. The masses are the field Negroes. When they see this man's house on fire, you don't hear these little Negroes talking about 'our government is in trouble.' They say, 'The government is in trouble.' Imagine a Negro: 'Our government!'"[65]

Malcolm's discussion of the House Negro and the Field Negro is a telling and revealing look into the radical critique he brought to bear on Cold War liberalism. On the one hand, Malcolm's discussion served to critique Black political culture and the possibilities of freedom within the context of the Cold War and worldwide anticolonialism. But by invoking this powerfully symbolic trope, Malcolm also revealed the legacies of slavery that continue to persist, spatializing the ideological differences in order to make them more apparent and using them as analogs to the current predicament of Black peoples in the United States. For Malcolm, his signifying suggested that the master's house was the United States, and he strongly implied that Black peoples should see themselves as "field Negroes," as separate from this American nation, at least ideologically and politically. When Malcolm's argument is understood in the context of his larger analysis of Third World struggles, and Black peoples' relationships to them, he was suggesting, as he did throughout the speech, that the Third World was where the possibilities for freedom lay for Black peoples.

As a powerful document that exists somewhere between song and speech, epic poem and manifesto, "The Message to the Grassroots" brilliantly reveals Malcolm's dynamic political vision that challenged Cold War liberalism, the Civil Rights movement's containment of Black freedom within the United States, and Black complicity with the expansion of U.S. empire in the Third World. For what gave the speech its ideological framework, internal logic, and political urgency was the Bandung Conference, which he invoked and which deeply inspired Black radicals in the 1950s and on into the Black Power era of the late 1960s. This "spirit of Bandung" was what Malcolm invoked later in his life when he linked European and America forms of racist power, claiming, "It has been since the Bandung Conference that all dark people on the earth have been striding towards freedom . . . but there are 10 million Blacks here in America yet suffering the worst form of enslavement . . . mentally blinded by the white man, unable now to see that America is the citadel of white colonialism, the bulwark of white imperialism . . . the slave master of slave masters. . . . At Bandung they had to agree that as long as they remained divided a handful of whites would continue to rule them. But once our African [and] Asian brothers put their religious and political differences into the background, their unity has had sufficient force to break the bonds of colonialism, imperialism, Europeanism . . . which are all only diplomatic terms for the same thing, white supremacy."[66]

The iconic place that Bandung held for Malcolm X and within the Black radical imagination is indicative of the larger influence that the Muslim Third World played within Black political culture and of the historical trajectory of the Muslim International. In "The Message to the Grassroots," Malcolm's use of Bandung to frame and contextualize his discussion of armed struggle, the "Black revolution and the Negro revolution," and the "field Negro and the house Negro" gave his ideas an internationalist and anticolonial contour, for he framed Black destiny as a choice between imperial power and the Third World, whiteness and freedom. While "The Message to the Grassroots" and the "spirit of Bandung" are a central part of the Muslim International, Malcolm X would elaborate on his political vision as the Muslim Third World continued to shape and define him.

"What Do We Care about Odds?"
Ballots, Bullets, and the Prospects for Freedom

From Bandung to Detroit, Harlem, and beyond, Malcolm X's speeches, interviews, and travels enlarged his political imagination as the Muslim Third World of Egypt, Palestine, Algeria, and elsewhere continued to play a central part in defining his political vision of internationalism. The political, ideological, and spiritual links he forged with the Muslim Third World and the continents of Africa and Asia through the formation of two organizations, Muslim Mosque Inc. and the Organization of Afro-American Unity (OAAU), were a compelling contribution to the history of the Muslim International, for in his speeches and interviews in the last years of his life, Malcolm continued to argue for the necessity of Third World solidarity across religious, racial, and national lines, in order to challenge European and U.S. power.

Even upon leaving the Nation of Islam and making his pilgrimage to Mecca, Malcolm continued to center race as a fundamental part of his political project. Traveling extensively throughout the Muslim Third World and the African continent on two separate occasions after his break with the Nation of Islam, Malcolm visited Saudi Arabia, Lebanon, Egypt, Sudan, Nigeria, Senegal, Morocco, Ghana, Algeria, Tanzania, Guinea, and several other countries and met with various leaders and heads of state, including Julius Nyere of Tanzania, Kwame Nkrumah of Ghana, Milton Obote of Uganda, Jomo Kenyatta of Kenya, Gamal Abdel Nasser of Egypt, and Ahmed Sékou Touré of Guinea, as well as several other elected officials and ministers in Africa and the Middle East. In developing his insurgent Muslim Internationalism and his developing Pan-Africanism, Malcolm's central concern was to internationalize the suffering of Black peoples in the United States by taking it to formal channels, such as the United Nations, a space through which Malcolm felt that the Third World could then be a more just arbiter than the United States of Black justice and dignity.

Upon leaving the Nation of Islam, Malcolm sought to define his political agendas more clearly, so he formed Muslim Mosque Inc. and the OAAU as vehicles to connect his burgeoning Muslim Internationalism and Pan-Africanism. Muslim Mosque Inc., according to Malcolm, was a means of establishing "religious authenticity with the Muslim world," and once that was established, he "set up the Organization of Afro-American Unity and took immediate steps to make certain that [U.S.-based Blacks] would be in direct contact with our African brothers on the African continent."[67] The OAAU was based on Kwame Nkrumah's Organization of African Unity, with Malcolm clearly borrowing from anticolonial frameworks and histories from the African continent as a means of harnessing Black peoples' political desires in the Americas. For Malcolm, the OAAU was a hemispheric organization, for he saw "Afro-Americans" as a hemispheric term, not confined to just the United States, but including the geographies of South America, Central America, the Caribbean, and the entirety of North America.

As Malcolm would say about Muslim Mosque Inc. and the OAAU, "The first step has been taken, brothers and sisters, since Garvey died, to actually establish contact between the twenty-two million Black Americans with our brothers and sisters back home [and it] was done by two organizations. Done first by Muslim Mosque, which gives us direct ties to our brothers and sisters in Asia and Africa who are Muslims. You know you've got to unite with them, because there are 700 million Muslims and we sure need to stop being the minority and become part of the majority. So as Muslims, we united with our Muslim brothers in Africa and Asia. And as members of the Organization of Afro-American Unity, we set on a platform to unite our people on this continent with our people on the mother continent." According to Malcolm, these two organizations "frightened many interests in this country" who didn't want to see "the successful regrouping or organizing of any faction in this country whose thinking pattern is international rather than national. Whose thought patterns, whose hopes and aspirations are worldly rather that just within the context of the United States border, or the borderline of the United States." He goes on to say, "This has been the purpose of the OAAU and the Muslim Mosque: to give us direct links, direct contact, direct communication and cooperation with our brothers and sisters all over the earth. And once we are successful in uniting ourselves with our people all over the world, it puts us in a position where we are no longer a minority who can be abused and walked upon. We become part of the majority."[68]

The centerpiece of Malcolm's political project was to internationalize the condition of Black peoples in the United States. In one of his most powerful speeches, titled "The Ballot or the Bullet," Malcolm X unequivocally laid out the futility of Black electoral participation, saying, "The government has failed us." While acknowledging that the Black vote can influence elections, Malcolm pointed out that despite this influence, Black peoples have received absolutely nothing for it, as the legislative, judicial, and executive branches use all manner and means to undermine Black electoral power, including the lack of enforcement of legal protections, filibuster, and gerrymandering. As a result, Malcolm argued, Blacks are "trapped, double trapped, triple trapped," adding that to vote under these conditions, "you're not only a chump, but you're a traitor to your race." Malcolm's clear rejection of Black electoral participation and the Civil Rights paradigm led him to the conclusion that Black freedom will come only by using what he called "new methods."

In making his case, Malcolm argued that the United States is "just as much a colonial power" as England or France ever was and that just as countries in Africa and Asia are seeking liberation, Black peoples in the United States should as well. Malcolm pointed out that revolutions, armed struggle, and guerrilla warfare are what has succeeded against white power in other parts of Africa and Asia and that Black youth in the United States "are disillusioned": "They've become disenchanted. They've become dissatisfied, and in their frustrations they want action . . . they don't want to hear anything about the odds are against us. What do we care about odds?"[69] In framing the United States as a colonial power, Malcolm linked Black youth with the popular uprisings of the Third World in their struggles for national liberation against colonial regimes by any means, and he suggested that Black peoples in the United States should internationalize themselves by moving from a Civil Rights framework to a human rights framework in order to get out from under "the jurisdiction of Uncle Sam" and into the Third World, "where our African brothers can throw their weight on our side, where our Asian brothers can throw their weight on our side, where our Latin-American brothers can throw their weight on our side."[70]

Malcolm's distinction between "Civil Rights" and "human rights" was really a coded distinction between Cold War liberalism and internationalism, between the United States and the Third World, which Malcolm saw as a more just arbiter of Black claims to dignity and justice. As a critique of the Civil Rights movement, Malcolm's desire to shift to a human rights perspective fundamentally challenged Cold War liberalism, which sought to contain Black liberation within the framework of U.S. nationalism. In Malcolm's dismissal of the possibility that Black peoples in the United States would be granted full equality through the electoral process or by legislative and judicial decree, his embrace of "human rights" imagined Black freedom into the Third World and also challenged the very basis of the United States' legal, political, and moral framework of democracy and rights. In addition, as Malcolm said in his "Ballot or the Bullet" speech, "You don't take your case to the criminal; you take the criminal to court."[71] For Malcolm X, the internationalization of the plight of Black peoples in America into a broader forum would force the United States to undergo scrutiny and challenge from the Third World. Malcolm felt that the pressure the United States would have to face would tilt the balance of power to Africa, Asia, and Latin America, as it would reveal U.S. hypocrisies, undermine the country's foreign policy objectives in the Third World, and expose the country's own brutal extension of European colonial racism.

For Malcolm then, the remapping of Black liberation was not just an ideological gesture. It was a tactical one as well and was central to his political vision in forming the Muslim Mosque Inc. and his Organization of Afro-American Unity. In his numerous travels throughout Africa and the Muslim Third World, Malcolm sought to gain support abroad from heads of state to bring the plight of Black peoples in the United States to the United Nations, in the same way that apartheid South Africa was being discussed in the United Nations. As Malcolm told an audience in Rochester, New York, in 1965, African leaders understood that as a Civil Rights issue, the circumstances of Black peoples in the United States could not be discussed at the United Nations, because it would violate the laws and the rules of protocol within that forum. But if the issue were to be framed as "human rights," then it would become international and fall under the jurisdiction of the U.N. Charter. For Malcolm, the central mission of his OAAU was to "come up with a program that would make our grievances international and make the world see that our problem was no longer a Negro problem or an American problem, but a human problem. A problem for humanity."[72] Echoing Du Bois's claim that the Black condition in the United States is but a local phase of a global problem, Malcolm took his appeal to that iconic

site of ancient Black greatness, Egypt—that country of the Muslim
Third World that was also a beacon of hope for Black and Third World
peoples worldwide for its defiant stand against colonial powers over the
Suez Crisis, and a country that Malcolm would use as a stage upon
which to express his internationalist vision for Black liberation.

In Cairo, Malcolm attended what was billed as "the African Summit," the second meeting of the Organization of African Unity, which
had been formed by Kwame Nkrumah in 1963. At this meeting, which
was attended by nearly all of the thirty-four African heads of state, with
the Egyptian president Gamal Abdel Nasser giving the welcome address,
Malcolm issued an eight-page memorandum on his own OAAU let-
terhead asking for African unity and for the case of Black peoples in
the United States to be taken up by an African country in the United
Nations. As the head of the Organization of Afro-American Unity, Malcolm implored the delegates to be aware of the "imperialist wolf" that is
America and to recognize the plight of twenty-two million Black peoples
who were trapped within America's borders after having been brought
there "forcibly in chains from this mother continent."[73] He explained to
the delegation that if apartheid South Africa could be discussed at the
United Nations, then so too should the plight of Black peoples in the
United States. For Malcolm, it was vital that he challenge the United
States Information Agency (USIA) and the State Department's programs
to manage America's image abroad, particularly around race, so as not
to impact African and Asian nations negatively. In so doing he brought
up the issue of the recently passed Civil Rights Act in the United States,
saying, "Many of you have been led to believe that the much publicized,
recently passed civil rights bill is a sign that America is making a sincere
effort to correct the injustices we have suffered there. This propaganda
maneuver is part of her deceit and trickery to keep African nations from
condemning her racist practices before the United Nations."[74]

As Malcolm detailed the delays in the enforcement of the legislation that resulted from *Brown v. Board of Education*, having been passed
ten years earlier, he asserted, "These are nothing but tricks of the century's leading neo-colonialist power. Surely, our intellectually mature
African brothers will not fall for this trickery." Malcolm implored the
heads of state to support the internationalization of the plight of U.S.-
based Black peoples in the United Nations, explaining, "Our freedom

struggle for human dignity is no longer confined to the domestic jurisdiction of the United States." He concluded that not to do so would be a threat to global stability, because Black peoples in the United States were ready to use armed struggle in order to achieve their equality. Malcolm closed by sounding a sage warning: "No one knows the master better than his servant. We have been servants in America for over 300 years. We have a thorough, inside knowledge of this man who calls himself 'Uncle Sam.' Therefore you must heed our warning. Don't escape from European colonialism only to become more enslaved by deceitful, 'friendly' American dollarism."[75]

Not only did Malcolm defiantly and poignantly call for African unity to challenge America's Cold War designs in the Third World, but he also laid bare the extension of white supremacy in the post–World War II moment, using the metaphor of slavery to caution the delegation not to "escape" from Europe only to be "enslaved" by America. The OAU followed up by passing a resolution that on the one hand recognized "the enactment of the Civil Rights Act designed to secure for American Negroes their basic human rights" but on the other hand stated that the OAU was "deeply disturbed by continuing manifestations of racial bigotry and racial oppression against Negro citizens in the United States of America."[76] For Malcolm, this was a success, which he told his supporters, writing to them while he was in Cairo and explaining that what he was trying to do was "very dangerous": "It is a direct threat to the entire international system of racist exploitation. It is a threat to discrimination in all its international forms. Therefore if I die or am killed before making it back to the States, you can rest assured that what I've already set in motion will never be stopped. . . . our problem has been *internationalized.*"[77] Malcolm clearly recognized the stakes involved, saying in an interview in Cairo that his appearance at the OAU meeting had created "a great deal of controversy . . . and apprehension on the part of the powers that be in America, because they realize that if any direct contact, communication, and understanding and working agreement are ever developed between the 22 million to 30 million Afro-Americans and the Africans here on the continent, there's nothing we couldn't accomplish."[78]

And Malcolm was right, both about the potential of internationalizing Black suffering and also about the shock waves his Cairo address to the OAU had sent throughout the corridors of power in the State Department. An August 13, 1964, article in the *New York Times* reported that the State Department and the Justice Department were concerned about Malcolm's participation at the African Summit in Cairo and the meeting of the OAU and his attempts to convince African heads of state to initiate a U.N. discussion of the persecution of Black peoples in the United States. According to the article, "Officials said that if Malcolm succeeded in convincing just one African government to bring up the charge at the United Nations, the United States government would be faced with a touchy problem . . . [and] find itself in the same category as South Africa, Hungary and other countries whose domestic policies have become debating issues at the United Nations. The issue, officials say, would be of service to critics of the United States, Communist and non-Communist, and contribute to the undermining of the position the United States had asserted for itself as the leader of the West in the advocacy of human rights."[79] In addition, another *New York Times* article published in January 1965 reported that Malcolm had convinced African delegates to the United Nations to use "the racial situation in the United States as an instrument of attack in discussing international problems," because "such a strategy would give the African states more leverage in dealing with the United States and would in turn give American Negroes more leverage in American society."[80]

As the United States continued to manage its image abroad, and at home for that matter, Malcolm continued to reveal a different reality of U.S. power to the suffering masses in his speeches and writings. In Cairo, Malcolm also continued to make the links between U.S. power and European colonialism and between the Muslim Third World and Black peoples in the United States. In September 1964, Malcolm wrote a piece in the *Egyptian Gazette*, making the treatment of Palestinians an issue of greater concern for Black activists in the United States. Criticizing Zionism and arguing that the State of Israel is "more firmly entrenched even, than that of the former European Colonial Powers," Malcolm went on to write, "European imperialists wisely placed Israel where she could geographically divide the Arab world, infiltrate and sow the seed of dissension among African leaders and also divide the Africans against the Asians."[81] Malcolm's critique of Zionism was framed as a European strategy to divide the nonwhite world of Africa and Asia while also challenging the postwar support of Israel from many Black activists in the United States. In fact, Malcolm mentions that Ralph Bunche had helped to negotiate the formation of the Israeli state, highlighting and critiquing Black Cold War liberals whom Malcolm saw as both undermining Black freedom in the United States and also helping to extend white supremacy and the subjugation of the Third World.

Upon Malcolm's return to the United States, the Muslim Third World would continue to influence his political imagination and the connections he forged between Black communities in the United States and those in the Third World. Just as Mecca, Bandung, Cairo, and the broader Muslim Third World shaped Malcolm's internationalist perspectives, his travels to Algiers did as well, providing him with an imaginative geography through which to discuss the connections between the circumstances of Black peoples in the United States and the struggles taking place in the Muslim Third World. Malcolm had talked about his visit to Algeria several times, including his meetings with the Algerian president Ahmed Ben Bella, who had also hosted Che Guevara, Gamal Abdel Nasser, and other Third World dignitaries when they defeated the French in 1962. Then in a talk at the Militant Labor Forum after his break with the Nation of Islam, Malcolm expanded on his experiences in Algeria in response to several reports that were circulating about a Harlem group called the Blood Brothers, who, with the support of the Nation of Islam, were allegedly assaulting whites and the police. Malcolm addressed that possibility and the panic it caused. But instead of assuaging the fear, Malcolm invoked his visit to the Casbah in Algiers as a means with which to contextualize the possible existence and actions of the Blood Brothers in Harlem. According to Malcolm, during his trip to Algeria, he went to the Casbah with some "blood brothers": "They took me down into it and showed me the suffering . . . that they had to live under while they were being occupied by the French." Malcolm continued, "The first thing they had to realize was that all of them were brothers" and that oppression, exploitation, discrimination, and segregation unified them. "Once all of them realized that they were blood brothers, they also realized what they had to do to get that man off their back." Malcolm explained, "Algeria was a police state. Any occupied territory is a police state; and that is what Harlem is. Harlem is a police state, the police in Harlem, their presence is like occupation forces, like an occupying army. . . . the same conditions that prevailed in Algeria that forced the people . . . to resort to terrorist-type tactics that were necessary to get the monkey off their backs, those same conditions prevail today in America in every Negro community."[82]

Just as he had done at the Bandung Conference, Malcolm used the anticolonial struggles in the Muslim Third World of Algeria as an analog for interpreting the conditions of Black peoples in the United States. As Malcolm said, "Everybody's wondering why I've been going back and forth to Africa. Well, first I went to Mecca to get closer to the orthodox religion of Islam. I wanted firsthand views of the African leaders—their problems are inseparable from ours. The cords of bigotry and prejudice can be cut with the same blade. We have to keep that blade sharp and share it with one another." Malcolm continued, "Strangely enough, listening to leaders like Nasser, Ben Bella, and Nkrumah awakened me to the dangers of racism. I realized racism isn't just a Black and white problem."[83] Malcolm believed that white supremacy's tentacles were global in reach and that in order to combat its penetrating depths, powerful alliances would have to be forged.

By placing Black communities within a global framework of white supremacy and by enlarging the scope of their allies and the scale of their struggle, Malcolm linked the violence of colonial racism with the policing of Black bodies in the United States. Malcolm's insights proved prophetic in more ways than one. For not only did Algeria become an anticolonial epicenter for Black radicals during the Black Power era, but a wave of urban rebellions would also be unleashed within the next year beginning in Watts as the insurgency that was Black Power began to take hold.

But more powerful than that was the influence of Malcolm and his ideas on future generations of revolutionaries in the United States and throughout the world. Forged through the prism of U.S. racism and Third World decolonization, Malcolm's Muslim Internationalism reveals a lasting body of work that deeply influenced the younger Black radicals who would identify with Black Power. As Huey Newton said, "The Black Panther Party exists in the spirit of Malcolm. . . . the Party is a living testament to his life work."[84]

Although the bullets finally caught up to him, they couldn't touch the enduring contributions that Malcolm made to the future of Black radical thought and the imaginative geography of the Muslim International.

From Mecca to Bandung, Cairo to Algiers, and Harlem to Palestine, the Muslim Third World became both a literal and ideological backdrop to the narrative of resistance he wove within the Muslim International. For it was on this stage of overlapping diasporas and shared histories of struggle that Malcolm X's unfolding drama of Black internationalism was narrated, a history of tragedy and triumph that sought to situate for Black and Third World peoples a more dignified and just place in the world.

2

TO THE EAST, BLACKWARDS
Black Power, Radical Cinema,
and the Muslim Third World

We must internationalize our struggle, and if we are going to
turn into reality the words of Che to create two, three, or more
Vietnams, we must recognize that Detroit and New York are
also Vietnam.

> —Stokely Carmichael, in "Carmichael Urges a 'Vietnam'
> in U.S."

In 1970, Gil Scott-Heron released the song "Whitey on the Moon"
from his album *Small Talk at 125th and Lenox.* As a response to U.S.
astronauts setting foot on the moon on July 21, 1969, Scott-Heron,
whose poignant songs about personal loss and public failure would continue throughout his brilliant career, saw this national adventure as
the epitome of hubris amid raging Black discontent and a brutal imperial war in Vietnam. He asked in song form, "A rat done bit my sis-
ter Nell with Whitey on the moon. Her face and arms began to swell
and Whitey's on the moon. . . . No hot water, no toilets, no lights
but Whitey's on the moon. . . . Was all that money I made last year for
Whitey on the moon?"

Scott-Heron's ironic yet biting commentary on white supremacy
and national arrogance was emblematic of the larger criticisms of and
challenges to U.S. power by Black activists domestically and Third
World revolutionaries globally. In fact, though Scott-Heron's critique of
the moon walk came a year after the event, cosmic forces almost seemed
in order, for on that day of July 21, 1969, other monumental historical
events were taking place as well. As the United States imagined possibility by looking to outer space while profoundly and criminally neglecting

racial injustice and imperial power, Black radicals in the United States looked to not-so-faraway places, such as Africa, Asia, and Latin America, for hope and possibility. In fact, July 21, 1969, the very day that U.S. astronauts actually set foot on the moon, was also the first day of the landmark Pan-African Cultural Festival in Algiers, Algeria, where internationally recognized artists, writers, musicians, and revolutionaries from all over the African diaspora and the Third World gathered. And on that same twenty-first day of July 1969, thousands of miles from Algiers and many more miles from the moon, three thousand people gathered in Oakland, California, at the opening of the Black Panther Party conference "United against Fascism," an assembly of activists who sought to forge an anti-imperialist front in the United States to challenge racist state violence both domestically and globally.

While the United States sought to conquer outer space and to expand its already broad dominion over the Americas, Africa, and Asia, U.S.-based Black activists, artists, writers, and others joined forces with like-minded radicals from throughout the Third World to challenge imperial power and to support national liberation struggles that the United States and Europe were hell-bent on destroying under the banner of the Cold War. Having just fought a successful but brutal anticolonial war against the French that captured the hearts and minds of revolutionaries in both the Third World and the United States, Algeria became a flashpoint for revolutionary internationalism that connected Oakland to Algiers and Black peoples in the United States to the Third World.

But this connection between Black peoples and the Third World was not new. Malcolm X, Lorraine Hansberry, Robert Williams, and others had already challenged U.S. Cold War liberalism and placed Black struggles in the United States within a global context of white supremacy. And their use of the Third World and colonialism as lenses to better understand and situate Black suffering persisted into the mid- to late 1960s and 1970s as Black Power erupted across the country. Known for her 1959 play *A Raisin in the Sun*, Hansberry was deeply committed to challenging colonial rule in the Third World while also underscoring the significance of decolonization to the plight of Black peoples in the United States. In fact, she wrote in the journal *Freedom* (and also later in *Freedomways*) about her support of the Nasserian Revolution in Egypt, the Mau Mau in Kenya, and other anticolonial insurgencies. Robert

Williams, the former head of the Monroe, North Carolina, chapter of the NAACP, had a profound influence on Black radicals and became a lightning rod for controversy in the late 1950s for his advocacy of Black armed self-defense. Forced to flee to Cuba and then to China after being framed for kidnapping in the United States, Williams said, "I'm interested in the problems of Africa, Asia and Latin America. I believe that we all have the same struggle, a struggle for liberation."[1]

Just as Harold Cruse had said, "What is true of the colonial world is also true of the Negro in the United States,"[2] Max Stanford, of the Revolutionary Action Movement, saw Black peoples in the United States as part of the Bandung world of Africa, Asia, and Latin America. Stanford (who later converted to Islam and became Muhammad Ahmad) was deeply inspired by Malcolm X and Robert Williams, and he organized conferences and wrote articles about the Black revolution's links to the Third World, his "Bandung Humanism" becoming the rubric and central theme for defining Black politics and solidarities with national liberation struggles taking place in Cuba, Algeria, Vietnam, China, and elsewhere.

Stokely Carmichael, the former chairman of the Student Nonviolent Coordinating Committee (SNCC), picked up the fiery baton where Malcolm left off and repeatedly underscored the links between U.S.-based Black peoples and the Third World in his writings and speeches. In Havana, Cuba, at the 1967 meeting of the Organization of Latin American States (OLAS), Carmichael asserted, "Black Power means that we see ourselves as part of the Third World; that we see our struggle as closely related to liberation struggle around the world." And he went on to argue, "Our people are a colony in the United States; you are colonies outside the United States. It is more than a figure of speech to say that the Black communities in America are victims of white imperialism and colonial exploitation."[3] In his writings, Carmichael also warned of the pitfalls of solidarity with whites while arguing, "Black people in this country [the United States] form a colony and it is not in the interest of the colonial power to liberate them."[4] Carmichael's geography of rebellion connected anticolonial struggles with Black liberation in the United States. And he was far from the exception. Black Panther Party member Kathleen Cleaver said, "From its inception, the Black Panther Party saw the condition of Blacks in an international context, recognizing that the same racist imperialism that people in Africa, Asia, Latin America were fighting against was victimizing Blacks in the United States."[5] Like Carmichael, Huey Newton, Angela Davis, and others, Eldridge Cleaver also saw Black peoples as a colony in the "white mother country" of the United States, a vocabulary that echoed throughout the Black Power era as the rhetoric of grassroots rebellion culminated in academic theory. Sociologist Robert Blauner described U.S. Blacks and other racial minorities by using an "internal colonial" model that was emblematic of the times.[6]

As national liberation movements in the Third World continued to occupy a significant place within the Black radical imagination, the Nation of Islam, Muhammad Ali, and especially Malcolm X provided a conduit for a profound trafficking of ideas between Black radical thought and the Muslim Third World in the post–World War II period, ideas that were deeply inflected with the politics of decolonization and anti-racism. For it was Malcolm X who said, "Islam is the greatest unifying force in the Dark World today,"[7] and for whom the Muslim Third World was not only the link between Africa and Asia but also the bridge with which he connected Black liberation struggles in the United States to the worldwide rebellions taking place in the Third World.

Whether it was the spiritual and political compass that Mecca provided or the influence of Bandung on his political thinking, Malcolm spoke defiantly in support of the anticolonial struggles in Egypt, Algeria, Palestine, and elsewhere. In fact, Palestine would reemerge within Black Power consciousness when the Student Nonviolent Coordinating Committee issued its 1967 article "Third World Round Up: The Palestine Problem: Test Your Knowledge" and when Huey Newton wrote "On the Middle East" in 1970, in which he expressed the Black Panther Party's criticism of Zionism and its support for the Palestinians.

As the widely recognized architect of Black Power and the Black Panther Party, Malcolm's Muslim Internationalism was forged through the prism of U.S. racism and Third World decolonization, and he left an indelible imprint on Black radical thought that deeply influenced the younger activists who would identify with Black Power. As Huey Newton would say, "The Black Panther Party exists in the spirit of Malcolm . . . The Party is a living testament to his life work."[8] As a result of Malcolm's influence, the shared histories between Black Power and the

Muslim Third World forged powerful visions of political radicalism and antiracist possibility, sharing strategies and solidarities as they engaged larger ideas about the nature of power and the means of resisting it.

As Black Power continued to take shape under the boot of U.S. state repression, it also continued, in the tradition of Malcolm X, to be influenced by the politics of the Muslim Third World. Although the Algerian anticolonial struggle influenced Black political culture from the 1950s into the early 1970s, it was through the revolutionary theorist Frantz Fanon and the film *The Battle of Algiers* that Algeria came into Black Power consciousness. As a groundbreaking visual achievement and the cinematic embodiment of Fanon's book *The Wretched of the Earth*, *The Battle of Algiers* poetically captured the Algerian resistance to French colonialism and was profoundly influential throughout the world, but particularly within Black radical circles in the United States, where it significantly influenced debates about the relationship of Black cinema to political struggle and revolutionary praxis.

But just as Algeria influenced Black Power politics and culture, so too did the Muslim Third World of Iraq. Sam Greenlee's two novels, *The Spook Who Sat by the Door* (1969) and *Baghdad Blues* (1976), poignantly explore the relationships between Black liberation struggles in the United States and the anticolonial movements of the Muslim Third World. Stationed in Iraq in the late 1950s, Greenlee witnessed the overthrow of the British- and American-backed monarchy there. This event inspired Greenlee to write both of his novels, one of which (*The Spook Who Sat by the Door*) became a film of the same name in 1973 and was pulled from theaters after three weeks due to pressure from the F.B.I. because of its incendiary politics. Greenlee revealed a racial internationalism in his work, one in which the Muslim Third World and Black Power found common cause.

As part of the Muslim International, these political and cultural histories between Black Power and the Muslim Third World provided an alternative grammar of resistance and a unique language of revolt with which to speak truth to power. Probing the relationships between art and politics, solidarity and struggle, the overlapping histories between the Muslim Third World and Black Power provided a lens with which to explore larger questions about the global nature of white supremacy, the scale of their foes, and the scope of their friends.

The Year of the Boomerang

Black radicalism in the United States has been deeply influenced by Frantz Fanon and his book *The Wretched of the Earth*.[9] As a psychiatrist, revolutionary, and writer, Fanon spent a great deal of time in the Muslim Third World of Algeria, using his experiences there and his sympathies for the Algerian cause as the basis for most of his writing. Fanon has been arguably the most influential thinker on race and colonialism, and *The Wretched of the Earth* would become his most famous work. Written just before he died and based upon his activities in the Algerian struggle, *Wretched* explored the possibilities and pitfalls of revolutionary violence, the poetics of armed struggle, the creation of a new national culture, and Fanon's critiques and warnings of an indigenous national bourgeoisie who would betray the popular will.

Fanon's influence came not only because he was closely linked with the Algerian anticolonial movement but also because he was seen as the voice and theorist for revolutionary violence, national liberation, and Third World solidarity. Influencing guerrillas, artists, and intellectuals in the United States, Latin America, Africa, the Middle East, South Asia, and beyond, Fanon became synonymous with the righteous indignation of the Third World in response to European and U.S. power.

His analysis and his positions on colonial domination, armed struggle, and internationalism and his distaste of nationalist elites struck many a chord throughout the Third World, as well as in the United States among an emerging generation of Black Power advocates who arose in the shadow and aftermath of Malcolm. For not only did the nascent Black Panther Party gain influence and inspiration from Stokely Carmichael's call for "Black Power," but as the analogies to the Third World and colonialism continued to be used as a lens to interpret Black suffering in the United States, the Black Panther Party became heavily influenced by the internationalism of Malcolm X, Kwame Nkrumah, Mao Tse-tung, Che Guevara, and Fidel Castro. But it was Frantz Fanon's ideas in particular that the Black Panther Party crafted into its vision for Black liberation.

As Kathleen Cleaver wrote, in the view of the Black Panther Party, Black peoples in the United States were "analogous to colonized people," leading Eldridge Cleaver to frame their condition in the United States in such a way that whites were the "mother country" and Black peoples were "the colony" and victims of "community imperialism."[10] As a result of this view, Fanon's analysis of the colonial situation and his solutions for eradicating it had a profound effect on adherents to Black Power in the United States. In particular, Fanon's analysis of the segregation inherent between colonizer and native in colonial space echoed the conditions of Black peoples in the United States, segregated as they were in ghettos throughout the country. For Fanon, the colonial world was a segregated one based upon race, a world in which the "cause is the consequence, you are rich because you are white, you are white because you are rich."[11]

More pointed, though, was Fanon's prescription for ending colonial domination. For Fanon, violence was inherent and endemic to the whole colonial project of control, so much so that, for Fanon, the native would have to reclaim violence in order to reclaim her dignity. As Black insurrection raged in the United States throughout the 1960s, Fanon's articulation of the poetics of violence seemed to give ethical and existential sanction to Black rebellion, suggesting even that these insurgencies were part of a broader revolutionary movement overtaking the United States. Fanon's analysis, according to Cleaver, "provided radical Blacks in America with deep insights—into both their own relationship to a world-wide revolution underway and to the profound kinship between their status in America and that of colonized peoples outside of America."[12]

Fanon's embrace of armed struggle, his analysis of colonial segregation, and his criticism of a nationalist bourgeoisie found tremendous traction among Black radicals in the United States, who exhibited a deepening frustration with entrenched U.S. racism and with the calls for nonviolence on the part of the establishment Civil Rights movement. As Cleaver wrote,

> Adapting Fanon's analysis helped to clarify the historical relationship between subjugated Blacks and dominant Whites. . . . viewing Blacks as colonized subjects, instead of so-called second class citizens, defined the political course the Black Panther Party proposed as a legitimate alternative to the assimilationist thrust of the Civil Rights movement, and justified organizational strategies designed to liberate, instead of integrate, Blacks.[13]

As Fanon's influence grew, so too did the influence of Algeria within the Third World imagination. In fact, through a heightened racial internationalism, the Algerian resistance to French colonialism, and the work of Fanon, Algeria was brought into the orbit of Black and Third World consciousness throughout the 1950s and 1960s and into the early 1970s in a variety of different ways and by a broad cross section of activists, critics, artists, and others. The violent war of resistance and the solidarities with the Algerian people served to situate Black freedom struggles within an international context, a vitally important strategy as the Cold War liberalism of the era sought to contain these Black anticolonial impulses. A broad and diverse range of interactions and encounters characterized U.S.-based Black peoples' engagements with and understanding of the relationship between their struggles and the Algerian anticolonial resistance.

In 1965, Algeria hosted the Afro-Asian Conference days after Malcolm X was assassinated. Malcolm had been expected to be there and to share the podium with Che Guevara, and though that never happened, Che addressed the gathering with his demand for anti-imperialist struggle throughout the Third World, saying, "Few settings from which to make this declaration are as symbolic as Algiers, one of the most heroic capitals of freedom. May the magnificent Algerian people—schooled as few others in sufferings for independence, under the decisive leadership of its party, headed by our dear *compañero* Ahmed Ben Bella— serve as an inspiration to us in this fight without quarter against world imperialism."[14]

Later, Kwame Nkrumah's Organization of African Unity declared Algeria to be the home to the first Pan-African Cultural Festival, which was to take place in 1969. Hosting hundreds of delegates and representatives from over thirty independent African countries, as well as from several countries then experiencing liberation struggles, the festival was also attended by Black artists from the United States, such as poet Haki Mahdubuti (Don Lee), jazz musician Archie Schepp, singer Nina Simone, Black Panther minister of culture Emory Douglas, and various other writers, artists, painters, and musicians from throughout the diaspora. The festival also became the moment when Eldridge Cleaver revealed that Algeria had been his home-in-exile from U.S. persecution, and the expat Stokely Carmichael and Miriam Makeba, his wife and a singer who was exiled from South Africa, also attended the festival. In fact, Cleaver, Carmichael, and Makeba were only some of the revolutionaries who saw Algeria as a kind of home-in-exile, for throughout the 1960s the country became that for other revolutionaries from around the world, including those from Palestine, Vietnam, Brazil, the United States, Canada, and various African liberation movements.[15] In fact, Algiers became the site of the first International Section of the Black Panther Party and was used as a platform to link Black liberation struggles in the United States with other Third World liberation struggles around the world. Referred by Kathleen Cleaver as the "Embassy of the American Revolution," the International Section lasted roughly four years, until about 1973, and ended mainly because of increasing instability in Algeria. Throughout its existence though, the International Section provided a space for the Black Panther Party to seek the international support of other Third World revolutionaries and movements for the Black revolution taking place in the United States, much in the way that Malcolm had at the Organization of African Unity in Cairo a few years earlier.

Though Algeria played a more prominent and visible role within Black Power in the late 1960s and early '70s than it had before, the earlier Algerian struggle against the French had already resonated within Black political culture. In fact, Hoyt Fuller, famed editor of the *Negro Digest* (and later *Black World*), traveled to Algeria in the late 1950s and said, after his visit to the Casbah in Algiers—the center for the insurgency against the French—that Algerians and Black peoples in the United States were "fighting the same war."[16] Harold Cruse, whose influential writings in the early 1960s made him a prominent figure within Black radical circles, had also spent time in Algeria, during World War II, and according to Cynthia Young, Cruse's shift to the radical Left occurred after his time in Algeria and his experiences witnessing the colonial relationship between the French and the Algerians.[17]

In addition, William Gardner Smith's 1963 novel, *The Stone Face*, explores the experiences of Simeon Brown, a Black man who escapes Jim Crow segregation and the racism of the United States and lands in Paris. Initially naïve about France and believing it to be a race-free utopia, Brown soon comes to realize the racist treatment given to Algerians in France. Unlike the other U.S. Blacks in Paris, Brown sympathizes with the Algerians' cause and their anticolonial struggle against France as he begins to view white supremacy as a global phenomenon and not simply confined to the United States. As a criticism of the refusal of Richard Wright and other U.S. Black expats to speak on the French colonial war in Algeria, *The Stone Face* seeks to reimagine Algerians in France as Blacks in the United States and, in doing so, positions U.S. Blacks in Paris as honorary whites. Smith uses the infamous October 1961 Papon Massacre of Algerians in Paris, which he had witnessed firsthand, to highlight Brown's decision to defiantly support the Algerians against French colonial violence, only to return to the United States to struggle on behalf of Black peoples there, whom he now refers to as "American Algerians."[18]

James Baldwin also commented on Algeria and France's brutal colonial war. On his many trips to Paris, Baldwin discussed the existential crises that he grappled with as a Black man who was nonetheless seen as an American in France, a colonial power. He often made references to the violent mistreatment of Algerians in Paris, the fact that they were rounded up, tortured, and put into camps outside the city, and he discussed Algerians disappearing, being killed, and thrown into the river Seine. He wrote:

> Algeria, after all is part of Africa, and France, after all is part of Europe: that Europe which invaded and raped the African continent and slaughtered those Africans whom they could not enslave—that Europe from which, in sober truth, Africa has yet to liberate herself. The fact that I had never seen the Algerian casbah was of no more relevance before this unanswerable panorama than the fact that the Algerians had never seen Harlem. The Algerian and I were both, alike, victims of this history, and I was still a part of Africa, even though I had been carried out of it nearly four hundred years before.[19]

In addition, when Ahmed Ben Bella, the iconic first president of Algeria, made a visit to the United States, it was headline news in numerous Black papers, including the Nation of Islam's *Muhammad Speaks*. But it was in the *New York Times* that his now famous sit-down with Martin Luther King Jr. took place. Ben Bella, King said, "believed that there was a direct relationship between the injustices of colonialism and the injustices of segregation," and King agreed that these struggles, both in the United States and abroad, were "part of a larger worldwide struggle" to end the racisms of colonialism and Jim Crow violence.[20] King went on to write a piece in the *New York Amsterdam News*, a prominent Black newspaper, titled "My Talk with Ben Bella," in which he wrote about the broad range of issues that they had engaged in their meeting. Possibly attempting to capture some of the anticolonial energy sweeping Black communities in the shadow of Malcolm, as well as providing himself with the legitimacy that comes from meeting a head of state (and an iconic one at that), King wrote, "It was on the question of racial injustice that we spent most of our time," and he concluded, "The battle of Algerians against colonialism and the battle of the Negro against segregation is a common struggle."[21]

Malcolm X would also reference the Algerian resistance several times, whether it was in discussing his travel there, his meetings with Ahmed Ben Bella, or in his famous speech "The Message to the Grassroots." The most poignant reference was made in 1964 at the Militant Labor Forum in New York, when Malcolm drew connections between Algiers, Harlem, and other Black ghettos in the United States:

> Algeria was a police state. Any occupied territory is a police state; and that is what Harlem is. Harlem is a police state, the police in Harlem, their presence is like occupation forces, like an occupying army. . . . The same conditions that prevailed in Algeria that forced the people, the noble people of Algeria, to resort to terrorist-type tactics that were necessary to get the monkey off their backs, those same conditions prevail today in America in every Negro community.[22]

Just as Malcolm, King, Cleaver, Cruse, Baldwin, and the larger tapestry of Black Power advocates explored the Algerian resistance as a lens for understanding the depth and breadth of white supremacy, Francee Covington explored it in a piece she wrote for the seminal 1970 anthology *The Black Woman*. In the essay, titled "Are the Revolutionary Techniques Employed in *The Battle of Algiers* Applicable to Harlem?" Covington reveals the incredible influence that the film and the Algerian resistance had on Black radicalism. In her piece, Covington asks, "What are some of the reasons for the success of the Algerian revolution? Can those reasons be transported and used in the United States, Harlem, Watts, Howard University? What are the parallels between Algeria and Black America, between the French colonialist army's approach and that taken by the U.S. army and national guard?"[23] Covington's piece in *The Black*

Woman was emblematic for recognizing the widespread influence that the Algerian struggle and, in particular, *The Battle of Algiers* had within Black political cultures in the late 1960s and early 1970s.

In fact, *The Battle of Algiers* has arguably become the seminal text for political cinema. By stunningly capturing the Algerian resistance to French colonialism, the film became the visual accompaniment to Fanon's *Wretched of the Earth*, for it not only gave cinematic voice to the colonized but it also filled in some of the gaps in Fanon's text about the forms of Muslim anticolonialism that were present in the Algerian resistance. *The Battle of Algiers* challenged established modes of filmmaking, marking a paradigm shift in film art that forced critics and creator to contend with the issues of both *what* to film and *how* do it. As a result, *The Battle of Algiers* influenced the emerging theoretical frameworks of what came to be known as Third Cinema, a cinematic movement that emerged in the Third World and sought to wed film art and production to popular people's struggles by challenging dominant (read: Hollywood) cinematic practices. Through the influence of the Muslim Third World, the Algerian anticolonial struggle and Fanon had a profound effect on Black radical circles in the United States. As a result, *The Battle of Algiers* and the movement known as Third Cinema, which the film was so closely tied to, became very influential within debates about Black cultural politics, Black representation, and the possibility of revolutionary and transformative art in the face of U.S. state repression, revealing the Muslim International as a space of shared histories of struggle and contestation over art, politics, and redemption.

The Camera as Gun

As decolonization swept the globe and national liberation movements gained traction, artists, intellectuals, activists, and others sought to define the newly emerging nations of the Third World in relationship to both their colonial past and their hopeful future. While discourses and debates occurred about national identity and the formation of a national culture, filmmakers, intellectuals, and artists saw film as a tool to be used in newly emerging nations, which led to the birth of Third Cinema.

Emerging initially out of Brazil, Argentina, and Cuba and spreading throughout Africa and Asia as well, Third Cinema arose not just as an alternative but as a challenge to dominant cinematic practice, whether it was Hollywood cinema or the commercial industrial cinemas in Europe and even in the Third World itself. Taking various forms, Third Cinema's films have been grand epics, pseudodocumentaries, avant-garde expression, and social realism, and initially its main impetus was to complement the national struggle by heightening a revolutionary ethos around national identity and highlighting the residues of colonial power and the continued repression of minorities, women, and the poor within the nation itself. Seeking to create alternative visions of the past, present, and future, Third Cinema blended genre, aesthetics, and visual stylistics not solely for the purposes of artistic excellence but also to mobilize popular people's movements within and across borders. Many of the films narrate national liberation struggles, express the complexities of nation building, and also seek to close the gap between artists and the people by creating dialogue through a cinematic practice that engaged popular struggles.

Along with the films came a culture of resistance around cinema, including productions, conferences, criticism, and, of course, manifestos. The early foundational texts included Glauber Rocha's 1965 essay "Aesthetics of Hunger," Fernando Solanas and Octavio Getino's 1969 piece "Towards a Third Cinema," and Julio García Espinosa's "For an Imperfect Cinema," also published in 1969. Muslim countries wrote their versions, including "Jamaat al-Cinema al-Jadida" (The New Cinema Group), published in Cairo in 1967–68, where cineastes founded the journal *Al-Sinima*, which explored Arab, Egyptian, and international cinemas. In addition, the Moroccan journal *Cinema 3* explored film from the Third World, just as various Arab writers and scholars in the Egyptian journal *At-Tariq* wrote "Cinima al badil" (Alternative Cinema), and the "First Manifesto of Palestinian Cinema" was published in 1972 at the Damascus Film Festival, with the "Second Manifesto" published in the next year.[24] In addition, Teshome Gabriel's highly influential "Towards a Critical Theory of Third World Films" would come later.

Concerned with decolonization and cultural struggle, the seminal texts within Third Cinema were, not surprisingly, deeply influenced by the work of Fanon, in particular *The Wretched of the Earth*. His ideas on the formation of national culture, the role of armed struggle, and the creation of revolutionary consciousness were seen not only in the writings that formed the foundation of Third Cinema but also in the seminal films that came to define the movement, as their artists and writers sought to bridge the gap between radical artistic practice and militant anti-imperialism.

Rocha's "The Aesthetics of Hunger" lays claim to a terrain cultivated by Fanon and his militant anticolonialism. Rocha asserts that colonial control was a violent encounter and that redemptive violence on the part of the colonized is the "moment when the colonizer becomes aware of the existence of the colonized." For Rocha, cinema is a weapon that reveals what colonial power conceals, and he argued that the new cinema of the Third World would "reveal that violence is normal behavior for the starving" and that "the aesthetics of violence are revolutionary rather than primitive."[25] While Rocha used Fanon as a means to give aesthetic dimension to Third Cinema, Solanas and Getino employed Fanon to give literal force to Third Cinema, opening their treatise with an epigram of Fanon: "We must discuss, we must invent."[26] With this, they laid claim to a terrain where anti-imperialist cinema would fundamentally challenge the political and economic order that made Third Cinema a necessity in the first place. Gabriel's "Towards a Critical Theory . . ." uses Fanon's analysis of the three stages of national culture to argue that Fanon's final "combative phase" defines Third Cinema praxis.

Fanon's influence was also seen in a number of Third Cinema films as well, including Solanas and Getino's *La Hora de los Hornos* (*The Hour of the Furnaces*, 1968), which explicitly quotes Fanon, and Glauber Rocha's *Deus e o Diabo na Terra do Sol* (*Black God, White Devil*, 1964), which reflects Rocha's "aesthetic of hunger" and mobilizes Fanon's ideas on revolutionary violence. In addition, Ousmane Sembene's *Xala* (1975) embodies Fanon's penetrating criticism of the corrupt nationalist bourgeoisie. But while these filmmakers and numerous others embraced Fanon's ideas, no film is more closely associated with Fanon than Gillo Pontecorvo's 1965 film *The Battle of Algiers*.

Even though elements of its institutional and production history suggest a mixed inheritance of European and Algerian support, *The Battle of Algiers* still remains a template for Third Cinema that, if anything, forces a reconsideration of what exactly is Third Cinema's relationship to radical politics. Despite its hybrid history, *The Battle of Algiers* maintains the radical liberationist thrust of Third Cinema while also leveraging its European support to reach a broader audience. Although the films were conceived by and based upon the writings and experiences of Saadi Yacef, who was in charge of military operations for the National Liberation Front (FLN) from the Casbah during the resistance, the final script was cowritten by Frank Solanos and the film's director, Gillo Pontecorvo, an Italian Marxist deeply influenced by Italian neorealism. Italy, as the largest producer of films in Europe at the time, outproduced all other European countries in the 1960s, because its films were well positioned for export and distribution deals. *The Battle of Algiers* was a joint venture between Yacef's Casbah Films and Italy's Igor Films, having received not only support from Italian financiers but also funding from private sources through Casbah Films as well as Algerian state support (which included access to locations and the use of extras, uniforms, and military equipment such as tanks and guns). For Saadi Yacef, who was the mastermind behind the film, this kind of coproduction and financing structure would expand the audience and market for the film, giving it international distribution, including to European art-house cinemas and to the United States.

Though it was somewhat dependent on European institutional support for funding and festivals, the film also embodies Third Cinema practice in seeking to heighten the sense of realism and immediacy through the use of several different techniques and certain aesthetic choices. For instance, in portraying an event that actually took place (the Algerian struggle), particularly in black-and-white film stock, *The Battle of Algiers* employs a docudrama style that blurs the line between fiction and documentary and embodies what Cuban filmmakers and others have privileged as Third Cinema praxis.

In addition, because the revolution had just ended three years prior to shooting and was fresh in the collective memory of Algerians, the use of nonactors was also a powerful device, for it suggests that actual participants in the struggle were a central part of the cast and did not even have to *act* but only be themselves, including Brahim Hadjadj, who played Ali La Pointe, and Saadi Yacef, who played Djafar (a character patterned after himself). This choice, as well as filming in locations where fighting had actually taken place—both in Algiers and more particularly in the Casbah—and the use of actual French people still living in Algiers, furthered the immediacy and realism that Third Cinema so poetically sought to achieve.

More specifically, the film seeks to challenge colonial representations of Otherness by revealing the complexity of Muslim and Arab lives. It not only utilizes the Arabic language to give the characters integrity and authenticity but also gives voice and even empathy to the Algerian resistance to colonial oppression. In addition, unlike conventional Hollywood and First Cinema practice, *The Battle of Algiers* does not center the use of an individual protagonist who forces audience identification with that individual. Instead, the film privileges a larger collective as the protagonist—the Algerian people. In this way, the film challenges dominant cinematic modes and also suggests that social change and the engines of history are the product not of individuals but of collectives, be they communities or even countries. While Ali La Pointe is one of many recurrent characters, and it is his capture around which the narrative arc is structured, the film shows that even after his death, the Algerian resistance to French colonial violence continued unabated.

Through Frantz Fanon and films such as *The Battle of Algiers*, the impact of Third Cinema was broad and far-reaching, including its influence on Black criticism and filmmaking in the United States. Just as the politics of the Muslim Third World influenced Black radical political mobilization in the United States in the 1960s and '70s, ideas about Third Cinema influenced critics and filmmakers to redefine Black representation, art, and aesthetics as vehicles for the creation and fomenting of political struggle and agitation. In fact, as Blaxploitation cinema emerged in Hollywood at the same time that Black Power reached a fever pitch, the stakes around Black art and politics got exponentially higher. Whether it was Lerone Bennett's criticism of Huey Newton's embrace of Melvin Van Peebles's landmark film *Sweet Sweetback's Baadasssss Song* or the emergence of Black independent filmmakers of the "L.A. Rebellion," such as Haile Gerima and Charles Burnett, the Black image on the screen became a lightning rod for debate. As a result, the politics of the Muslim Third World, *The Battle of Algiers*, and specifically Third Cinema, more broadly, informed influenced heated debates about the relationships between Black art and aesthetics to the politics of liberation and repression.

It's the American Dream, Well Ain't It?

As Black militancy grew in the late 1960s and saw hundreds of Black cities in flames, the hunger and thirst for more empowered Black art that spoke to the insurgent Black masses of that time also played out within the mainstream film industry, as Black audiences demanded more empowered and multidimensional images that challenged Hollywood's long-standing degradation of Black images and histories on the big screen.

The tectonic shift from Civil Rights to Black Power also witnessed a similar shift within the desires of the Black viewing public as Black communities sought new images and ideas on the screen that resonated with their increasingly insurgent attitudes. Much of the rancor and dissatisfaction centered on Sidney Poitier. Representative of the Civil Rights establishment, Poitier was the biggest box office draw in Hollywood until about 1967, with films such as *In the Heat of the Night*, *To Sir with Love*, and *Guess Who's Coming to Dinner*. But by the late 1960s, as Black militancy reached a critical mass, Poitier's image in his films did not speak to the rising discontent and desires of Black communities. As Ed Guerrero notes in his landmark text *Framing Blackness*, many Black critics began to openly question Hollywood's representations of Blackness, seeing them no longer as the crude "Rastus," "Mammy," and "Coon" caricatures of Hollywood's past but rather as "dialectic opposites," characters who were "sterile paragons of virtue that were completely devoid of mature characterization or of any political or social reality." For Guerrero and these critics, these characters of the "social problem" films in Hollywood were simply inverted "positive" stereotypes that were just as one-dimensional as the previous "negative" representations, leading critics and audiences "to perceive the neutered or counterfeit sexuality of Poitier's roles as obsolete and insulting, especially when contrasted with rising black nationalist calls for a new, liberated black sense of manhood and self." In his critique of films such as *The Defiant Ones* (1958), *The Bedford Incident* (1965), *Duel at Diablo* (1966), and especially *The Long Ships* (1964), in which Poitier plays a Moorish prince with a harem, Guerrero notes that Poitier was "castrated" in order to "uphold the protocols of white masculinity."[27]

At the time, writers and journalists commented on Poitier's place within the popular culture of the 1960s. Clifford Mason wrote in a 1967

New York Times piece titled "Why Does White America Love Sidney Poitier So?" that Poitier was a "good boy in a totally white world with no wife, no sweetheart, no woman to love or kiss, helping the white man solve the white man's problems."[28] Larry Neal, the Black Arts theorist, also wrote in a piece titled "Beware of the Tar Baby" that Poitier was "a million dollar shoe shine boy." Neal, who's critical cultural perspective was shaped by the Black Arts Movement, had cut his teeth on radical forms of representation, and he lamented that Black peoples were locked in the vicious system of Hollywood, a cinematic prison "of distorted symbols and images [and] the very attempt to extricate ourselves only leads to more confusion."[29] Guerrero himself goes on to note that while some critics openly embraced and supported Poitier, others, such as James Baldwin, focused less on Poitier and placed more blame on Hollywood for its insatiable desire for demeaning Black images. For critics Mason, Neal, and others, the film industry was firmly rooted within America's centuries-long racial drama and even complicit with it. The urgency of the militant moment demanded that Hollywood's exigencies for complacent Black figures and representations be transcended and transgressed rather than accommodated.

Guerrero points to *Guess Who's Coming to Dinner* as the turning point in the question of Black representation. As a film that won two Oscars and was a commercial success, it marked a shift for Poitier, as he tried to respond to the critics and the streets by playing more empowered and assertive characters, but to no avail. Instead, "the revolution in black consciousness very quickly rendered Poitier's saintly roles as laughably out of touch with the rising demand for assertive, realistic black images on the screen."[30]

When Hollywood began to shift and contain the impulses and desires for strong assertive characters, "macho men" characters played by Jim Brown and Fred Williamson were the precursors to the Blaxploitation era films such as *The Mack*, *Dolemite*, and *Shaft*, which attempted to capture "the life" of the underworld on-screen. With Hollywood's deepening financial crisis (and, as a result, its increased dependence on independent productions), mounting pressures from Civil Rights organizations to integrate its studios and the unions, and its realization that a vibrant Black moviegoing audience existed, Blaxploitation became a genre unto itself when Hollywood recognized the thirst among Black communities for empowered images and rebel figures. With the low production costs of these films and Blaxploitation's emphasis on portraying central protagonists as drug dealers, pimps, and gangsters who wear flashy clothes, have several women, and drive fancy cars, many saw this as another deliberate attempt to create Black caricatures and not Black characters, thereby undermining the political impulses of collective struggle taking place in the streets. According to Guerrero, these films "underscore[d] Hollywood's insistence on stunting the development of a black political voice and emancipated consciousness. . . . As well, these changes trace dominant cinema's implicit contribution to a destructive shift in the black community away from collective political struggle of the 1960's and toward such individualist, self indulgent activities as drug consumption and the single minded pursuit of material gain."[31]

Major Civil Rights organizations such as the NAACP and PUSH (People United to Save Humanity) protested the demeaning images, criticizing Hollywood for its degrading Black images and for negatively affecting Black youth. But these organizations mostly sought "positive" images that rarely, if ever, challenged the status quo and ultimately affirmed a liberal narrative of race at the height of Black Power. But as these debates raged, an alternative group of Black filmmakers emerged from UCLA in the late 1960s and early '70s. Known as the Los Angeles School of Black Filmmakers, or more simply the L.A. Rebellion, these filmmakers were deeply committed to challenging Blaxploitation cinema while seeking to recenter the potentially powerful relationship between Black art and politics.

This influential and significant film movement was composed of Haile Gerima, Charles Burnett, Larry Clarke, Julie Dash, Ben Caldwell, and others. Inspired by an eclectic but empowering range of writings, films, and artistic and political movements, these filmmakers explored everyday working-class Black life through a broad lens of influences that included Malcolm X, Amiri Baraka and the Black Arts Movement, the anticolonial movements taking place in the Third World, and the writings of Mao, Che Guevara, Amil Cabral, and Frantz Fanon, as well as the writings of Third Cinema, including Rocha, Solanas and Getino, and Gabriel (who was their professor at UCLA). Their influences in film included the work of Oscar Micheaux, as well as Third Cinema classics from Brazil (*Barravento, Black God, White Devil,* and

Vidas Secas), Argentina (*The Hour of the Furnaces*), and Cuba (*Memories of Underdevelopment, The Last Supper*), as well as *The Battle of Algiers*, to name a few.[32]

Seeking to combine film with their leftist politics, the L.A. Rebellion openly rejected Hollywood cinema, particularly Blaxploitation film. For these filmmakers, Blaxploitation was anathema, a counterrevolutionary cinema that belittles Black humanity and struggle. As Charles Burnett said, "We were all influenced by the idea that either you're part of the problem, or you're part of the solution. And to us it was quite obvious that exploitation films were part of the problem."[33] The films the L.A. Rebellion created—*Bush Mama, Killer of Sheep*, and *Passing Through*, among others—focus on melodrama with a documentary feel that centers on the working class and the everyday struggles of Black peoples amid poverty and chaos. As Cynthia Young argues, especially for *Bush Mama* and *Killer of Sheep*, Gerima and Burnett wanted to "reposition black Americans as members of an internal colony subject to some of the same forces terrorizing Third World colonies."[34]

As Black rebellion continued to rage across the country, and Blaxploitation films filled the theaters, many saw a deep tension between the screen and the streets. Instead of accepting the recycled images of Blackness that define the overwhelming majority of Blaxploitation films, Black artists and critics saw another frontline: the theaters of war that were the movie houses all across the country. As the tension between the war on the streets and the images on the film screen increased, there was a call to reanimate Black film practices in order to produce a more direct relationship between art and politics, as had occurred in Third Cinema and previous moments of Black creative flourishing. Not surprisingly, Malcolm X's Muslim radicalism, the politics of the Muslim Third World, and *The Battle of Algiers* became ideological touchstones, making the debates around what constitutes Black revolutionary cinematic praxis part of the cultural history of the Muslim International.

"I Say You're Afraid to Bleed!" or *"He Won't Bleed Me"*

If there is one film that sparked the debate and the whole movement known as Blaxploitation, it would have to be Melvin Van Peebles's 1971 independent classic *Sweet Sweetback's Baadasssss Song*. Written, directed, produced, edited by, and starring Melvin Van Peebles, *Sweetback* tells the tale of a Black man on the run from police authority in Los Angeles after being framed for a murder he did not commit. Beginning with the words "Dedicated to all the brothers and sisters who had enough of the man," the film chronicles his escape from white authority into Mexico, foregrounding Sweetback's sexual prowess as a means of escaping. Using avant-garde and experimental techniques with striking images of burning police cars, the film generated tremendous controversy, not the least of which was its use of sexuality and its racially redemptive conclusion with the words "A Baadasssss Nigger Is Coming Back to Collect Some Dues."

Controversial and compelling, Van Peebles's film was a box office success, ultimately and unwittingly crafting a formula that Hollywood would soon capitalize on as Blaxploitation and that would radically alter the debate around Black representation. Huey P. Newton, the Black Panther Party chairman, embraced Van Peebles's film as a "revolutionary" film in a lengthy essay titled "He Won't Bleed Me: A Revolutionary Analysis of *Sweet Sweetback's Baadasssss Song*" and made it required viewing for all Black Panther Party members, which added fuel to the already smoldering fire around the film. All of this ultimately led to a response by Lerone Bennett titled "Emancipation Orgasm: Sweetback in Wonderland," in which Bennett challenged Newton's assertion that *Sweetback* is a revolutionary Black film.

Bennett framed the discussion of revolutionary film practice with the new militancy of Black communities. In recognizing the new militant moment in which *Black* has replaced *Negro*, Bennett argued that, prior to this, "in the pre-black days, Negroes generally reacted to the white image . . . becom[ing] opposite of what white people said Negroes were. This symbolic strategy is being abandoned by post-Watts blacks who are defining themselves . . . as the opposite of what Negroes said Negroes were." Bennett cautioned, however, that this reaction to the Poitier image of Civil Rights respectability could also be a trap and that Black peoples would "end up in an old harbor of white clichés, with the mistaken impression that they are discovering new land."[35]

With the commercial success of *Sweetback*, Bennett astutely anticipated the spate of "Sons of *Sweetback*" (as he called them), which would ultimately spawn the Blaxploitation era, and he argued that this "symbolic confusion" finds itself most clearly in "the cult of poverty, which roman-ticizes rats, roaches, heroin, and misery. Instead of painting poverty realistically as an evil imposed by an evil system, instead of probing deep into the root causes of poverty, and presenting the appalling human costs of malnutrition, poor houses and lack of capital, some men paint a Rousseau-like picture of poverty as the incubator of wisdom and soul. . . . Some men foolishly identify the black aesthetic with empty bellies and big-bottomed prostitutes." Bennett argued that this symbolic confusion leads some to identify "black people with the degradation of the con-ditions imposed on them," using the example of the elevation of the "pimp to the status of folk hero."[36]

In contrast to the "symbolic confusion" of Blaxploitation, Bennett pointed to the fictional situation of a hypothetical Black character strug-gling with urban poverty and the deep psychic wounds it inflicts. Ben-nett argued that, instead of portraying how "cool he looks standing on the corner with a wine bottle, dying in broad open daylight" or doing the opposite and "condemn[ing] a man whose society condemned him to poverty," cinema should "condemn that society and create images and symbols that will lead him to his manhood and to his enemies. You don't do that from afar in the mean spirit of American charity. You take your stand with him, realizing that he is not only your brother but that he is, in literal fact, you."[37]

Bennett argued that the way out was neither a reaction to the white stereotype nor a reaction to the "Negro" reaction to the white stereo-type. He made the case for "directive images—large and dynamizing images that shape and mold behavior in desired directions," adding that they were the "short hand symbols of the ideals and aspirations of a cul-ture. They tell people who they are, they define roles and they apportion tasks . . . they project ideal images of the ideal relationships between man and man, between man and woman, between man-woman-child. . . . Without such a core of images, an oppressed community cannot make a revolution or anything else. Without such a core of images, a nation cannot be built, Africa cannot be revisited, and African-Americans can-not survive."[38]

Bennett highlighted the imagery promoted by the Nation of Islam as an example of what he'd like to see in films, arguing, "The direc-tive images of the Nation [of Islam] emphasize that to be black is to be productive," and they "neither praise nor romanticize victims." In fact, Bennett argues, the Nation "pays victims the highest compliment by asking them to pick up their beds and walk to the front lines of the battle against their tormentors."[39]

Bennett continued his critique of *Sweetback* by challenging Van Peebles on the notion that film cannot both entertain and engage and by arguing, "A real work of art created an audience instead of seeking one." And he ultimately said that if *Sweetback* is a revolutionary Black film, then "the problem of the Black Revolution is the question of vision,"[40] an appropriate and compelling metaphor to invoke when linking cinematic and artistic work with revolutionary praxis.

Bennett then challenged Huey Newton's assertion that *Sweetback* is revolutionary or Black and countered that, instead of creating imagery about Black rebellion, "it drags us into the pre-Watts days of isolated acts of resistance, conceived in confusion and executed in panic." He went on to argue that *Sweetback* "does not pose revolutionary questions, and it does not point to revolutionary solutions. . . . It poses no questions of social structure. The movie does not show us the enemy. It does not show us the system. It doesn't show us the forces that control the black community." Bennett argued that revolutions are won by relying not on individual acts, panicked responses, or sexual skill but rather on "organized and deliberate responses of the masses, on their level of consciousness, their organization, their will." And in making this point, he tellingly compared the character Sweetback to the hustler Ali La Pointe in *The Battle of Algiers:* "[Pontecorvo] shows us, Malcolm said, a hustler swinging, becoming a revolutionary and a man. He shows us that revolutions are not made in bed and that oppressed people do not triumph or love by the phallus alone."[41]

In *Sweetback* there is no clear sense of how or when the protagonist became a revolutionary, Bennett said. "There is no such ambiguity in *The Battle of Algiers.* The male hustler in that movie turns himself inside out, like a glove, like Malcolm in fact. And like Malcolm, he confronts his former companions with the errors of their way." Bennett "wishe[d] that van Peebles had confronted black pimps and prostitutes, as Malcolm confronted them in his Autobiography and his life."[42] Most tellingly and strikingly, Bennett raised a potential objection that is worth quoting at length:

Some will say: "you are criticizing the man for not filming *The Battle of Algiers*. How could he film *The Battle of Algiers* when there had been no battle of Algiers in America?" But that is precisely the point. There has been a Battle of Watts in America, and a Battle of Newark, and a Battle of Detroit. A Malcolm lived in Harlem, a King in Atlanta, and Angela Davis is in a California prison. And it is impossible to make a revolutionary black film in America without taking these realities into consideration.[43]

Bennett's wide-ranging critique of *Sweetback* and the vexed nature of Black representation in a white supremacist culture was a defining moment. His use of the anticolonial politics of the Muslim Third World as part of the ideological backdrop of his argument speaks to the significant and penetrating role the Muslim Third World played within the broader terrain of Black radicalism and Black cultural politics. Bennett supported his argument about "directive images" not simply by invoking the Nation of Islam or by using the Algerian anticolonial struggle as an analog for Watts, Newark, and Detroit. He also used Ali La Pointe in *The Battle of Algiers* and Malcolm X as the figures that should motivate radical Black representation. Both of them Muslim, Malcolm and Ali La Pointe went from street hustler to revolutionary and ultimately to martyrdom—a transformation that not only became the paradigmatic arc for Black Power adherents but was also embodied in Frantz Fanon's *The Wretched of the Earth*.

By challenging dominant cinematic modes that dehumanize racial others, *The Battle of Algiers* not only gave voice and dignity to the oppressed but also revealed that a collective and communal struggle against injustice is the only way to victory. In centering Ali La Pointe and his radical transformation amid degradation and racist violence, Bennett provided a template for revolutionary film practice and challenged Newton and his limited vision of *Sweetback*. By situating these debates about Black politics and art within a global context of anti-imperialist struggle, Bennett was suggesting that the debate was not simply about film but rather about film practice in urgent times. In conjuring the anticolonial struggle of the Muslim Third World, *The Battle of Algiers*, and Malcolm's own defiant and enduring Muslim radicalism, Bennett's compelling critique placed these debates about cinema, cultural politics, and redemptive possibility within the overlapping histories of the Muslim International.

But despite Bennett's critique and warning, the "Sons of *Sweeetback*" did emerge, and Blaxploitation was born, limiting Black cinematic and political possibilities. As the L.A. Rebellion of Gerima, Burnett, and others sought to challenge Hollywood through independent productions, Ivan Dixon's *The Spook Who Sat by the Door* (1973) cleverly and brilliantly walked the line between independent and studio production, commenting on white expectation and control, only to undermine it. Not surprisingly, the politics of the Muslim Third World continued to shape the contours of Black radical politics, cinema, and art, as the anti-imperial struggle in Iraq became a lens through which to imagine Black political possibility.

"Because It's War, Honky!"

Sam Greenlee's two novels, *The Spook Who Sat by the Door* (1969) and *Baghdad Blues* (1976), powerfully explore the possibilities between Black liberation struggles in the United States and anti-imperialist movements of the Muslim Third World during the Cold War. Greenlee provocatively revealed the international dimensions of race by mapping the politics of the Muslim Third World onto the United States and the politics of Blackness in the United States onto the Muslim Third World.

Through the work of Greenlee, we get another glimpse of how Black cultural activists in the Civil Rights and Black Power era positioned themselves, their art, and their politics in relation to the anticolonial and anti-imperialist movements taking place in Asia, Africa, and Latin America. The Cold War inaugurated a new phase in American power that simultaneously sought to contain both the anticolonial impulses emanating from the Third World and a burgeoning Civil Rights and Black Power movement domestically. As such, Greenlee and other cultural activists in the United States imagined Black identities diasporically and internationally, particularly in relation to the popular struggles taking place in the Muslim Third World.

While working for various U.S. government agencies in the Muslim Third World of Iraq, East Pakistan (now Bangladesh), and Indonesia in the late 1950s and early 1960s, Greenlee experienced the anti-imperialist movements sweeping the globe, particularly Gamal Abdel Nasser's overthrow of the British in Egypt and the immense impact it had throughout the region. Stationed in Iraq in the late 1950s, Greenlee witnessed first-hand the impact of the Nasserian Revolution there, which culminated in the overthrow of the country's British- and American-backed monarchy. These events inspired Greenlee to translate the politics of anticolonialism in the Muslim Third World into the burgeoning Black Power movement in the United States in his first novel, *The Spook Who Sat by the Door*. Greenlee's second novel, *Baghdad Blues*, is based upon his direct experience in Iraq at the time of the overthrow of the Anglo-American monarchy, though in this book, Iraq, not the urban centers of America, is the backdrop for exploring the global dimensions of Blackness, race, and imperialism.

The thematic and ideological relationships between the film version of *The Spook* and the film *The Battle of Algiers* are particularly compelling. As a groundbreaking visual achievement, a flashpoint in anticolonial politics, and the cinematic embodiment of Frantz Fanon's *Wretched of the Earth*, *The Battle of Algiers* poetically captures the Algerian resistance to French occupation and colonialism and has been profoundly influential throughout the world, but particularly within Black radical circles in the United States. As flip sides of the same insurgent coin, these two films provide a great deal of possibility in exploring the relationships between Black diasporic radicalism, the anticolonial politics of the Muslim Third World, and the international dimensions of race; as Greenlee says of both films, "We reached the same conclusions traveling on parallel lines."[44]

Just as *The Battle of Algiers* radically redefined the art of film and gave cinematic voice and empathy to decolonization and the burgeoning movement known as Third Cinema, *The Spook* emerged during the era of Blaxploitation in Hollywood, where Black representation often consisted of deeply racist clichés that undermined the politics of Black Power taking place in the streets. As a result, *The Spook* sought to challenge Blaxploitation and was more ideologically aligned with the emergence of the Black independent cinema of Haile Gerima, Charles Burnett, and others who were deeply influenced by radical politics, internationalism, and Third Cinema in seeking to challenge Hollywood's degradation of Black life.

Exploring the films *The Spook Who Sat by the Door* and *The Battle of Algiers*, as well as the novel *Baghdad Blues*, provides an opportunity to explore the relationship between cinema and politics, art and aesthetics, and the cultural politics of representation while revealing the overlapping histories and shared territories of struggle that define the Muslim International in the post–World War II era as U.S. empire building, Third World decolonization, and Black liberation struggles took shape.

Greenlee's return to the United States weeks after the Watts Rebellion in 1965 gave him flashbacks of his experiences in Iraq—he saw in Black peoples in the United States what he had seen in Iraq: "attitudes on faces that were ready to explode."[45] His experience of watching the buildup to the overthrow of the monarchy in Iraq gave him a way of imagining how racism could be resisted and challenged, and he wondered how the Iraqi insurgency against the United States and the British and the Nasserian Revolution in Egypt and Syria could be used as blueprints for Black liberation in America. As Greenlee stated, "I always saw 'The Spook' as colonial rebellion, akin to the fight against imperialism abroad. What a lot of people don't want to deal with is that our revolution is a part of a [bigger] global anti-racist, anti-imperialist rebellion; and many of the same things that were happening in Kenya, Ghana, South Africa, South America, Asia was going on in the U.S. because the same means of suppression was practiced in every one of those places. So, I look at 'The Spook' as colonial rebellion that takes place in the U.S."[46] As Greenlee's observation clearly suggests, the links he made between the imperial control of Iraq and the history of Black peoples in the United States were based upon his understanding that they shared similar histories around racial and economic injustice. And so he set out to complete *The Spook*, a novel he says he wanted to be a handbook for guerrilla warfare, explaining, "I was more useful as a propagandist than holding a gun."[47] Although the novel was released in 1969, it wasn't until 1973 that the Ivan Dixon–directed film was released, but not without challenges, controversy, and censorship. Christine Acham has brilliantly detailed the production history of the film and its aftermath in her scholarship and a documentary film, and according to her research, the film was pulled from theaters within three weeks for its incendiary politics after the FBI put pressure on exhibitors and theaters throughout the country.[48]

The Spook centers on a Black man, Dan Freeman, who works within the confines of elite white power. Having been challenged as being racist by a senator who is running for reelection and needs the Black vote, the CIA embarks on a recruitment of Black people that is designed for them to fail, so as to provide the CIA with the claim that Blacks are not qualified. But one man, Freeman, passes the battery of intellectual and physical tests and is reluctantly brought into the CIA. The novel plays off the multiple meanings of the word *spook*, suggesting a spy, a racial epithet for Black peoples, and also a haunting figure.[49] Greenlee brilliantly employs all these possibilities, portraying Freeman as the dutiful servant to his white masters in the CIA—deferent and accommodating for years, until he decides to leave and go back to Chicago to "work" with youth in the rough South Side. There, he recruits some of the most hardened gang members, teaching them the tactics of urban guerrilla warfare and insurgency, propaganda and disinformation, sabotage and weapons training—all skills he learned from working for the CIA. The radicalized youth begin to spread their training to other urban centers, and as the film ends, urban rebellions have struck throughout the country, leaving the United States under siege.

Based upon Greenlee's time in Iraq during the country's anticolonial rebellion, the film *The Spook Who Sat by the Door* strikingly resonates with *The Battle of Algiers*. Both explore—whether implicitly or explicitly—the politics of the Muslim Third World, and in different ways, both films have influenced and inspired Black radical politics and cultural practice here in the United States. Upon their release, both films were also ostensibly banned for their radical politics, and they both explore the means of resisting and challenging racist power. Both films are also imbued with deep Fanonian undertones particularly around space and racial violence, *The Battle of Algiers* centers on the colonial segregation of the Casbah from the French Quarter, and *The Spook* centers on the activity within the segregated space of the ghetto. In the films, both the Casbah and the ghetto serve as spatial tropes and sites of isolation, repression, and ultimately resistance.

Just as *The Battle of Algiers* centers on the Algerian people as a collective protagonist, *The Spook* attempts to do the same with Black peoples in the United States. Like Ali La Pointe and even Djafar in *The Battle*, Freeman is the narrative center as *The Spook* seeks to privilege the notion of—and the hope for—a collective solidarity and the reality that political change occurs because of social movements and not the actions of any one individual. Despite the ideological and class-based tensions and debates that occur between Freeman and the initial group of trainees at the CIA, between Freeman and his police friend Dawson, and between Freeman and his former girlfriend (who ultimately leads to his blown cover), the scenes around these themes are what give the film complexity and texture, with the emergence of an upwardly mobile post–Civil Rights Blackness that is in opposition to Freeman's Black Power politics. And though these tensions reveal the ideological divisions that would mitigate any possibility of Black unity, the film's conclusion suggests that social change is a collective struggle that transcends any single figure or cinematic protagonist. For when Freeman is shot by the cop Dawson, the film ends with a voice-over explaining that the urban insurgency that Freeman set in motion has spread across the country and sparked a national rebellion.

In addition, *The Spook* utilized cinematic techniques and received state support similar to *The Battle of Algiers*, which utilized Third Cinema techniques of hand-held cameras and on-location shooting, as well as receiving friendly Algerian state support (that provided uniforms, military equipment, locations, etc.). As Acham writes and reveals in her documentary on the film, *The Spook* utilized numerous guerrilla filmmaking techniques that echoed those of the L.A. Rebellion films of Gerima and Burnett. Just as this emerging Black independent film movement was influenced by Third Cinema praxis and a desire to challenge Hollywood's historical degradation of Black images, most recently seen with Blaxploitation, *The Spook* sought to challenge dominant cinematic conventions while probing the politics of Black representation. As a result, guerrilla filmmaking techniques were employed in *The Spook*, such as location shooting without permits and the use of hand-held cameras to heighten realism. And when the film budget tightened, the production moved to Gary, Indiana, where the first ever Black mayor, Richard Hatcher, who was very sympathetic to the film, allowed the crew to shoot exteriors, use city services such as the fire department, utilize explosives and fires, orchestrate the intense riot scene, and also use a helicopter to capture panoramic overhead shots of the postriot neighborhoods.[50]

Combining support from mainstream Hollywood cinema and private financing, *The Spook*, like *The Battle of Algiers*, had a complex and hybrid production and financing history. While initial shooting began with private investment, studio after studio turned down the film, forcing director Ivan Dixon to travel outside the United States and to the continent of Africa to seek independent funding for the film. Visiting Ghana, Algeria, and other places, he was offered four hundred thousand dollars by financiers in Nigeria, who told him to return the next day. When he returned, his investors had changed their minds, telling Dixon that, "some white men came and told us not to do business with Ivan Dixon," suggesting that knowledge of the novel and the film remake was gaining momentum and was seen as threatening to powerful interests.[51] But Dixon persisted, and while initial funding began to dry up, he put together a reel of action clips from the film and, along with the script, sent it out to Hollywood studios to try to get more funding. This attracted the attention of United Artists, who decided to help provide finishing funds. As Greenlee recounts, "They thought they had a Blaxploitation film. When they saw the final cut, a deathly silence descended over the room."[52]

In fact, just as *The Battle of Algiers* was arguably the cinematic equivalent of Fanon's *Wretched of the Earth*, the film *The Spook Who Sat by the Door* (in addition to complementing *Wretched* itself) seemed also to conjure and catalyze Fanon's *Black Skin, White Masks*. According to Greenlee, both he and Dixon knew *The Spook* would be treated and perceived by the studio as a Blaxploitation film, simply because the characters in it were Black. While it was this perception of *The Spook* as a Blaxploitation film that ultimately led United Artists to put up some financing, it also reveals the limited vision and understanding of Black humanity and artistic possibility that exist in Hollywood. And ironically this perception of *The Spook* as Blaxploitation is the central point of the film itself. Although Freeman surprises the CIA when he passes their battery of tests, which reflect both his intellectual and physical abilities, he is grudgingly hired and given a position as "reproduction station chief"—a glorified photocopier. Freeman's job as a copier, the role expected of him as the acceptable Negro, suggests something about his role as a mimic and a copy of white expectation and desire, both within the film's narrative and as a comment on Hollywood and broader American society. For Freeman's character not only subverts this white desire by "spooking" and ultimately training Black youth for insurrection, but he also offers a metacritique of America's representations of

Blackness, whether they be the cardboard imagery of a Sidney Poitier or the stock caricatures that dominated Hollywood's Blaxploitation cinema. As either side of the same coin, both the noble Negro and the accommodating Negro empty Blackness of any humanity, complexity, and nuance, just as the updated "Black brute" in Blaxploitation cinema did as well. So *The Spook*, at both the level of its narrative, with Freeman as "obedient," and the level of its financing history, in being perceived as Blaxploitation, brilliantly seeks to use white desire for Blackness to garner legitimation, attention, and support, only then to seek to radically subvert it.

In performing the dutiful servant during his time at the CIA, Freeman, through his "spooking," provides a mirroring and even mocking critique of the conventional role of obedient Blackness within Hollywood history. Equally important is that he works at the CIA, the preeminent institution that defines and enforces—through covert operations, violence, and destabilization—U.S. statecraft throughout the Third World. By having Freeman working at the CIA, reappropriating their techniques and tactics, and training Black militants in the United States to undertake a guerrilla war, *The Spook* is suggesting the deep connections between the tactics of repression in the Third World and the potential for liberation for Black peoples in the United States. In fact when asked by a trainee why they are making explosives and whether this approach will work in their rebellion, Freeman says, "If you don't think it can work, you check out Algeria, Kenya, Korea, and Nam." For the very means by which Cold War liberalism was destroying the national liberation movements in the Third World—war, covert operations, and subterfuge—are the means that Freeman is using to teach Black youth to challenge the domestic side of Cold War liberalism that sees "Negroes as Americans" rather than as part of a global struggle against white supremacy. In fact, as he says to one of the Black youth, "We force whitey to make a choice between two things he digs most of all. There is no way that the United States can police the world and keep us on our ass too, unless we cooperate." This "cooperation" sits at the heart of the Cold War liberal consensus that came to define mainstream Black politics in the United States and fractured domestic Black freedom struggles from those in the Third World. In fact, *The Spook* is replete with references to the international dimensions of race and the anticolonial rebellions taking place in the Third World. As was emblematic of the time, Freeman tells one young man, "What we have now is a colony; what we want is a new nation." In explaining their predicament, Freeman uses colonialism and "nationhood" as a metaphor for understanding Black repression and suffering in the United States, and though limited, this metaphor suggests at the very least an attempt to situate Black struggles within a global structure of white supremacy and also suggests the possibility of a larger community of struggle and belonging. Clearly, as was the case with the Black Panther Party, the Revolutionary Action Movement (RAM), and other organizations, Black communities in the United States had their own particular history, strategies, and tactics for dealing with the persistence of anti-Black racism, but as a sign of the times the national liberation struggles in the Muslim Third World influenced and inspired Black liberation struggles in the United States.

The Spook (both as the film and as the novel) is deeply informed by the logic of the Cold War, containing several references to Cold War U.S. statecraft and the paranoia about communist infiltration. As U.S. domestic politics came to be interpreted through the logic of Cold War liberalism, *The Spook* reveals the presence of that outlook through the typically racist logic that was employed against Black activists. In the film, both the CIA and law enforcement interpret the urban rebellions taking place to be a result of Soviet supervision, not Black intelligence, strategy, and vision. In fact, Dawson asks Freeman at the film's climax, "Are you working with the Commies as they say? Who's behind you? . . . The FBI says this is the most sophisticated underground movement in the Western hemisphere. The work of an expert!" to which Freeman responds, "And expertise is a white man's monopoly? Well, I am an expert!" Not only does Freeman reject the racist assumption of "Commie" influence, but also, in doing so, he aligns himself with those countries in the Third World who met at the iconic and monumental Bandung Conference in seeking to imagine their own liberation without U.S. or Soviet assistance.

By situating Black liberation within this global context of the Cold War and the age of Bandung, *The Spook Who Sat by the Door* explores the influence of decolonization in the Muslim Third World on Black radicalism in the United States. Greenlee's second novel, *Baghdad Blues*, is in many ways a prequel to *The Spook Who Sat by the Door*, for it is based upon his direct experience in Iraq at the time of the overthrow of the Anglo-American monarchy. Though in this novel the Muslim Third World of Iraq, and not the urban centers of the United States, becomes the stage for exploring the global dimensions of Blackness, race, and U.S. imperialism. Greenlee's experiences abroad made him well aware of what he called the "global struggle of antiracism," and he explains, "This is what I wanted to inject in my work."[53]

Baghdad Blues begins in 1956, the year after the Bandung Conference of Afro-Asian unity in Indonesia—a historic moment that informs much of the novel's politics and the connections it seeks to make between Black freedom, the Muslim Third World, and the politics of anti-colonialism. For U.S.-based Blacks such as Malcolm X, RAM, and others, Bandung was a seminal moment in the global struggle against white supremacy. As Malcolm X said, "It was the first ever unity meeting in centuries. . . . All of them were Black, Brown, Red or Yellow."[54] Malcolm would go on to say that at Bandung, the conference attendees realized that "the same man that was colonizing our people in Kenya was colonizing our people in the Congo. The same one in the Congo was colonizing our people in South Africa, and in Southern Rhodesia, and in Burma, and in India, and in Afghanistan, and in Pakistan. They realized all over the world where the dark man was being oppressed, he was being oppressed by the white man. . . . So they got together on this basis."[55] As a response to centuries of colonialism and the emergence of a Cold War superpower rivalry that sought to influence and, in many ways, suppress the democratic aspirations and national hopes for decolonizing African and Asian countries, the Bandung Conference became a symbol of possibility not only for the Third World but also for Black peoples in the United States who saw the links between Jim Crow segregation and colonialism in the Third World.

While *Baghdad Blues* narrates the interconnected histories of Iraqis and Black peoples in the United States, it is in essence a literary complement to the Bandung Conference. In tying the political fates of Iraqis and U.S.-based Blacks together, Greenlee foregrounds how the struggle of African and Asian nations for independence during the Cold War was also about the struggles for racial justice in the United States. That is, American imperial culture really involved a struggle to define how race was going to operate in a new historical period in which anticolonialism and antiracism became the defining features of twentieth-century national liberation movements.

Though published in 1976, the year of the U.S. Bicentennial, *Baghdad Blues* embodies much of the internationalist impulse that drove early twentieth-century Black thought within the Pan-African Congress Movement, the African Blood Brotherhood, the CAA (Council on African Affairs), and other internationalist organizations and individuals who sought to connect the histories of oppressed peoples with their critiques of race and capitalism. In many ways, Greenlee's novel is an attempt not only to narrate the relations between the domestic and the foreign, slavery and colonialism, and U.S.-based Blacks and the Muslim Third World, but also to reclaim the terrain of U.S.-based Black anticolonialism and Third World internationalism that was compromised by the politics of the Cold War.

Baghdad Blues is framed by Cold War history, placing Dave Burrell, a Black man in the USIB, within the context of Cold War Iraq, a client state ruled by a monarchy supported by Britain and the United States. After arriving and interacting more with the Iraqis, Burrell begins to see sides and complexities of Iraq and its people that others in the USIB and the American Embassy either don't see or refuse to see, and he becomes aware of the anger and resentment of the Iraqis toward the American support of a corrupt and repressive government. Like Burrell, Greenlee talked about how during his time in Iraq, he was "socially ostracized" by the white staff members in the USIB and the American Embassy because he was Black. This ostracism motivated him to meet with various parts of Iraqi society. As he says, "Iraqis were the only social contact I had."[56] And because of these contacts, Burrell is not surprised at the eventual overthrow of the American-backed government.

What drives the narrative and what reveals so much of the novel's power are Burrell's relationships with both the Americans and the Iraqis. In the novel, Baghdad becomes the site upon which the American empire will define its Cold War national identity, particularly in the Muslim Third World, as numerous U.S. Embassy staff highlight the importance of Iraq as a "bedrock of our Middle East policy" and the "most stable government in the region."[57] But it is through the figure of Burrell that America's imperial ambitions are challenged and its domestic politics on race are revealed. For Burrell's presence violates and challenges the assumptions and clear distinctions made between the colonizer and the colonized, "civilization" and "savagery," and race and nationhood.

In both the novel and an interview, Greenlee mentions that he was constantly made aware of his Blackness, both by Iraqis and by the white U.S. government staff. On numerous occasions in the novel, white Americans confront Burrell about his skin color. For some, his skin color and presence in Iraq as part of the American staff are proof of Cold War American liberalism and progress—a kind of moral legitimacy and sanction of American foreign policy—which explains why he is always being policed and disciplined by American officials and told that he has great "representational potential."[58] At one point, Carl Taylor, the head of the USIB, talks to Burrell about the "image of the American race problem in Iraq" and how it is "overblown in the European and Arab papers." He instructs Burrell to talk about it to the Iraqis, explaining, "They don't know about Ralph Bunche and people like that . . . so don't be hesitant to discuss it . . . your own accomplishments are as good an example that it is possible for Negroes to progress if they want to in our country." Here Taylor, like others at different times in the novel, tries to project an idea of America meritocracy, invoking Ralph Bunche and Race Man politics to Burrell as examples of American equality.

While Burrell is sometimes silent, exposing his thoughts only through internal monologue, at other times he is outspoken. When asked, "Do they ask you any questions about the race problem in the States?" he replies, "Not often. They seem to feel it's a white man's problem."[59] On another occasion, Taylor confronts him, "Do you sometimes feel uncomfortable here because of your color?" Burrell replies, "There are more people here of my color than yours. Why should I feel uncomfortable because of my color?"[60] In these responses, Greenlee reveals the role of race within the current global order, for Burrell's responses challenge the legitimacy of the American presence in Iraq by calling attention to both the invisibility of whiteness and the place of Blackness within a "liberal" vision of American national identity—a challenge that had far-reaching implications in Cold War America. As Burrell says through narration, "I had already realized that a black skin was an asset in Iraq, and after living in the States all my life, that sure as hell was new."[61]

This challenge to the Cold War liberalism that dominated American politics is profound, highlighting the central tension around race that brought together the intimate connections between the domestic politics of race and the imperial reach of empire. Greenlee brilliantly highlights these tensions in the beginning of the novel, when Burrell, while taking a two-week course in "Communist world conspiracy" prior to going to Iraq, goes to lunch with his white colleagues and is not allowed to enter a restaurant in Virginia because he is Black. Upon leaving, Burrell says, "I remember thinking as I passed the Lincoln Memorial that Virginia was quite a place to teach a nigger about Communist tyranny."[62] By invoking the mythic Lincoln and reminding the reader of a segregationist America consumed by the specter of communist takeover, Greenlee ironically underscores the ever-present tyranny of race and the Cold War liberalism that not only haunted the domestic front but also no doubt projected itself onto and drove American foreign policy concerns.[63]

In making the links between the domestic politics of race and its projection onto the imperial adventures in Iraq, Greenlee challenges the Cold War liberalism and orthodoxy that came to dominate the Civil Rights movement in the 1950s and '60s. Throughout the novel, as Burrell befriends two Iraqis, Ali and Jamil, he spends more time with both the working class and intellectuals, and we are presented with a diverse group of Iraqis. And as the revolution against the American-backed government unfolds, the embassy staff try to make use of Burrell's contacts with various Iraqis to find out who may be responsible. But Burrell doesn't cooperate, for Greenlee presents him as sympathetic to the Iraqi cause, as his interactions with embassy officials concerning his Iraqi friends reveal not only a powerful critique of Orientalism and Cold War liberalism but also the powerful alliances that Burrell and the Iraqis are imagining and forging in the shadows of Bandung and other Third World internationalisms.

The Cold War liberalism of the late 1940s and 1950s severely influenced antiracist struggles in the United States by "domesticating" U.S.-based Black anticolonial impulses that sought to create links and forge solidarities among U.S. Blacks and between them and other oppressed peoples around the world. By nationalizing Black identity and collapsing Blackness and Americanness, the Cold War had a tremendous impact on the Civil Rights movement and Black support of American foreign policy objectives in the name of anticommunism. While *Baghdad Blues* explores the projection of race onto the imperial desertscape of Iraq at the height of the anticolonial moment and the Cold War, Greenlee also sought to explore the place of Blackness within a global framework. As the revolution unfolds, Burrell begins to define his relationship to U.S. nationalism more clearly. On one occasion, when asked about his close friend Jamil, he thinks to himself, "It'll be a cold day in hell . . . when I tell any of you anything of any importance about Jamil or any of the others. I didn't give a shit what kind of passport I carried: I knew who my friends were."[64] Later when confronted by Jim, another embassy official, and asked whether he is bothered to see Americans and Englishmen humiliated, Burrell tells him, "I dig what's happening to the Iraqis since those tanks moved in the other night. They're walking a lot taller out in those streets today." Jim asks, "Do you identify with those Iraqis, then?" Burrell says, "Hell yes. Who am I going to identify with, Adrian Prescott [a senior embassy official]? I couldn't if I wanted to and he wouldn't let me if I could. You think they [the American staff] consider me any different from the Arabs in the embassy?" Jim says, "And suppose you had to choose?" to which Burrell replies, "Don't ask, baby."[65]

The Iraqis also raise the question of race to Burrell. After the overthrow, Jamil tells Burrell he is ecstatic that Iraqis will no longer have the Americans and the British as overseers. Instead, "We will make our own mistakes, solve our own problems, create our own nation. To hell with the Americans and the British!" to which Burrell first reveals to the reader, "I loved him, envied him, identified with him. To build a nation . . ." and then replies to Jamil, "Well man, you know I'm American." Jamil responds by saying, "But you're different, you understand," to which Burrell replies, "There are a lot like me at home," and then he reveals to the reader, "As I said it, I wondered if it were true."[66] For the Iraqis, as for Burrell, a distinction is made between Blackness and Americanness, to the dismay of the insecure embassy staff, who want to ensure that Burrell maintains his loyalty to the American imperial project. And although Burrell tells Jamil that there are many like him "at home," his ambivalence about this underscores the powerful role of the Cold War liberalism that cemented itself in the United States, where Black anticolonialists such as Robeson and Du Bois became further marginalized within political discourse and targets of the McCarthy witch hunts.

In challenging the nationalist assumptions underscoring U.S. race relations and their projection onto the global terrain of empire building, the novel further heightens its internationalist dimensions through its critiques of Orientalism. "I saw myself through the eyes of Arabs and Asians," said Greenlee of his time in the Muslim countries of Iraq, East Pakistan (Bangladesh),[67] and Indonesia, a comment that has profound implications for how he explored the complexities of race, imperialism, and internationalism. This perspective is a radical reversal of classic Orientalism, in which the empire's racial Others—Arabs, Asians, and Africans—are seen through the eyes of whiteness, frozen in the gaze of colonial power. But Greenlee felt forced to see himself—and "American" Blackness—through *their* eyes, ultimately sharing a vision rooted in a common history of white supremacy that centers on the experiences of the colonized. This forced him to reject the possibility of an imperial citizenship in the United States, which made one complicit with the subjugation of other oppressed peoples at the hands of American foreign policy, as when in *Baghdad Blues*, Burrell challenges the assumptions of viewing the world through American/white eyes when an official begins blaming Gamal Abdel Nasser, Egypt's charismatic leader, for what is happening in Iraq, saying, "Nasser. Oh that man is a devil. He must be stopped. . . . If we lose Iraq, we lose the Middle East." To which Burrell replies, "Since we didn't own Iraq, I didn't see how we could 'lose' it."[68]

How else does *Baghdad Blues* use the Muslim Third World differently from the Orientalizing histories of much of European and American literature, as detailed by the works of Edward Said and others who explore how European power and empire are projected and represented? Orientalism is ultimately a discourse of racial difference that has served to situate whiteness and its power over nonwhite peoples and places, particularly in the Muslim Third World. Critiques of and challenges to Orientalism, then, are also critiques of white supremacy and the relationships it creates between imperial powers and the nonwhite world.

The challenges to Orientalism in *Baghdad Blues* come in various forms, but most forcefully through Burrell as the novel's protagonist. Utilizing Blackness to challenge the authority of Orientalism has profound possibilities, because it can reveal white supremacy's constructed nature of both of these identities—"Blackness" and the "Oriental"— and also allow for the possibility of revealing the profoundly liberating potential of solidarity and alliance against white supremacy. While the use of a Black protagonist instead of a white one does not automatically resolve all of the possible Orientalizing tropes that can plague any work that places itself within the outposts of empire in the Muslim Third World (see Richard Wright's *The Color Curtain*, for instance), Greenlee's novel avoids these traps and provides a fundamental critique of Orientalism itself.

In the conventional Orientalist narrative, the Muslim Third World, or the "exotic East," is the backdrop against which the West or the white Westerner redefines and entrenches the power of whiteness by presenting the people and society in which the narrative is situated as uncivilized, irrational, eternally despotic, and decadent. The country or place that the narrative explores is usually presented as benignly existing in a powerless and naturalized condition and as being eternally "backward" or "poor." While Orientalism also works in much more complex and nuanced ways to cement white authority and legitimacy, it is important to note that the representation of Otherness within the conventional narrative is almost always naturalized.

But in *Baghdad Blues* something different is happening, because whiteness and its authority are not being celebrated but rather critiqued. While numerous white characters exhibit classic Orientalist ideas about the Iraqis (laziness, unsuitability for democracy, etc.), the novel, through the voice of the Black Dave Burrell, works in multiple ways to challenge these ideas. Most prominent is how the relations of power are represented. Iraq, in Greenlee's work, is positioned as *subjected* to imperial power and is not invisibly situated, with its struggles somehow normalized and decontextualized from colonial history. Instead, the Iraq in *Baghdad Blues* is represented as having been brought to this position precisely *because* of its relationship to American and imperial power and the long legacy of European colonialism, not as benignly existing in powerlessness and so naturally or eternally impoverished.[69]

In addition, the power of *Baghdad Blues* comes from its positioning of Iraqis, as well as Arabs and Muslims in general, primarily as racial subjects who have been *constructed* as Other by white supremacy. By not reductively representing the Iraqis in the conventional Orientalist fashion, as people whose religious identities overdetermine their existence and experiences, *Baghdad Blues* represents them instead as more complex beings who are part of a broader global system structured by race. Their presentation as racialized subjects of colonial violence, then, provides the possibilities for a shared experience of racialization with others who have also been victims of white supremacy around the world.

When the revolution occurs, Burrell is asked by Nelson, the CIA operative in Iraq, about whether his friend Yussuf, who may hold a ministry position in the new government, would be friendly to the United States, Burrell says, "No, he doesn't like Americans at all." To which Nelson responds, "But he saw you regularly, had you to his home several times." Burrell replies, "Yeah, but he overlooked the fact that I'm American because I'm black. He insists that makes a difference, because my people have been the victims of the same kinds of things as the Iraqis. You know he went to the Bandung conference? He was real hung up on Afro-Asian unity."[70] Here Greenlee presents the Iraqis not as Orientalist clichés that are reactively anti-Western, but rather as people who have been subjected to a broader system of racial violence and who recognize their affinities with other victims of white supremacy and Euro-American control, like Burrell and other Black peoples in the United States. Yussuf's attendance at the Bandung Conference speaks volumes to the kinds of internationalist consciousness woven through the Iraqi resistance and the novel itself.

Toward the very end of the novel, Burrell is with Jamil and Yussuf, who has just been appointed to a ministry in the new government. Yussuf mentions his optimism for Iraq, telling Burrell, "There is no incompatibility between Islam and democracy," and he continues to talk about the ways in which the new government will give women equal rights as well as protecting the rights of minorities, the Kurds, Christians, Shia, and Sunnis. This initiates an exchange between Yussuf and Burrell:

Y: Why do you work for the Americans?

B: I'm an American.

Y: According to your passport, but do your colleagues agree? We are not blind. They think of you as they think of us; they despise us equally. . . . We know what they say behind our backs, they call us "ragheads." We know their hypocritical manner toward you at the official functions, but they ignore you when there are no Iraqis to impress. We know how they treat your people in the United States, in spite of their propaganda here and on the VOA [Voice of America Radio]. When Jamil asked me to meet you, I was reluctant, expecting a fawning sycophant. What is the expression Jamil?

J: Uncle Tom.

Y: We've had experience with our own Uncle Toms.

Yussuf continues:

Y: Is it important for you to be in Baghdad?

B: Yes. I've had an education here. They lie about you too in the States. And I've learned many things about myself, and even more about white Americans.

Y: But are you not needed at home now? Are not important things happening there for your people?

B: I sure hope so Yussuf. I hope the marches and demonstrations will make a difference.

Y: But you are not optimistic?

B: Did you pray the Turks, British and the Americans off your backs?

Y: And you believe you can learn from our struggle; perhaps use it in your own.

B: Yes.

Y: From Islam?

B: That too.[71]

Emblematic of the internationalism that sits at the heart of *Baghdad Blues*, this exchange challenges the Orientalist notions about the incompatibility of Islam and democracy while also highlighting that Iraqis have also had their own experiences with "Uncle Toms." In doing so, Yussuf and Burrell highlight how U.S. policy around race in the post–World War II era both domestically and internationally co-opted anti-racist impulses through the installation of U.S.-backed dictators abroad and by placing Black faces in high places domestically.

Through their exchange, Burrell and Yussuf discuss the realities that await both the Iraqis and U.S.-based Blacks in their struggle against white supremacy and for self-determination. In doing so, Yussuf recognizes the limitations and erasure of Black dignity embedded within an American passport as he highlights his own awareness about American hypocrisy toward Black peoples and the attempts by the United States government to project a vision of an egalitarian America to Iraq and other Third World countries through media propaganda. And in their discussions of the racial politics in the United States, Burrell highlights the iconic Civil Rights methods of marches and demonstrations to underscore the nature of antiracist struggle there, revealing that the hegemony of Cold War liberalism over Black struggle in the United States has created a Civil Rights–dominated movement, whose efficacy he wonders about in comparison to the methods the Iraqis undertook to gain self-determination. In addition, Burrell's response—"That too"— to Yussuf's query about learning from Islam is a clear suggestion of the powerful role that Islam came to play within Black political discourse in the post–World War II era, through the Nation of Islam, Malcolm X, Muhammad Ali, and others—organizations and figures who forged strong ties with liberation struggles in the Muslim Third World.

Greenlee explained that in Iraq, "whites used terms like ragheads and slopes, which was another way of calling them niggers."[72] In suggesting the central role of white supremacy in determining both domestic and foreign policy, Greenlee, in *Baghdad Blues*, reveals Iraqis who are firmly aware of the relationship among race, colonialism, and slavery, as Yussuf tells Burrell, "They think of you as they think of us. They despise us equally."[73] In presenting these kinds of understandings among the Iraqis about race, Greenlee represents them not as the fanatic, irrational zealots that an Orientalized Muslim resistance is perceived to be based upon, but rather as participants in a resistance and insurgency who understand and recognize the deep histories and relationships of race that anticolonial national liberation struggles are rooted in.

Landscapes of Power, Rebel Held

Greenlee's work and the contributions it has made to the broader fabric of Black internationalist writing have expanded the frontiers of possibility by linking Black freedom to the Muslim Third World. By providing a template and lens with which to interpret Black suffering, Greenlee's work, like *The Battle of Algiers*, also provided the creative means through which to remedy that suffering, as ideas and frameworks for Black artistic and cinematic practice have been influenced by the political and cultural histories of the Muslim Third World and beyond.

For it was through the anticolonial struggles of Algeria and Iraq, the influence of Malcolm X's own Muslim radicalism, and the emergence of Black Power that the Muslim International became a site of contact and difference within and across national boundaries—a space through which to probe the global dimensions of white supremacy and to imagine new possibilities for politics and new frontiers for freedom. Through political histories and cultural struggles, the Muslim International has also been a space in which the relationships between politics and art can be engaged, in which ideas about tactics and strategies, aesthetic choices and thematic concerns, can be debated, shaped, and also created.

The challenge to America's Cold War liberalism was made plain as Black Power raged on American streets and the winds of Third World rebellion fanned its flames. For it was only through the most violent forms of state power—the FBI's COINTELPRO and the emergence of the prison—that the United States was able to contain and seek to destroy Black radical politics and its internationalist impulses. But Malcolm had been in prison, and his conversion to Islam and his relationship to the Muslim Third World became a source and site for redemption in the face of unbridled racism and unimaginable horror. So it's no surprise that in the post–Civil Rights era, in which mass incarceration became the new paradigm of racial control, that Malcolm X and the politics of the Muslim Third World would profoundly influence a new generation of Black youth, becoming a definitive presence in the cultural revolution now known as hip-hop. In connecting geographies of violence and what Aimé Césaire referred to as "a compass of suffering," hip-hop culture has provided eloquent testimony to the resilience of the Muslim International and Black Islam in keeping alive the enduring memory and defiant histories of Black and Third World peoples who had integrity where there shouldn't have been any and found dignity in the struggle for a better world.

3

RETURN OF THE MECCA
Public Enemies, Reaganism, and the Birth of Hip-Hop

> Man what happened to us?
> Geographically they moved us from Africa
> We was once happiness pursuers
> Now we back stabbing, combative, and abusive
> The African and Arab go at it they most Muslim
> We should be moving in unison.
> — Nas and Damian Marley, "Tribes at War"

NEW YORK CITY, and by extension the United States, got remixed by the influence of Islam well before the idea of 9/11. But this time it was through hip-hop culture. For Muslim MCs in the 1980s, New York City and its surroundings were reclaimed by its Black inhabitants in more ways than one. In the lexicon and imagination of Black Islam, New York was rechristened via Islam's holiest sites, with Harlem becoming Mecca and Brooklyn becoming Medina. Harlem was named Mecca for many reasons, one of which had to do with Black Islam's prophetic voice—Malcolm X—making Harlem sacred ground, where he, through Islam, would connect Black peoples in the United States to the larger Third World of Africa and Asia as he cast his verbal stones at the evils of white world supremacy. It is no surprise, then, that Malcolm X would also become hip-hop's prophetic voice, as his influence and the embrace of Black Islam in hip-hop culture were forged out of a crucible of post–Civil Rights America and the expansion of U.S. empire abroad, a volitile period when the "Black criminal" and the "Muslim terrorist" became the domestic and foreign threats, respectively, to U.S. national security.

As Black Power raged and urban rebellions roiled U.S. cities in the mid- to late 1960s, U.S. state agencies saw these rebellions as the domestic front in a broader war against popular people's movements throughout the Third World. During this period, marked by retrenchment and a backlash against the perceived gains of the Civil Rights movement, U.S. federal, state, and local authorities mobilized a broader campaign to silence and destroy these movements and any possibility of their reemergence in the future. From the 1960s and into the twenty-first century, COINTELPRO, Nixon's "law and order" mantras, and Reagan-Bush-Clinton policies in the "War on Crime" gave birth to an urban police state, while a new "carceral imagination" gave shape to the "Black criminal" as a defining threat to U.S. domestic security.[1]

And as U.S. empire extended European colonialism into the Muslim Third World and intensified its already existing dominion in the late 1960s, the emergence of the "Muslim terrorist" within mainstream political discourse and popular culture defined Islam and the Muslim Third World as a fundamental threat to U.S. national security. As a kind of "prehistory" to the current "War on Terror," U.S. foreign policy in the Muslim Third World of Palestine, Iran, Iraq, Lebanon, Afghanistan, Pakistan, Egypt, Saudi Arabia, and elsewhere constructed Islam and the figure of the "Muslim terrorist" as a fundamental threat that came to haunt U.S. political discourse beginning in the 1970s and 1980s and extending into the 1990s with Samuel Huntington's "Clash of Civilizations" thesis and, of course, the post-9/11 era.

When the hypernationalism of the post–Civil Right backlash created the "Black criminal" and the "Muslim terrorist" as threats to U.S. national identity, it was through the presence of Malcolm X and the embrace of Black Islam that hip-hop artists responded, using their collective exclusion as both Black *and* Muslim to tap into a deep vein of Black internationalism that not only challenged domestic racism but also imagined Black belonging beyond the United States, into Africa and the Muslim Third World. By crafting an alternative community of belonging that has given contour to the Muslim International, Black cultural activists in hip-hop challenged U.S.-based racial control and domination, and they also linked these struggles with the expansion of U.S. empire abroad, extending and inflecting a long-standing tradition of internationalism that has been a hallmark of Black radical practice and Black political thought in the post–World War II era.

Hip-hop culture, then, stands as a powerful example of what Amiri Baraka referred to as the "changing same" of Black music.[2] For it was through the historical influence of Islam and Malcolm X within Black political culture that Black artists in the post–World War II era invoked Islamic themes and symbols in their radical Black cultural practices, giving shape and contour to the cultural politics of the Muslim International. Like jazz and the Black Arts Movement before it, hip-hop culture, especially its "Golden Age," became a space in which Black radicalism, Islam, and the politics of the Muslim Third World had a powerful impact on the lyrical imaginations, sonic landscapes, and political visions that were being expressed by artists such as Rakim, Public Enemy, Mos Def, Ice Cube, Gang Starr, and Lupe Fiasco, to name a few. In forging the aesthetic and political dimensions of the Muslim International through sound, hip-hop became a space for Black artists to express what the official language of politics proved incapable of translating, as they imagined Black freedom beyond America's borders. Using the language of the unheard, Muslim artists in the age of empire and mass incarceration turned the possibility of prison bars into musical bars of rebellion and hope, as hip-hop became a powerful site of redemption and deliverance, mapping a new imaginative geography in the post–Civil Rights era, a geography that was forged through the cultural and political histories of Black Islam, the Muslim Third World, and Black internationalism.

Sound of Da Police

Brilliantly captured in Cle Shaheed Sloan's 2005 documentary *Bastards of the Party*, hip-hop's emergence from urban America in the 1970s was a result of a host of political, economic, and racist state forces that can be traced back to the rise of Black Power in the 1960s and to the profound shifts in the U.S. economy that began at roughly the same time. As capital and commerce left the urban centers and crossed borders into the Third World in the second half of the twentieth century, cities in the United States came to embody and represent something radically different from what they had before. No longer the engine of progress and prosperity or the center of American sophistication and modernity, the city instead came to embody decline, fear, and danger.

In order to displace the fears caused by global capital, America's political discourse portrayed the country's "decline" not as a result of the larger contradictions in capitalism but rather as a result of the moral decay and degeneracy that the city—and its inhabitants—supposedly represented, as racial anxieties and economic insecurities once again became cemented in the American imagination. From the mid- to late 1960s on, as a result of repression, white flight, and the erosion of local tax bases due to corporate flight across borders, the "city" was demonized to embody fear, danger, and crime within the mainstream imagination, all of which became code words in justifying a full frontal assault on the Black and Brown communities that lived there.[3]

In the immediate aftermath of urban unrest and heightened Black discontent, Lyndon Johnson's Great Society programs in the mid-1960s were one of the first in a long line of initiatives that claimed to address the condition of the nation's cities. As Black anger intensified over white resistance to racial justice, Johnson's programs failed. Under the banner of "law and order" after the presidential election of 1968, Nixon and his proxies, including the FBI and local police forces, used covert programs such as COINTELPRO and other "legitimate" means to destroy the political unrest that was taking place all across urban America. With hundreds of urban uprisings that set American cities ablaze and sent smoke signals of Black Power rising, Nixon used the mantra of "law and order" to mobilize what he called the "Silent Majority" (his white constituencies) to generate the political will and national consensus he needed to destroy the Black Panthers and other Black (and Brown) liberation and antiwar organizations. As Black communities challenged policing, poverty, and U.S. imperial desire around the world, Nixon repeatedly returned to his "law and order" mantra in order to contain and destroy the domestic unrest that ultimately made America's actions in Vietnam untenable.

As the 1970s wore on, the rhetoric of "crime" captured the national imagination. And it was New York, specifically the Bronx, that came to represent a kind of national symbol of urban decay, the ashes from which the phoenix of hip-hop would arise. All over America, the movement of factory jobs abroad exacerbated the conditions set in motion by Nixon's politics of aggression. As employment, tax bases, and economic opportunities shrank, both federal and state governments began to shift their focus from education and infrastructure to the eradication of "crime," fattening police budgets and triggering the passage of punitive laws (such as the notorious 1973 Rockefeller Drug Laws) in order to calm the national fears about "crime" in the city.

As white fears deepened throughout the 1970s in the shadows of Black Power, the defeat in Vietnam, the post-Watergate discontent, the economic stagflation of the decade, and the Iranian hostage crisis of 1979, the widespread perception of whites was that "their America" was in decline. This sentiment found coherence in the figure of Ronald Reagan, who, with the emergence of the New Right, sought to comfort white America through a resurgent U.S. nationalism that was predicated upon the creation of both domestic and foreign enemies of the state.[4]

A telling moment occurred on August 4, 1980, when Reagan chose to launch his presidential campaign in the small town of Philadelphia, Mississippi. As the symbolic first stop on his campaign for the White House, Reagan's choice was a harbinger of things to come, for this was the town where, in 1964, Civil Rights activists Michael Schwerner, Andrew Goodman, and James Chaney were murdered by white supremacists. In his speech there in 1980, Reagan openly declared, "I believe in states' rights"—a not-so-subtle support of the southern segregationist mantra that dated back to slavery and had become a white rallying cry against the Civil Rights movement. This was essentially the flip side of Reagan's deeply coded attack on "big government" and distrust of D.C., which echoed throughout his campaign and tenure as president, as his appeal to not only the conservative white upper class but also working-class whites (known as Reagan Democrats) tapped into a rich vein of white resentment about the perceived gains of the Civil Rights and Black Power movements.[5] Reagan aligned himself with deeply racist currents in the United States, tapping into the prevailing perception among whites that, through the passage of Civil Rights bills and related policies, the U.S. government had betrayed the interests of "real Americans" and was instead beholden to minorities, giving special treatment to Blacks, women, immigrants, and other aggrieved groups.

What Nixon had begun under the banner of "law and order," Reagan repackaged as the "War on Drugs" and the "War on Crime" as part of his "Morning in America" crusade in the 1980s. But it was *mourning* in America for urban communities. Reagan's far-right-wing politics and attacks on Civil Rights gains went big time under the lights of the new Hollywood–Beltway axis, as his "War on Drugs" and "War on Crime" slogans captured the white imagination, and he used "welfare queens," "crack dealers," "gang wars," and "illegals" as supposed threats to domestic order and the very essence of his view of America.[6]

Reagan sought to link the idea of America to an implicit idea of whiteness that leaned heavily upon notions of tradition, family, responsibility, work ethic, and character, molding all of these into a larger conception of citizenship. Against this backdrop, Reagan made coded and not so coded appeals to whites by distinguishing them from and contrasting them with the inhabitants of urban centers, as he played on the sensationalized fears of supposed Black criminality. In doing so, Reagan tapped into a deep historical vein of white supremacy that marks the distinction between "citizen" and "criminal" as a racial one, in which whiteness is linked to the nation, and Blackness is coded as un-American. Reagan manipulated these ideas as a resurgent whiteness retook center stage with a vehemence, pitting supposedly hard-working Americans against the "criminal" element in the cities, who were not only accused of draining the resources of hard-working taxpayers but were also seen as moral failures and a collective shackle on America's feet. In Reagan's doublespeak, the inner cities kept America captive and prevented the nation from reaching its destiny, a powerful narrative that encouraged the demonization of Blackness in mainstream television, newspapers, and popular culture.

Reagan's legacy and his deep connections to Hollywood strengthened the complicity between the bright lights and the Beltway, and the hysteria-generating sequels that were the George H. W. Bush and Clinton administrations furthered the narrative about the inherent dangers of the inner city. Both Bush and Clinton continued to use "crime" to generate political capital as the mainstream media continued to utilize the logic of Reaganism. Bush I grabbed the mic from Reagan and spat the same rhymes, using Willie Horton to get elected the first time and the Los Angeles Uprisings of 1992 to try to get reelected. And though Bush failed at that reelection, Clinton's subsequent "tough on crime" policies resulted in the largest increase in the prison population during any presidency in American history, and his passage of the repressive 1994 Violent Crime Control and Law Enforcement Act added thirty billion dollars to build more prisons and put a hundred thousand more police officers on the streets.[7] So if Clinton was a friend to Black folks, imagine the enemies.

This was indicative of a larger pattern that had begun in the late 1960s under Nixon, in which Black discontent and political mobilization resulted in U.S. state-sanctioned repression that included huge cutbacks in education and infrastructure and drastic increases in funding the formation of an urban police state and the building of prisons. As a result, the prison population in the United States skyrocketed by 500 percent between 1970 and 2000, with the United States having a higher rate of prisoners per one hundred thousand of its population than any other country in the world.[8] This has culminated in what Michelle Alexander has referred to as "the New Jim Crow," in which, according to her, "racial caste has not ended in America: we have only redesigned it."[9]

As the distinction between the citizen and noncitizen revealed itself once again to be a racial one in the United States, the post–Civil Rights moment further entrenched this distinction by marking the difference between the "citizen" and the "criminal," making Blackness the domestic marker of exclusion from the national family.[10] This national family of America also had supposed global threats that sought its demise, and from the 1970s on, the Muslim Third World complemented the domestic menace of Blackness to the American national family.

On the international front, the hypernationalism of Reagan and the desire to "restore greatness" to America were predicated upon the fears stoked by the administration of the Cold War and the racial panics caused by the fears of "Islamic terrorism." The New Right's embrace of evangelical Christianity framed U.S. foreign policy such that "godless" communism and "militant Islam" were viewed as threats to the United States. With anticommunist battles being pitched in Central America and covert wars being fought everywhere, the Muslim Third World also fell under an expanding U.S. orbit, making Iran, Lebanon, Libya, Egypt, Saudi Arabia, Palestine, Pakistan, Afghanistan, and other countries witnesses to a deepening U.S. military and political presence.

In fact, the fears of "Islamic terrorism" that proliferated in the 1980s had their roots in the previous decade, for the 1970s had witnessed the beginning of the rise in the "terrorist threat" to U.S. and Western interests when the politics of the Palestinian–Israeli conflict deepened, and the United States and western Europe provided more diplomatic, financial, and military support to Israel. With Palestinians seeking to bring international attention to their plight, they and their allies across the globe struck at various targets around the world, but none more visible than the 1972 Olympics in Munich, Germany, where they stormed the dormitory for Israeli athletes, which led to eleven of those athletes being killed. Broadcast all over the world, this event and its unfolding drama brought the figure of the "terrorist" to living rooms in the United States, an image and idea that was solidified as the politics of the Muslim Third World became a more prominent part of the American public's collective awareness. Anti-Muslim sentiment deepened as the Arab oil embargo in 1973 shook the U.S. economy and as economic anxieties, racist rhetoric, and xenophobia congealed in the belief that Muslims were holding America hostage economically, which intensified the racist rhetoric in the United States, a rhetoric that was clearly ignorant of the United States' imperial role in the region and its demand for a continuing flow of oil and regional control.[11]

But no event did more to harness the widespread discontent of the 1970s than the Iran hostage crisis in 1979. As a result of American intervention in Iran, including the CIA's "Operation Ajax," which overthrew the democratically elected Mohammed Mossadegh in 1953 and immediately installed a brutal dictator in the shah, Iranian students stormed the U.S. Embassy in Teheran and took sixty-five Americans hostage. Lasting for 444 days, the Iran hostage crisis gripped the United States and sparked hypernationalist sentiments as television, newspaper, and other media covered the story intensely, constructing a narrative in which an innocent America was under siege from ruthless and maniacal Muslims.

Coincidentally, the hostages were released on the day that Reagan was being inaugurated in 1981, giving truth to the lie of his "Morning in America" slogan, as it symbolized a newly redeemed America that had to be ever mindful of the threats that were posed to it. Catapulting from the nightly news coverage of the Iran hostage crisis, a steady diet of television programming, news media coverage, and Hollywood films throughout the 1980s portrayed a constant threat of "terrorism" against the United States. And with increased U.S. involvement in the region, several events in the late 1970s through the 1980s and into the early 1990s figured the Muslim Third World as a threat to U.S. interests, linking "terrorism" to Islam and Muslims and further justifying U.S. control and dominance in the region. In addition to the Iran hostage crisis, there was also an increase in U.S. intervention in Lebanon, which resulted in the 1983 bombing of an American military barracks in Beirut, killing 243 U.S. soldiers. The United States also began fighting a proxy war against the Soviet Union in Afghanistan, which necessitated deeper dependence and control of neighboring Pakistan and the use of Saudi Arabia to assist in weapons deals. In addition, the increasing tensions of the Palestinian–Israeli conflict, the Iran–Iraq war, in which both sides were given U.S. funding and arms (as revealed in the Iran–Contra Affair), the U.S. attacks on Libya in 1986, and the Gulf War against Iraq in 1990, just to name a few, all created a national hysteria about the fear around "terrorism" and the perceived menace of the Muslim Third World to the United States.

With the "Black criminal" and the "Muslim terrorist" becoming the twin pillars of U.S. state formation in the post–Civil Rights era, it is deeply ironic that Malcolm X would become the iconic figure for Black radicalism and hip-hop culture late in the twentieth century. For not only had he been incarcerated and labeled *criminal* at an earlier time, but he also converted to Islam and became a radical Black internationalist who challenged U.S. anti-Black racism and linked these struggles with those in the Muslim Third World. In addition, as the figure of the "Muslim terrorist" dominated mainstream discourse, it served to undermine the historical role of Islam within Black political culture by isolating and stigmatizing those Black activists and artists who aligned themselves with Islam and the politics of the Muslim Third World. Despite these attempts to fracture Black Islam from the Muslim Third World and also to undermine the politics of the Muslim International, Malcolm's role as iconic figure was a testament to the enduring political vision that he had crafted, for Black Islam in hip-hop culture reclaimed the interpretive authority over Black destiny in the United States and imagined a different community of belonging with very different possibilities for freedom, in which Black peoples would be seen not as national minorities but as global majorities.

Follow the Leader: Reframing X

Malcolm's resurgence in hip-hop in the 1980s and into the 1990s was due to a host of different factors, not the least of which was the increasing significance of Afrocentricity, Black Nationalism, and the resurgence of Black Islam. As a result of these direct responses to the massive repression of the post–Civil Rights backlash, the Reagan–Bush policies of the "War on Crime," massive incarceration, and the racist appeals and rhetoric of Reagan, Malcolm's resurgence signified the renewed desire and longing of a new generation of Black youth to seek answers to the probing questions they had about their place in U.S. society and how to resist it. And what they found was what others before them had found: that white supremacy and Eurocentrism were alive and well, having shape-shifted into a U.S. nationalism that was predicated on containing Black freedom struggles at home and an expansionist politics abroad. As a result, there was a tremendous resurgence of interest in the history of Black Power, Afrocentric thought, and Islam as forces that could potentially empower and challenge the prevailing dogmas of post–Civil Rights repression. And if one figure could harness most of these energies, it was Malcolm X, who became the icon for the hip-hop generation as his voice was sampled, his ideas were referenced, and his influence shaped ideas about Black resilience and resistance. Culminating in Spike Lee's 1992 biopic titled *Malcolm X*, interest in Malcolm was widespread, from his presence in hip-hop music and video to sales of his autobiography, which rose 300 percent from 1988 to 1991, while sales of four of Malcolm's books from Pathfinder Press increased 900 percent from 1986 to 1991.[12] In addition, Malcolm became a cottage industry after Lee's marketing campaign, as "X" caps, T-shirts, and other merchandise made Malcolm a mass-market commodity.

Malcolm's resurgence in urban America in the mid-1980s also spoke to the profound failure of and disillusionment with the Civil Rights project. Put plainly, the mountaintop was not reached. And Malcolm became an enduring reminder of that failure, for no one sounded the warning about the limitations of Civil Rights more so than Malcolm. It was no surprise that when hip-hop embraced Black radicalism and Islam that Malcolm became the iconic image of the culture. It wasn't only Malcolm's embrace of Black radicalism, his conversion to Islam, and his Pan-Africanist and Third Worldist politics that appealed to a younger generation. For Black youth facing down the barrel of the Reagan–Bush backlash, the hip-hop generation and Malcolm shared a great deal in common. Just as the hip-hop generation did, Malcolm represented the idea of an "authentic" Blackness that did not sell out or compromise to white America. Both Malcolm and hip-hop also gave voice to the poverty and difficulties of urban existence while also speaking truth to power against the Black bourgeoisie, white power, and state authority. Both Malcolm and the hip-hop generation faced accusations of reckless violence, while, ironically, both were also subject to incarceration and the constant threat of imminent violence and death as Black bodies in white America. Malcolm had transcended the violence and despair of the ghetto and incarceration, providing a redemptive possibility to Black youth who had already been locked up or were constantly subjected to that possibility in the era of mass incarceration, which defined the post–Civil Rights era. And just as Malcolm had, hip-hop during this period celebrated an enduring valorization and sanctity of Blackness as a source of pride, redemption, and resistance. Finally, and possibly most important, like Malcolm, hip-hop was deeply invested in the power of words as a weapon, and, like Malcolm, it used its rhetorical rebellion to speak its truth to power.

Through the long shadow cast by Malcolm X, the sometimes strident but always determined challenge to U.S. power was also seen in the influence on hip-hop culture of the Nation of Islam and Louis Farrakhan, who galvanized Black youth and the hip-hop generation in the late 1980s and throughout the 1990s. Having broken away from Wallace Muhammad, who had taken over after the death of his father, Elijah, and moved the Nation of Islam toward Sunni Islam, Farrakhan went on a trip to Africa and the Middle East and returned to revive and lead the Nation of Islam. Farrakhan would travel frequently throughout Africa and Asia in the 1980s and '90s, continuing that tradition within the Nation of Islam of linking Black struggles in the United States with those in the Third World. As a result of his travels, his rhetoric, and his influence, Farrakhan faced tremendous political pressure from all sides and from the highest levels of the U.S. government, including when he received a five-million-dollar loan from Libya's Muammar Gaddafi to assist in the economic development of urban America. Farrakhan would become a lightning rod for controversy, as the news media attacked him incessantly. A 1995 special issue of *Newsweek* magazine, for instance, put Farrakhan on the cover just after his Million Man March on the Mall in Washington, D.C., with the nebulous headline "The Two Faces of Farrakhan."[13] His influence on hip-hop culture would continue, not only when he played the peacemaker of "beefs" between several artists, but also when he held the Hip-Hop Summit in 1997 following the murders of Tupac Shakur and Biggie Smalls. This summit brought together a number of well-known and respected hip-hop artists. In fact, Farrakhan has become the second most influential figure within hip-hop culture behind Malcolm X, having been sampled and mentioned in songs by artists such as Public Enemy, Ice Cube, Big Daddy Kane, Biggie Smalls, Brand Nubian, Queen Latifah, Digable Planets, the Fugees, and numerous others. More recently, in 2008 Nas, on his controversial *Untitled* album, stated in a refrain, "They did not have the power to stop Louis Farrakhan, a testament to the Nation of Islam's influence on hip-hop culture."

But Lee's *Malcolm X* was, for better or worse, a signal moment, because it sought to capture, and catapult from, the renewed interest in Malcolm among the hip-hop generation and the deep discontent that existed in urban America. Lee's film framed an exploration of three different Malcolms—the hustler, the Nation of Islam devotee, and the post-Mecca Black leader. In seeking to tell Malcolm's story, Lee firmly situated him within a conventional Hollywood logic of individual heroism and tragedy and, in doing so, catered to Hollywood's expectations about Blackness by spending a great deal of time on Malcolm as a hustler and "criminal." In portraying the arc of Malcolm from street hustler to prisoner to revolutionary and finally to martyr, Lee's film almost completely ignored Malcolm's Muslim Internationalism and his linking of Black liberation in the United States with Third World liberation struggles, a radical position that was a central part of Malcolm's politics both while he was in the Nation of Islam and especially after he left. Absent were Malcolm's poignant insights into the global nature of white supremacy, the relationship of U.S. empire to European colonialism, and the role of Black peoples in the United States in dismantling racial injustice nationally and internationally. By not exploring how Malcolm situated his criticism of U.S. racism within a broader struggle against white world supremacy (to reference Malcolm), Lee domesticated Malcolm's politics and undermined Malcolm's radical Third Worldist ideal under the banner of a liberal universalism. Tellingly, the film's opening showed the iconic "X" in red, white, and blue, burned out of an American flag, which suggested that Malcolm was merely part of a larger tradition of American liberalism and dissent. In true Hollywood biopic form, Malcolm was framed as an American hero worthy of recognition, and not the Third World militant that he truly was.

What made Malcolm so powerful was his radical and redemptive vision for Black liberation. But Lee's film overlooked and undermined this, especially at a time when the Muslim Third World was in the crosshairs of U.S. empire, as the first Gulf War in Iraq had just been "won." Through the prisms of domestic racism and Third World decolonization, Malcolm shaped his Muslim anticolonialism into an enduring legacy that deeply influenced a younger generation of activists immediately following his assassination, including RAM, the Black Arts Movement, the Student Nonviolent Coordinating Committee (SNCC), and of course the Black Panther Party, who saw themselves as "a living testament to his life work."[14]

But in order to understand the significance of the resurgence of Islam and Malcolm X in hip-hop in the 1980s and '90s, when the "Black criminal" and the "Muslim terrorist" were the violent specters threatening U.S. national identity, it is important to understand the historical context of the rise of the Nation of Islam and Malcolm X in America in the 1950s and '60s, when desegregation battles were taking place in the United States and decolonization was overtaking the Third World of Africa and Asia.

As the widely recognized architect of Black Power and the Black Panther Party, Malcolm X traveled throughout Africa and the Muslim Third World of Africa and Asia, seeking to link U.S. Black struggles with the worldwide rebellions taking place against European colonialism. Linking the struggles of Vietnam, the Congo, Cuba, and other nations to those of U.S.-based Blacks, Malcolm's own Muslim Internationalism not only sought to link Black Muslims in the United States with the larger movements of decolonization in the Muslim Third World, but in doing so, he also sought to link the struggles of U.S.-based Blacks in general with the Bandung world and the global struggles against white supremacy taking place throughout Africa, Asia, and Latin America.

In the immediate aftermath of World War II, as U.S. empire expanded, Black intellectuals and activists who were being influenced by the anticolonial movements taking place in Africa and Asia began to look at the Middle East as an emerging battleground upon which to negotiate their own political identities, affiliations, and agendas. As scholar Melani McAlister has written, while "the tendency has been to see the transnational elements of Black culture in the United States as focused exclusively on identifications with Africa," she argues that for Black activists, intellectuals, and writers, they "looked not only to Africa but also to other areas, and particularly to the Middle East, as site and source for explorations of blackness and the recovery and reconstruction of black history."[15] As McAlister details, for Black Christians and the emerging Civil Rights movement, the religious narratives of Exodus, slavery, and suffering were powerful tropes and analogies for translating biblical histories into contemporary struggles around racism—all of which served to create and forge ties to the Middle East through religious narratives of liberation and redemption. But Black Islam in the United States also laid claim to the region and its histories, including but not limited to Islam's holiest sites, Mecca and Medina. In fact, during this same period through the Nation of Islam and Malcolm X, Islam came to be seen as an alternative form of radical Black consciousness that was quite distinct from what was perceived to be the integrationist goals of Black Christianity—a consciousness that was internationalist in scope and one that more clearly aligned itself with the revolutionary nationalism that was overtaking the Third World. Because of Christianity's association with whiteness, Islam, as echoed by James Baldwin and others, came to be understood as "the Black man's religion."

For the Nation of Islam and Malcolm X, Islam became the focal point for redefining a new Black identity that built upon earlier periods of Black anticolonial sensibilities and that tied their vision of Black liberation to the larger Muslim Third World, forging links and trading upon the fact that Islam was a major world religion. A central part of this alternative narrative of origin and sense of belonging for Black peoples in America was how the Nation of Islam respatialized Black identity without exclusively looking at Africa as the site for the recovery of Black history. As a result, the NOI redefined and expanded Black identity beyond the United States and in relation to the Third World, using terms such as the *Asiatic, Asian black nation, Afro-Asiatic Black Man,* and the *Asiatic Black Man,* all of which echoed Elijah Muhammad's claim in his seminal text that "we are descendants of the Asian black nation . . . the rich Nile Valley of Egypt and the present seat of the Holy City, Mecca, Arabia."[16] As a result, the Nation of Islam "provided an alternative to—and in some sense a fundamental critique of—the nation-state. [For] African-American Muslims could claim a symbolic counter-citizenship, an identity that challenged black incorporation into the dominant discourse of Judeo-Christian Americanness."[17] These alternative identities and the forms of countercitizenship that they made possible were powerful rhetorical mechanisms for Black converts to Islam to redefine themselves not only in relation to the United States but also to the larger Third World of Africa and Asia, for as Malcolm X said, "Islam is the greatest unifying force in the Dark World today."[18] As the presence of Islam witnessed a resurgence within Black political culture in the mid- to late 1980s, these ideas and histories became a means of reclaiming a narrative of resistance, expanding the scope of Black belonging, and redefining Blackness in the face of the politics of repression during the era of Reagan.

Malcolm, Mecca, and Black Art

Even in death, Malcolm was the ideological architect and radical theorist for groups such as RAM, SNCC, and the Black Panther Party. But while his influence is most often and most notably seen within the realms of Black political thought, Malcolm also had a tremendous influence on Black cultural production and artistic practices. Both Amiri Baraka and Larry Neal, two of the central figures in the formation of the Black Arts Movement, have discussed the impact of Malcolm on Black life. According to Baraka (then Leroi Jones), "The concept of Black Power is natural after Malcolm. Malcolm's legacy was the concept and will toward political power in the world for the Black man."[19] In addition Larry Neal said,

> But even though Malcolm's death—the manner of it—emotionally fractured young black radicals, there were two central facts that all factions of the movement came to understand. And they are: that the struggle for black self-determination had entered a serious, more profound stage; and that for most of us, nonviolence as a viable technique of social

change had died with Malcolm on the stage of the Audubon. . . . Malcolm's ideas had touched all aspects of contemporary black nationalism: the relationship of black America and the Third World, the development of a black cultural thrust, the rights of oppressed peoples to self-defense and armed struggle; the necessity of maintaining a strong moral force in the black community; the building of autonomous black institutions; and finally, the need for a black theory of social change.[20]

Although Malcolm's influence on Black political thought has been recognized, his ideas on Black cultural radicalism have not been explored at great length, in particular his influence on the Black Arts Movement and then hip-hop culture. One of Malcolm's more involved discussions on cultural politics came at the opening rally for his newly formed Organization of Afro-American Unity (OAAU). At the founding rally in 1964, Malcolm demanded that Black peoples "launch a cultural revolution," stating, "We must recapture our heritage and our identity if we are ever to liberate ourselves from the bonds of white supremacy. . . . our cultural revolution must be the means of bringing us closer to our African brothers and sisters. It must begin in the community and be based on community participation. Afro-Americans will be free to create only when they can depend on the Afro-American community for support and Afro-American artists must realize that they depend on the Afro-American community for inspiration."[21]

Malcolm's declaration on the founding of his OAAU, modeled after Kwame Nkrumah's Organization for African Unity, was part of a larger and broader framework for Black liberation. Forged from Malcolm's travels to Africa and Asia, his insurgent Third Worldism, and his Muslim Internationalism, Malcolm's statements on art and its role within social movements is a telling and revealing look not only into the power and promise that the Black Arts Movement offered but also into hip-hop culture. Echoing Fanon's famous declaration in "On National Culture" (from the *Wretched of the Earth*) about the role of culture in the formation of the nation, the idea of a Black nation that was forming in the post-Malcolm period saw cultural and artistic production as central to Black liberation.

Fanon argued that in the formation of national culture the final phase is the "fighting phase," in which "the native, after having tried to lose himself among the people, with the people, will rouse the people.

Instead of letting the people's lethargy prevail, he turns into a galvanizer of the people. Combat literature, revolutionary literature, national literature emerges. During this phase a great many men and women who previously would have never thought of writing . . . feel the need to proclaim their nation, to portray their people and become the spokesperson of a new reality in action."[22] Echoing Fanon's dictates about the formation of the nation, Baraka's famous phrase "its nation time" was also reflected in his vision of the role of the artist within the Black Arts Movement or other radical cultural practices. As Baraka said in an essay titled "The Black Aesthetic," "The purpose of our writing is to create the nation."[23] While Fanon warned against a national culture that reached into the romanticized past, he argued that the artist "who uses the past must do so with the intention of opening the future, of spurring them into action and fostering hope."[24]

Both Malcolm's and Fanon's ideas about the aesthetics and ideologies of insurgent art took as their root the demand to challenge Eurocentric and white supremacist ideas about the nature of art, radical politics, and the practice of liberation. For both of them, the new moment of Black and Third World radicalism held utopian possibilities that had to be seized, because both offered principled critiques of the destructive force of the West, Europe, and the United States on Black and Third World peoples. For Malcolm, "Black artists need to recapture our heritage and our identity if we are ever to liberate ourselves from the bonds of white supremacy,"[25] whereas Fanon saw European dominance as a psychically powerful foe:

> Let us decide not to imitate Europe. . . . Let us endeavor to invent a man in full, something which Europe has been incapable of achieving. Two centuries ago, a former European colony took it into its head to catch up with Europe. It has been so successful that the United States of America became a monster, where the flaws, sickness, and inhumanity of Europe have reached frightening proportions. . . . We must make a new start, develop a new way of thinking, and endeavor to create a new man.[26]

Rooted in the Muslim International, which grew out of Malcolm's conversion to Islam and his travels to Africa, Asia, and Muslim Third World as well as Fanon's lifework in Algeria, both Malcolm's and Fanon's proscriptions to resist European or white supremacist notions of art, truth,

and aesthetics became a fundamental tenet of Black Arts' cultural practice. The Black Arts imperative sought to challenge what were seen as
white-dominated ideas about art and literature and to replace them with
new literary conventions and thematics that were not only radical breaks
from white or Western ideas about art and aesthetics but were also distinctly different from previous eras of Black creative impulses, be it the
Harlem Renaissance, the Harlem Writers Guild, the Negritude Movement, or other artistic and literary movements. Black Arts sought to wed
aesthetics to ideology and writing to fighting. Congealing into a quasi-
coherent set of ideas around Black Arts, Blackness became the primary
pivot point on which the new cultural and political landscape would turn,
as Black artists sought to give creative expression to the racial pride
and "Black is beautiful" slogans of the post-Malcolm 1960s. Seeking to
purge Black peoples' minds of racial self-hate and the internalization
of anti-Black ideologies, Black artists emphasized the creation of new
models that were radical breaks from those of whiteness and the West.
Whether it was Larry Neal's pronouncement that "the main thrust of
this new breed of contemporary writers is to confront the contradictions arising out of the Black man's experience in the racist West,"[27] or
James T. Stewart's comment in his essay in *Black Fire*, titled "The Development of the Black Revolutionary Artist," in which he says, "We must
emancipate our minds from Western values and standards,"[28] Black Arts
writings are replete with references to and admonishments of Black
peoples to break from the West and its racial handmaiden, whiteness.

In response to Malcolm's assertion that in a revolution "you don't do
any singing" because "you're too busy swinging,"[29] Black artists sought
to bridge that gap by singing in order to inspire swinging—that is, to
create radical art that would foment revolutionary action. And in doing
so, the Black Arts Movement became rhetorical rebellion and exile from
the lands of Black respectability, as it sought to create a community-
based art that invented new forms and conventions in poetry, theater,
and literature.

But the critical disposition of the Black Arts Movement toward the
West and whiteness that was influenced and informed by the theoretical frameworks of Malcolm X and Fanon carried with it the histories
of the Muslim Third World, whether through Malcolm's Muslim radicalism or Fanon's militant anticolonialism in Algeria. Not surprisingly,

because of the presence of the Muslim Third World within Black political culture in the postwar era, the Black Arts Movement was inflected by ideas and symbols of Islam and the Muslim Third World, for the artistic and aesthetic tradition that it forged was part and parcel of the Muslim International.

While jazz music was also a space for previous explorations of the Muslim International in the United States, through the work of numerous Black jazz musicians such as Ahmad Jamal, Yusef Lateef, and Art Blakey, the Black Arts Movement of the late 1960s was also a site for the Muslim International, as it employed Islam and Islamically themed symbols and ideas in their radical Black cultural practices of the time. According to Melani McAlister, "The Black Arts movement defined political struggle as cultural struggle; this cultural struggle required a new spirituality. In literary circles, Islamic symbolism and mythology were incorporated into the self-conscious construction of a new black aesthetic and a revolutionary black culture."[30] Amiri Baraka, whose play *A Black Mass* was based upon the Nation of Islam's myth of Yacub, as well as his Jihad record label, was one of the primary proponents of incorporating Islam into the Black Arts Movement, for Baraka believed that Islam offers "what the Black man needs . . . a reconstruction . . . a total way of life that he can involve himself with that is post-American in a sense."[31]

In addition, in her book *"After Mecca": Women Poets and the Black Arts Movement*, Cheryl Clarke reveals the profound influence and role that women had within the formation of a distinctly womanist Black Arts aesthetic that challenged the oftentimes patriarchal order forged by both Black Power and the Black Arts Movement. Seizing on the trope of "mecca," Clarke argues, "'Mecca' resonates with Black consciousness movements of the 1960's and 1970's in the United States, a demand to turn away from the (white) West. In turning away, black artists created a new lexicon of prescriptive and proscriptive blackness." Borrowing from Gwendolyn Brooks's poetry book *In the Mecca*, Clarke argues that "mecca" became a signifier with which to define and redefine Black peoples' relationships to dominant white society. For Clarke, "mecca" became "a trope of deliverance from Western oppression" and also came to "represent the struggle of black people, during the late twentieth century, to envision a world in which African American culture occupied the center. This 'Mecca' is as much to be struggled toward as struggled for—much like Malcolm X's 'hadj' and Martin Luther King's 'mountaintop,' one is always getting there."[32]

While Islam and the embrace of Muslim identities by some Black peoples in the United States were becoming a kind of salvation and reorientation both politically and spiritually, the influence of Islamic iconography and Muslim themes could be seen within Black Arts literature, making its cultural and aesthetic struggles part of the Muslim International. For example, in the seminal anthology *Black Fire*, by Amiri Baraka (Leroi Jones) and Larry Neal, poems include Gaston Neal's "Personal Jihad," Welton Smith's "malcolm," which concludes with the Nation of Islam allegory of Yakub, David Llorens's "The *Fellah*, the Chosen Ones, the Guardian," and Nathan Hare's "Brainwashing of Black Men's Minds," as well as the numerous poems and plays by writers who had changed their names, including Yusef Iman, Yusuf Rahman, and Ahmed Legraham Alhamisi. In addition, Ed Bullins's anthology *New Plays from the Black Theater* also featured Muslim-themed pieces, including *El Hajj Malik: A Play about Malcolm X*, by N. R. Davidson Jr., and *The Black Bird (Al Tair Aswad)*, by Marvin X,[33] as did Askia Muhammad Toure's "Tauhid" (meaning the oneness of Allah), Larry Neal's "Can You Dig It?," Alicia Johnson's "Tae (The Word)," and Marvin X's "Fly to Allah."[34] Also, as noted by Cheryl Clarke, numerous female poets and writers utilized Muslim symbols and themes, including Gwendolyn Brooks's *In the Mecca* anthology, while Umar bin Hassan and Jalaluddin Nuriddin, original members of the seminal group the Last Poets, converted to Islam, as did Amiri Baraka, Sonia Sanchez, and untold others. According to McAlister, "Even though the majority of Black Arts writers and readers were not Muslims, this myth and culture became part of the language and geography of black cultural identity. For a new generation, then, culture became the basis for constructing an alternative nation; and this (post)nation—with its own sense of spirituality and its own political vision—was the underlying utopian gesture of black nationalist thought and literature. Within this project, Islamic affiliations often functioned as both a site and source for those black identities, linking African Americans to the Arab and Muslim Middle East in ways both literal and metaphoric."[35]

Through the Black Arts Movement, the contours of the Muslim International were shaped by the demands for new forms of representation and revolutionary consciousness within Black radical circles. The

Black Arts Movement's imperative for a socially engaged art that would challenge Eurocentrism and white supremacy would resonate years later in urban America. Just as Black cultural activists sought to connect art to radicalism and ideology to aesthetics in the literature, theater, and poetry of the Black Arts Movement, the presence and influence of Islam and Muslim identities would reemerge in the Black art and politics of hip-hop culture almost two decades later, making hip-hop in the post–Civil Rights era another radical site for exploring the politics of the Muslim International.

Dawn of the Golden Age

"The Golden Age" (roughly 1986–94) is often referred to in nostalgic ways as a time when hip-hop was at its creative and political peak. And with few exceptions, that era's most significant artists embraced Islam, deeply influencing the rest of hip-hop history as well, so that a vast canon of songs expresses the relationship between Blackness and Islam, including Brand Nubian, Poor Righteous Teachers, X-Clan, Rakim Allah, Public Enemy, Ice Cube, Gang Starr, Big Daddy Kane, the Wu Tang Clan, Pete Rock and C. L. Smooth, A Tribe Called Quest, The Roots, Common, Mos Def, Lupe Fiasco, Beanie Segal, Freeway, Jurassic 5, Self Scientific, Oddisee, Shabazz Palaces, Jay Electronica, as well as numerous others. Forged through the violent crucible of the post–Civil Rights and Black Power eras, hip-hop sought to reclaim a history of Black radicalism and internationalism in the context of the criminalization of Blackness, mass incarceration, and what I have called the rise of the carceral imagination in the United States from the 1970s and into the twenty-first century. When the post–Civil Rights consensus demonized urban America and criminalized Blackness as "un-American" in the 1970s, the "Muslim terrorist" emerged within the larger U.S. imagination during the same period, as the politics of the Muslim Third World began to play an increasing role within U.S. foreign policy.[36]

As the "Black criminal" and the "Muslim terrorist" have served to give coherence and purpose to U.S. national identity, the recurring presence of Black Islam in U.S. political culture continues to reveal the unresolved contradictions around race and empire that sit at the heart of U.S. state formation. Rather than attempting to be incorporated or embraced by U.S. society, Black Islam, especially through hip-hop, has used its collective exclusion as both Black *and* Muslim to critique U.S. racial domination by challenging the master narrative of race and Blackness in the United States and the legacies of slavery, while also imagining an internationalism in relation to Africa and the Muslim Third World that challenges U.S. global power in those regions.

Marshaling the history of figures such as Malcolm X and the internationalist dimensions of Black Islam that he forged through his Muslim Mosque Inc. and his Organization of Afro-American Unity, these artists imagined Black belonging beyond the United States, and rather than assuming the logic of the New Right and viewing the Muslim Third World simply as "the enemy," hip-hop artists tapped into a deeper history of Black internationalism that had linked itself and its struggles with the continent of Africa and the Muslim Third World, mobilizing the struggles and iconography of South Africa, Egypt, Iraq, and elsewhere as a site and source of affiliation and solidarity. By crafting an alternative community of belonging that shaped and was shaped by the Muslim International, Black cultural activists in hip-hop not only challenged U.S.-based racial control and domination but also linked these struggles with the expansion of U.S. empire abroad, extending and inflecting a long-standing tradition of internationalism that has been a hallmark of Black radical practice and Black political thought in the post–World War II era, whether it was through Robeson, Du Bois, Claudia Jones, Malcolm X, Harold Cruse, Stokely Carmichael, Angela Davis, the Black Panthers, and numerous others.

Conjuring the history of Malcolm X and the radical redemptive vision that he outlined throughout his life, hip-hop was a cultural extension of Malcolm's internationalist vision. Just as Malcolm challenged the limits of the United States in determining Black destiny by connecting Black peoples with struggles in the Third World and providing a lens with which to view the global and entrenched nature of white supremacy, hip-hop also imagined Black possibility beyond America, as Africa and the politics of the Muslim Third World provided an alternative grammar of resistance and a unique language of revolt that was used to probe larger questions about the scale and scope of their friends and foes. With this presence of Islam and Malcolm X, hip-hop culture became a powerful way to explore how its poetry, aesthetics, and political imagination not only forged a redemptive vision of Blackness in the face of the remixed racism of the post–Civil Rights era, but also a radical alchemy of art and politics that shaped and contributed to the nuances and textures of the Muslim International.

Though Malcolm X became hip-hop's prophet of rage, his influence and that of Islam's are part of a longer history in which Black politics and art have been influenced and inspired by Islam and the Muslim Third World. Just as previous moments in Black history manifested diverse Muslim identities and interpretations—be they the Moorish Science Temple, the Nation of Islam, the 5% Nation of Gods and Earths, or the Ahmadi and Sunni Muslims—the age of hip-hop culture also reflected this diversity. But what is significant is that just as in the past, Islam became a means to root Black identity in the United States within the larger community of belonging that was global Islam, a move that most often connected Blacks to larger communities of resistance beyond the boundaries of the United States.

There is a vast canon of songs in hip-hop that reflect the history of Black Islam, whether it be the militant nationalism of Public Enemy, the bohemian blues of Black Star, the street swagger of Gang Starr, the cosmic chaos of the Wu Tang Clan, or the revolutionary street knowledge of early Ice Cube. By focusing on the work of Rakim, Ice Cube, Public Enemy, and Mos Def, we can consider the history of Islam and hip-hop within the broader context of the Muslim International, which was shaped and formed by post–Civil Rights repression and U.S. expansionism, when mass incarceration replaced segregation as the source of Black containment and the "Muslim terrorist" was seen as threatening U.S. security abroad.

Above the Clouds

As hip-hop became increasingly commodified in the early 1990s and "gangsta rap" became more prominent, the demand for hip-hop to return to its roots and to tap into its deeper legacies of Black resistance increased. Not surprisingly, it was the Black Arts Movement that was almost exclusively invoked as a standard and beacon for hip-hop's own potential and political purpose in the face of hypercommodification.

Gwendolyn Pough, Marcus Reeves, Marvin Gladney, and numerous others have discussed the relationships between the Black Arts Movement, Black Power, and hip-hop culture. Viewing hip-hop as an extension of that artistic and politicized moment, these scholars and critics explored not only how hip-hop aspired to define a new Black aesthetic but also how it raised social consciousness among Black communities in the post–Civil Rights and post–Black Power moment of the late twentieth century. To many, hip-hop came to be seen as the torchbearer for the Black Arts Movement, and just as that movement was seen as the cultural arm of Black Power, hip-hop was thought to be the cultural arm of a new social movement, if one existed, or, if not, then hip-hop was going to be the spark that would ignite one in late twentieth-century urban America.

Placing hip-hop within this longer arc of Black artistic resistance also served to disarm critics of the music, including those within the Black community themselves, who saw it as self-destructive, apolitical, and even counterrevolutionary. While most of the popular attacks on hip-hop characterized it as violent, misogynistic, and homophobic, these justifiable critiques often overlooked the liberatory intent of the genre and the deeply politicized ideas that, at its best, it embodied.[37] But if viewed as a cultural extension of the Black Arts Movement, hip-hop, instead of being dismissed, could be seen as part of a deep artistic, historical, and political legacy in which it would be taken more seriously, not only by critics and audiences, but also by the artists themselves, who many thought did not have a sense of the political possibility—or even responsibility—of the artist and the art form. The desire for a return to a Black Arts imperative, then, signified a longing for an uplifting and empowering art that could mobilize Black peoples, who were staring down the gun barrel of white America.

When hip-hop wasn't being compared to the Black Arts Movement, it was more often than not compared to itself, for many continue to invoke hip-hop's Golden Age as the genre's shining and defining moment, a period when hip-hop emerged as an aesthetic, lyrical, and also thematic force, marked by brilliant sampling styles, lyrically complex poetry, social uplift, and political protest around racial and economic injustice. Just as the Black Arts Movement was deeply influenced by Malcolm X and Black Nationalism and was loaded with the imagery and iconography of the Muslim Third World, so too was hip-hop's Golden Age. Whether it was Public Enemy's militant chaos, Rakim Allah, Brand Nubian, Poor Righteous Teachers, or any number of other acts, the Golden Age, with rare exception, wove through its songs of protest an embrace of Black Nationalism and Islam that rooted their critiques of U.S. state racism and injustice within a longer and deeper tradition of Black history and protest.

Afrika Bambaataa's Universal Zulu Nation, which emerged in 1973 in the immediate aftermath of the COINTELPRO-induced repression of Black Power, was formed in an attempt to use the arts as a vehicle to influence Black and Brown youth in the shadows of domestic war. Extending the Black Arts Movement's imperative to use art for social uplift and to connect it to community organizing, Zulu Nation is considered the founding ideological movement for hip-hop culture, as Bambaataa detailed a whole philosophical approach to Zulu Nation that was about social uplift, transcendence, and unity. Zulu Nation became more popular as Bambaataa's songs "Planet Rock" and "Renegades of Funk" became early b-boy anthems, and its founding "manifesto" borrowed heavily, and in some cases word for word, from the Nation of Islam's own statement "What the Muslims Believe," including opening with the refrain "We believe," in reference to the "mental and physical resurrection of the dead," calling for a reinterpretation of the Bible because it had been "tampered" with, stating its belief in the Qu'ran, and encouraging spiritual growth through "knowledge of self" (which became an existential mantra within hip-hop), as well as several other similarities. This early and influential blueprint for hip-hop was deeply informed by Islam and Black Nationalism, and it created an ideological paradigm out of which hip-hop and its relationship to Islam would continue to flourish.

Possibly the first hip-hop release that referenced Malcolm was the 1983 release by Tommy Boy Records, titled "No Sell Out," which featured Malcolm X speeches over an early hip-hop instrumental by Keith Leblanc. This song was sampled seven years later by Intelligent Hoodlum in his song "Black and Proud," in which he also invoked Malcolm X. By the late 1980s, the combination of Black radicalism and Islam in hip-hop had exploded. Lakim Shabazz, in his 1989 song "Black Is Back," also sampled Malcolm X on the difference between "the Black revolution and the Negro revolution" and then again on his 1990 song and video "Lost Tribe of Shabazz," in which he narrates the stolen legacy and history of Black peoples through slavery, an exile and displacement that were central to the Nation of Islam's theology, which imagined

Black peoples as the "lost tribe of Shabazz." Using the sampled voice of Stokely Carmichael saying, "Our people will survive America," Shabazz connected breakdancing and graffiti to Islamic worship practices and hieroglyphics. In the video, Shabazz uses the pyramids in Egypt as the backdrop to narrate the history of Black Islam and the origin of Black greatness, invoking a broader community of belonging that is central to the Nation of Islam's theology, as he says, "To them it's Africa, to us it's Asia," in reference to Egypt, connecting urban America with the Muslim Third World. Schooly D's 1989 song "Education of a Black Man" also samples Malcolm X, and King Sun's 1990 song "Be Black" (from his *Righteous but Ruthless* album) is replete with Islamic references to the Nation of Islam, Farrakhan, and others as he singles out those for whom activism and the embrace of Africa were style and not substance.

Also at this time came the powerful force of Brand Nubian, Poor Righteous Teachers, X-Clan, and Public Enemy, who all brought a defiant militancy and poetry to their fusion of Black radicalism and Islam. Brand Nubian, a group that comprised Sadat X (formerly Derek X), Lord Jamar, and Grand Puba, released *One for All* in 1990. Their song "Wake Up" samples Roy Ayers's classic "Everybody Loves the Sunshine," and it became one of the canonical songs about the Nation of Islam and the 5% Nation, detailing the specific cosmology and the redemptive power of the "knowledge of self" in the face of white supremacy and the destruction of Black history, asking, "Can a devil fool a Muslim?" They followed up this classic album with 1993's *In God We Trust*, with songs such as "Allah U Akbar," which is Arabic for "God is Great," and "Meaning the 5%," which samples Farrakhan as he details the history of Black Islam and its material critique of race and power, identifying 5 percent of the population as the poor righteous teachers and the "Black man of Asia." The group Poor Righteous Teachers took its name from this, as its members, Wise Intelligent, Culture Freedom, and Father Shaheed, became a foundation for Black Islamic teachings with their albums *Holy Intellect* (1989), *Pure Poverty* (1991), *Black Business* (1993), and also *The New World Order* (1996), whose songs such as "Rock Dis Funky Joint," "The Nation's Anthem," "Conscious Style," and "God, Earths and 85'ers" showcased their embrace of Islam and Black Nationalism as the means to critique Reagan-era racism and repression, the legacies of slavery, and the restoration of Black pride and dignity.

Another seminal group was X-Clan, whose members were affili-
ated with the community work of Blackwatch in Brooklyn, New York.
Deeply influenced and inspired by Malcolm X, the Nation of Islam,
Marcus Garvey, the Black Panthers, and Pan-Africanism more broadly,
Blackwatch became a community force based on the legendary work
of Sonny Carson, the celebrated activist from Brooklyn who was im-
mortalized in the 1974 film *The Education of Sonny Carson.* Along with
Brother J, Professor X (who was Lamumba Carson and the brother of
Sonny Carson), and others, X-Clan released two albums, 1990's *To the
East, Blackwards* and 1992's *Xodus,* both of which were laden with Black
Nationalist thought, Islamic iconography, and Black internationalist
ideals that imagined Black peoples in the United States within a larger
global context.

The Native Tongues, a collective that included the groups A Tribe
Called Quest, De La Soul, the Jungle Brothers, and others, combined
Afrocentricity and Islam with a bohemian aesthetic in the late 1980s and
into the 1990s. A Tribe Called Quest would more openly embrace Islam
in the mid- to late 1990s while also forming the Ummah, which takes
its name from the Islamic ideal of a worldwide community of believers
that transcends boundaries of any kind. As a loose collective of artists,
the Ummah included Jay Dee (Dilla), Q-Tip, D'Angelo, Raphael Siddiq,
and others. The Native Tongues would have a profound influence on
hip-hop, both aesthetically and politically. As the hip-hop equivalent to
the Black filmmakers of the L.A. Rebellion, the Native Tongues movement would influence other artists who embraced Islam, such as the
Roots, Mos Def, Common, and numerous others.

Grammy Award–winners Digable Planets, whose first album combined jazz-inflected sounds with esoteric rhymes, followed up their debut
with the more brooding and politicized 1994 album *Blowout Comb,* one
of hip-hop's most underrated albums, which combines Black Panther
ideology, Nation of Islam rhetoric, and Marxist philosophy into a unique
blend of avant-garde abstraction. As the incredible Ladybug Mecca raps
on the song "Dog It," "I raise everyday for the masses, tote my fist right
up against the fascists," and also "in my vein lives bell hooks, Derrick
bell . . ." and later "my tools, jewels, the Nation [of Islam]." On the same
song, rapper Butterfly raps, "We symbolize the blessed and represent
the rest," as well as "I'm makin bacon, still saying wa'asalaam alaikum,"

recognizing that money, which he refers to as "bacon" (a forbidden substance to Muslims), is a necessary evil, and he still maintains his commitment to principle with the Arabic greeting, "Peace be onto you."

Showing the deep influence of Malcolm X on hip-hop culture and the politics of a new generation of Black youth, the legendary group Gang Starr would continually mobilize Malcolm X as part of their Islamic iconography and street protest music. From their 1989 album *No More Mr. Nice Guy*, Gang Starr's video for the song "Manifest" reclaims Malcolm X for the hip-hop generation, as Guru dresses like Malcolm with glasses, kufi, suit, and tie and takes to the podium as he raps to the audience. Sampling Charlie Parker and Miles Davis's version of "Night in Tunisia," Gang Starr draws a powerful link between Malcolm's oratory and hip-hop's own potential to use language to mobilize and raise awareness, while also revealing that hip-hop is deeply connected not only to previous Black art forms such as jazz but also to a history of Black activism that is a direct extension of Malcolm X's vision for Black liberation.

In their 1990 song "Who's Gonna Take the Weight," on the album *Step in the Arena*, Guru opens with "I was raised like a Muslim, praying to the East," over a horn sample of Maceo and the Macks 1973 song "Parrty" and a chaotic siren-laden track by DJ Premier. The song's title is taken from a 1971 Kool and the Gang song of the same name, which opens with "People, the world today is in a very difficult situation, / And we all know it because we're the ones who created it, / We're gonna have to be the ones to clean it up." Gang Starr's song becomes hip-hop's answer to the situation, fusing central elements of Islamic teachings with street wisdom, which became emblematic of the kind of intergenerational dialogues taking place between the hip-hop generation and the Civil Rights and Black Power generation, be they political or aesthetic, through the sampling of jazz, soul, and funk music.

The video for the song is striking in that it features Guru (wearing a Malcolm X shirt) and DJ Premier dressed in fatigues as images of Malcolm X, Nelson Mandela, and others appear on screen. Prior to Guru's rapping, a sampled voice says, "Knowledge is power and knowledge can be the difference between life or death," a preface to and a suggestion of the power of "knowledge of self," which is so central to the Nation of Islam—as Guru says, "That's why I'm down with the Nation, spirituality supports reality, we gotta fight with the right mentality." And with the song's release just after the first Gulf War, Gang Starr connects the violence and death of urban America with the violence of the U.S. war in Iraq, revealing the group's solidarity with the people of Iraq by using various images and iconography throughout the video to show U.S. war planes bombing Iraq, women in Islamic clothing, Arabic script, Elijah Muhammad, U.S. military leaders, and Iraqi children in hospitals as victims of U.S. bomb attacks. By connecting urban America to Iraq, Gang Starr rhetorically asks, "Who's gonna take the weight?" a question that demands accountability and serves as a social protest against the forces of policing in urban centers and U.S. imperial power in the Muslim Third World.

Gang Starr would continue with these themes on 1992's album *Daily Operation*, whose cover features a framed image of Malcolm on a wall behind Guru and Premier and whose songs, such as "Conspiracy" and "2 Deep," are laden with Islamic references and ideas. On their next album, 1994's *Hard to Earn*, Gang Starr samples Malcolm X from his famous speech "The Message to the Grassroots" in the song "Tonz O' Gunz," highlighting the hypocrisy of the United States in asking Black men to be violent as American soldiers fighting for "democracy" in wars of empire abroad but then insisting that Black peoples be nonviolent in the United States in their demand for Black rights and dignity. On their 1998 album, *Moment of Truth*, the song "Above the Clouds" is loaded with Islamic references and language that opens with "I self lord and master [ISLAM] shall bring disaster to evil factors," as Guru provides his "ghettostyle proverbs" and Wu Tang Clan's Inspectah Deck conjures Nation of Islam and 5 percent mysticism with "the maker, owner plus sole controller," as they both meditate on incarceration, police surveillance, Black prophetic destiny, and the hope of transcending the wilderness of white America to go "above the clouds."

As the Afrocentric era of the Golden Age began to wane and the influence of West Coast street parables was on the rise, the Wu Tang Clan emerged with their own brand of Muslim metaphysics. With nine different members, all of whom espoused their own vision of Islam, the Wu Tang Clan made mic skills resemble sword styles. Their first hits, 1992's "Protect Ya Neck" and their 1993 song "C.R.E.A.M." (Cash Rules Everything around Me), were both recorded on their debut 1993 album, *Enter the 36th Chamber*, which combined obscure martial arts films, the supreme mathematics of the 5% Muslims, and street fables of survival into a rich alchemy of cosmic mayhem. "C.R.E.A.M." signifies on both the slang term for money and the central tenet of the Nation of Islam: that Black men are "the Asiatic Black man; the Maker; the Owner; the *Cream* of the planet Earth, Father of Civilization, God of the Universe," subverting the idea that capital or money ("cream") is the engine of the world, but rather that Blackness is.

Wu Tang Clan's second album, released in 1997, was the epic *Forever*. The album continues with Islamic references, including its opening track, "Wu-Revolution," a reflective monologue that focuses on the need for radical change and personal transformation and is replete with references to "the original man, Asiatic Black man" and "the supreme being, the Black man from Asia, otherwise known as Muslims," as well as chants of "Malcolm X! Malcolm X! Malcolm X! Rise Rise Rise!" and other Muslim metaphysics on the nature and existence of heaven and hell.

Their master text titled "Triumph" was the first single from the *Forever* album and is a manifesto that radically challenged the prevailing paradigm of corporate-controlled hip-hop with its nine-man soliloquy, with no chorus or hooks. Along with Cappadonna's English rap of the Arabic phrase "Alhamdulillah" ("All praises due to God") and references to Noble Drew Ali, Wu Tang member Inspectah Deck warns that the Wu Tang are "shackling the masses with drastic rap tactics," and Masta Killa points out the Wu Tang's brilliance amid mediocre and simplistic corporate hip-hop by saying, "Light is provided through sparks of energy, from the mind that travels in rhyme form, giving sight to the blind, the dumb are mostly intrigued by the drum."

Wu Tang member solo albums are just as loaded with Islamic iconography mixed with classic martial arts cinema and street fables of survival. Whether through Raekwon's *Only Built for Cuban Linx*, the GZA's *Liquid Swords*, or Method Man's *Tical* (on which he has a song entitled "PLO Style," in reference to the Palestinian Liberation Organization), members of the Wu Tang Clan spread the ideas and teachings of the Nation of Islam and the 5% Nation like no other hip-hop group or artist. The 2000 album of Wu Tang member Ghostface Killah, *Supreme Clientele*, has a song called "Malcolm," in which he samples Malcolm's condemnation of a "corrupt vicious hypocritical system that has castrated the Black man, and the only way the Black man can get back at it is to strike it any way that he know how." Over an eerie piano loop, Ghost-face starts rapping, "I'm like Malcolm, out the window with a joint, hoodied up, blood in my eye," and throughout the song as the Malcolm sample repeats, he says, "Teach brother Malcolm," while lamenting the condition of Black youth. Ghostface would continue to invoke Islamic ideas on his 2006 album, *Fishscale*, especially in the song "Underwater," a surreal odyssey in faith and despair, and then again on his 2010 album, *Apollo Kids*. He raps in its opening song, "Purified Thoughts," wonder-ing if he's a "good man or a fool," and goes on to say, "To free my mind on Friday I cleanse in the mosque. Let the imam pray over my head and wash thoughts, sterilized, purified, Godly," and also seeks to be buried in a "twenty-four-carat tomb" next to the prophets, naming Abraham, Jesus, and Muhammad.

By the late 1990s and into the post-9/11 era, a number of Muslim artists continued to emerge, some of them on more independent labels and others on midlevel or major labels. These include rappers Freeway and Beanie Segal, who emerged from Philadelphia and signed to Jay-Z's Roc-A-Fella Records. They both combined a more street-centered bra-vado with their Muslim-inflected redemptions, sprinkling their tales with existential laments about street life and the corruption of this world. For example, on Beanie Segal's 2005 song "I Can't Go on This Way," he raps, "I was taught trust in Allah but tie your camel, use your tongue as your sword and your books as your ammo." Later in the song, Segal contends with the contradictions of negotiating between the rap indus-try and family life and the personal failings that occur as a result: "My heart in the faith I don't practice, I still pray Allah forgive me for my actions, 'cause I spit gangsta, think Muslim and act Kaffar [unbeliever]." In this poetic ode to underclass existence, Beanie Segal reveals a poignant vulnerability about the impossibility of worshipping the divine amid suffering and despair.

Also, the artist known as Oddisee, a half-Sudanese, half-U.S. Black rapper who, on his 2009 song "Hip-Hop's Cool Again," raps, "I'm half Arab half nigga . . . in the mosque Friday, on Sunday the scripture . . . get harassed at the airport and the block, by the FBI, Interpol and the cops." Oddisee not only details his complicated background but also reveals that as a result of being both Black and "foreign" Muslim, he is subject to all manner of surveillance and harassment in post-9/11 America. And the Somali-born rapper K'naan, who gives poetic insight into his experience in his war-torn homeland and the plight of the African continent still under European and U.S. control, has also appeared on Nas and Damian Marley's *Distant Relatives* album, on which he raps in the song "Tribes at War."

Lupe Fiasco is a chart-topping rapper who has continued to invoke Islamic themes in his music and has used his belief to inform his political critiques of U.S. imperialism, capitalism, and inequality. In response to Kanye West's hit "Jesus Walks," which U.S. soldiers appropriated as a rationale for the invasions of Iraq and Afghanistan, Fiasco released his own "Muhammad Walks," in which he raps, "I ain't trying to profit off the prophets." On his 2011 album, *Lasers,* his song "Words I Never Said" explores media manipulation, poor educational systems, and the wars in the Muslim Third World, as he states, "I really think the war on terror is a bunch of bullshit, just a poor excuse for you to use up all your bullets." He also raps, "Limbaugh is a racist, Glenn Beck is a racist, Gaza Strip was getting bombed, Obama didn't say shit, that's why I ain't vote for him, next one either," and then, "Jihad is not a holy war, where's that in the worship? Murdering is not Islam! And you are not observant, and you are not a Muslim, Israel don't take my side 'cause look how far you've pushed them." In challenging Obama and the liberal veneer of his presidency, Fiasco details both the assault on Palestinian lives and U.S. complicity and apathy in it, as well as presenting a reflective critique of those who respond to state terror with violence.

Rebels without a Pause

Arguably the most influential group in all of hip-hop is Public Enemy. Their brand of militant Black Nationalism fuses Islam, Black Power ideology, Malcolm X, and others into a vision of Black liberation that combines a sonic amalgam of James Brown samples, sirens, screeches, and speeches into a chaotic assault on white America. Whether with "Rebel without a Pause," "Shut 'Em Down, " their anthem "Fight the Power," or "Welcome to the Terrordome," Public Enemy has single-handedly defined the benchmark of hip-hop's political radicalism. Through song and video, the members of Public Enemy have seen themselves as "media hijackers," and they've fully utilized the formats of song and video for their political possibilities, revealing their embrace of Malcolm X and other Black radical figures, for instance, in the video of "Fight the Power."

Their embrace of Islam is evident in their songs. Whether it be sampling Malcolm X, calling Farrakhan a prophet in "Bring the Noise," or referencing and utilizing the Nation of Islam's critiques on race and U.S. society, the rappers in Public Enemy have worn their allegiance on their sleeves. Known as "the hard rhymer," Chuck D said in an interview, "If people with African roots are connected to Islam, then you got a problem of taking your slaves away: 'We've lost our slaves—our slaves are international now'!"[38] Using this understanding as the basis for the group's political engagement, Public Enemy laid the foundation for some of the most intensely penetrating songs in the genre. Coming as they did in the shadows of the Reagan–Bush regime, Public Enemy has forcefully and poetically pushed the ideological edges of hip-hop with their politically conscious, historically informed, Nation of Islam–inspired lyrical and aural assault. With an empowered defiance unrivaled in hip-hop's brief history by the mid- to late 1980s, Chuck D's baritone flow and the Bomb Squad's chaotic and furious rhythms provided the soundtrack for the rise in Black militancy during that time. Their song "Black Steel in the Hour of Chaos" stands as a living testament to their political ideals and incisive critiques of American society.

Released on their landmark 1988 album, *It Takes a Nation of Millions to Hold Us Back*, "Black Steel in the Hour of Chaos" is one of hip-hop culture's most revolutionary anthems and a foundational song in what I call hip-hop's carceral canon. In this song, Chuck D creates a powerful narrative of imprisonment and redemption as he details the circumstances of his incarceration for refusing military service and national belonging, providing a powerful critique of the two defining institutions for urban Black communities in the era of Reaganism: the military and the prison.

In the song, Chuck D recounts the story of his incarceration from within the prison itself, as his rejection of induction into the United States military is the reason for his incarceration. In refusing to join the army, Chuck D reiterates his disavowal and rejection of American national belonging, foregrounding the ever-present gap that exists for

Black peoples between national allegiance through military service and the economic, political, and social promises that citizenship in the United States supposedly affords. As Chuck D says, "Here is a land that never gave a damn / about a brother like me and myself / because they never did." What makes Chuck D's defiance of military service so empowering is the conservative political climate that existed in the United States in the post–Civil Rights era of "law and order" and the "War on Drugs," during which the line between citizen and criminal was a racial one, with whiteness defined as quintessentially American and Blackness defined as a social menace to the national family, as Chuck D himself says in the song, "I'm not a citizen." In addition to Reagan's racialized claims to "Americanness" were the militaristic overtones of much of his political and social rhetoric. The conservative climate fostered by the Reagan–Bush regime with the themes of national identity and belonging pivoted around an axis of militarism and American power for protecting the nation from the external threats of "Muslim terrorists" and communists. The increases in defense spending and the rise of the military–industrial complex during the Reagan regime signified and underscored the heightened nativism and patriotism that were part and parcel of the conservative political agenda during that period.[39]

In light of this, "Black Steel in the Hour of Chaos" serves as a powerful response to the racially coded ideas about U.S. national identity. Later in the first verse, Chuck D drives this point home when he says, "They could not understand that I'm a Black man / And I could never be a veteran." In explicitly rejecting military service, particularly in the era of Reagan, Chuck D forcefully asserts the contradiction between Blackness and American national belonging, an ideological hallmark of the Nation of Islam that sought to define Black belonging outside the boundaries of the United States. In Chuck D's assertion of this empowered Black identity, his refusal to serve in the U.S. military conjures the history and figure of the iconic Muhammad Ali, who after his conversion to the Nation of Islam but prior to his refusal to serve in the Vietnam War said, "I'm not an American. I'm a Black man."[40] Ali elaborated on his position vis-à-vis U.S. imperial war in Vietnam, saying, "Why should they ask me to put on a uniform and go ten thousand miles from home and drop bombs and bullets on brown people in Vietnam while so-called Negro people in Louisville are treated like dogs and denied simple human rights?" And he continued, saying, "No, I'm not going ten thousand miles from home to help murder and burn another poor nation simply to continue the domination of white slave masters of the darker people the world over."[41]

Unlike Ali's, Chuck D's rejection of military service landed him in prison, the central institution that defined Black existence in the era of Reaganism. Calling incarceration "a form of slavery" in "Black Steel in the Hour of Chaos," Chuck D echoes what scholars of prisons such as Michelle Alexander have called "the new Jim Crow," because incarceration has led to legal forms of discrimination in housing, education, employment, and other realms of society. Though the song narrates a prison break, the video shows Chuck D, as the leader, hanged in the prison by the warden while the others escape, suggesting that Black leadership is constantly in peril and targeted by American institutional power.

In spite of this, there is still solace and sanctuary to be found in the possibility of resistance that is woven through "Black Steel," for fifty-two Black men *do* escape incarceration and the institutional violence of the prison. Like other prison narratives of resistance that have been central to shaping Black liberation struggles worldwide, such as those from George Jackson, Malcolm X, Mumia Abu Jamal, Assata Shakur, and Jamil Al-Amin among countless others, Public Enemy's "Black Steel in the Hour of Chaos" stands as hip-hop culture's defining contribution to the legacy of that carceral canon.

Damn, I Wanna Kill Sam

As the lyrical architect and political conscience of the group N.W.A., Ice Cube released his first solo album, *AmeriKKKa's Most Wanted*, which was a landmark moment in hip-hop, when the West Coast's most talented MC fused his militant street poetry with the production mayhem of Public Enemy's Bomb Squad, tackling Black oppression, the incarceration of Black men, and racial inequality, asking, among other things, "Why more niggas in the pen than in college?" His follow-up the next year, *Death Certificate*, was infused with the Nation of Islam's strident politics. The album cover showed Ice Cube standing in a morgue next to a dead body that was covered by an American flag and had a toe tag that read "Uncle Sam." While the album cover clearly suggests the meta-phorical death of America, the liner notes to the album more clearly associate him with the Nation of Islam, as he is shown standing between two groups of Black men, one group dressed in sweat suits and athletic sneakers and the other group in the Nation of Islam's standard ward-robe of suits and bow ties. Reading from the Nation of Islam's official newspaper, titled the *Final Call*, with the headline "Unite or Perish," Cube is shown in the middle, giving visual truth to his attempt to unite both elements. In addition, he writes in the liner notes about the histor-ical decimation of Black peoples in the United States, who are "mentally dead" and have "limited knowledge of self," a situation that Ice Cube suggests can be rectified, explaining, "The best place for a Black male or female is the Nation of Islam."[42]

Death Certificate is divided as the "Death Side" and the "Life Side," with the "Death Side" revealing the structural and systemic forces caus-ing the "death" of the Black community as Cube's incendiary critiques of white supremacy, policing, and economic injustice turned on the "Life Side" to what he sees as self-destructive behavior and Black complicity with the powerful forces allied against them. The song "I Wanna Kill Sam" is an incisive critique of the U.S. armed forces and their recruit-ment of Black men for imperial war as it serves as a sonic parable about the relationship between the slave trade and military service. Released just after the euphoria of the Persian Gulf War and the nearly decade-long hypernationalism and militarism of the Reagan–Bush administra-tion, Cube's "I Wanna Kill Sam" stands as a powerful and defiant song about the legacies of slavery, persistent Black suffering, and the role of the U.S. military in maintaining white domination both domestically and globally.

While *Death Certificate* reveals Ice Cube's relationship to the Nation of Islam, the lyrical content of this album—and that of his subsequent ones as well—features many references and allusions to the Nation of Islam that thematically reflect the philosophical underpinnings of its views on race and American history. This is most clearly evident in the song "When I Get to Heaven," which appears on Ice Cube's 1993 album, titled *Lethal Injection*.

Ice Cube's "When I Get to Heaven" is perhaps one of the three most searing indictments of Christianity's role within the Black community as expressed in popular music, the other two being Me'Shell N'Degeo-cello's "The Way" and KRS-One's "Why Is That?" In "When I Get to Heaven," which is heavily rooted in the liberationist eschatology of the Nation of Islam, Ice Cube poetically expresses a redemptive tale about what he perceives to be the hypocrisies of Christianity within Black communities, commenting on a variety of subjects such as slavery, materialism within the Church, the racial divisions that have existed within Christian practice in the United States, the incarceration of Black men, and ultimately the redemptive promise of the afterlife.

"When I Get to Heaven" cleverly and creatively uses a sample from Marvin Gaye's classic "Inner City Blues" to form a powerful and pensive backdrop for Ice Cube's ruminations on Black identity, American history, and social struggle. In invoking and evoking "Inner City Blues," Ice Cube creates a powerful cultural space of communal critique that forges a link among generations of Blacks in the history of their struggle as he connects the Civil Rights–Black Power lamentation of ghetto existence and inner city suffering in the late 1960s and early 1970s with the rage of the underclass produced by Reagan–Bush policies, Daryl Gates's policing, and the failure and complicity of institutions to remedy the conditions created by these approaches. While Marvin Gaye sings, "This ain't *livin'*, this ain't *livin'*" (italics mine), throughout "When I Get to Heaven," Ice Cube thematically underscores Gaye's refrain with a vividly compelling vision of social death within Black communities wrought by the history of institutional failure and the complicity of Christianity in it.[43]

Ice Cube's critique in "When I Get to Heaven" has profound historical resonance with larger claims made by Black communities regarding the relationship between American national identity and Christianity. The Nation of Islam reached its zenith in popularity in the late 1950s and early 1960s, when Malcolm X was its most visible minister, and it appealed to Black peoples through its resounding critiques of race and white supremacy, which deliberately and destructively built the edifice that is American society. Much of the Nation of Islam's rhetoric has employed highly racialized notions that served to challenge and rhetorically resist the power of white supremacy. In claiming that Islam is "the religion of the black man,"[44] the Nation of Islam has retold American history from the perspective of the aggrieved, detailing the devastation and dispossession of Black history and culture vis-à-vis the holocaust of slavery—a decimating process of erasure that many saw as accompanied and even legitimized by the introduction of Christianity into Black communities.

As a critique of the role of Christianity within the Black community, "When I Get To Heaven" reveals the various contradictions and hypocrisies of the Church and its clergy. Ice Cube claims his "whole neighborhood is comatose," and the second and third verses also make reference to the hypocrisies of the Church in relation to its materialism and lack of social outreach ("Mr. Preacher, if I can't pay my tithe, do I have to wait outside?" and "I just stare at the Church man, spending more money on the Church band"). While in these instances Ice Cube points to what he views as the misplaced priorities of the Church, these critiques of the contemporary moment also serve as rhetorical devices that allow Ice Cube to begin a discussion of what he—and by extension the Nation of Islam—believes to be the historical role of the Church in the process of Black political marginalization, economic debasement, and spiritual colonization. Ice Cube foregrounds this historical trajectory when he says, "Lookin' for survival / The devil made you a slave and he gave you a Bible / four hundred years gettin' our ass kicked / By so-called Christians and Catholics."

In the third verse, Ice Cube provides one of the most explosive indictments of white supremacy in hip-hop, at once artful in its emphasis on the historical continuity of white supremacy and poignant in Cube's critique of Christianity and what he perceives to be its incestuous relationship with racist terror. In the third verse, Ice Cube says, "The same white man that threw me in the slammer / He bombed a church in Alabama." Here Ice Cube connects white supremacist terror of the 1960s Civil Rights movement in the South with the contemporary imprisonment of Black men throughout the country in the era of Reagan and mass incarceration, highlighting the historical continuity between an era of enforced legal and social segregation and one reeling from the aftermath of Reagan–Bush conservatism, postindustrial decline, and continued state repression.[45]

By invoking the church bombings of the 1960s by white supremacists, Ice Cube underscores the violent racial rifts that existed within the supposed brotherhood of the Christian faith. In doing so, Ice Cube powerfully highlights the historical frustration of some Black communities with Black Christians who continued to seek brotherhood with whites despite the continued violence by white Christians against the nonviolent Civil Rights activists of the era. These frustrations formed the tensions that divided the Black community between the nonviolent Civil Rights movement of Dr. Martin Luther King Jr. and the more defiant posture of the Nation of Islam, associated with Malcolm X.[46] The church bombings in the 1960s, the most notorious of which involved the killing of four young girls in Alabama, sparked serious criticism by Malcolm X of the emerging Civil Rights movement. In his famous speech "The Message to the Grassroots," Malcolm X clearly distinguishes himself and the Nation of Islam from Dr. King's movement when he says, "As long as the white man sent you to Korea, you bled. He sent you to Germany you bled. You bleed for white people, but when it comes to seeing your own churches being bombed and little black girls murdered, you haven't got any blood." Malcolm continued, saying, "If violence is wrong in America, violence is wrong abroad. If it is wrong to be defending black women and black children and black babies and black men, then it is wrong for America to draft us and make us violent abroad in defense of her."[47]

By exposing this hypocrisy, Malcolm's linking of Black military participation in American violence abroad and the refusal of Black Christian leadership to use violence as a defensive tool against white supremacist terror was a powerful critique of the Civil Rights establishment and its enduring commitment to, and identification with, America. In "When I Get to Heaven," Ice Cube's insightful referencing of this social and political history raises a historical mirror to the contemporary conditions of Blacks, suggesting that Christianity, whiteness, and "Americanness" are intimately tied together still, so even though Black incarceration has replaced an earlier mode of racial terror, the repression of Blacks continues nonetheless, vis-à-vis "the same man" but in a different era and through different means. For this reason, later, in the second verse of the song, Ice Cube—like Malcolm X during his relationship with the Nation of Islam—makes an urgent call to Black communities, saying, "Black man you gotta make a decision," in reference to the vital necessity for Black peoples to choose to identify with what is viewed as a hypocritical Christianity rooted in white supremacist America or to identify with the alternative yet empowering Nation of Islam, which is more internationalist in its scope.

Despite Ice Cube's dystopic description of the secular suffering in "When I Get to Heaven," an abiding sense of hope still runs throughout the narrative, such as in its chorus, "They won't call me a nigger when I get to heaven." For despite the New Right attacks on the underclass and the constant criticism of the Black poor as societal "problems," Ice Cube's radical vision of the Nation of Islam's salvation for Black peoples trapped in a white world of racism, recrimination, and degradation suggests an alternative moral anchor and utopian vision for America's truly disadvantaged.

God by Nature

Known as "the God"—in line with Black Islam's deification of the Black body in response to America's demonization of it—Rakim Allah is arguably hip-hop's most gifted lyricist and its reigning poet laureate, for he has continued to express his Islamic mysticism in lyrically complex and metaphorically dense deliveries. Songs such as "Move the Crowd," on 1987's *Paid in Full* album, in which he raps "All praises due to Allah and that's a blessing," and 1988's *Follow the Leader*, in whose title track he raps, "God by nature, mind raised in Asia, since you was tricked, I have to raise ya, from the cradle to the grave, but remember, you're not a slave," and then continues, saying, "'Cause we were put here to be much more than that, but we couldn't see because our mind was trapped. But I'm here to break away the chains, take away the pains, remake the brains, rebuild my name," are iconic examples of Rakim's brilliance. His empowering odes to Black redemption and Muslim Internationalism continue in the song "In the Ghetto," from the 1990 album *Let the Rhythm Hit 'Em*. Sampling Bill Withers's 1972 song "Kissing My Love" and the 24 Carat Black's 1973 song "Ghetto: Misfortune's Wealth," from the brooding album of the same name, Rakim details a vivid narrative of time travel and memory, rapping, "Then I take a thought around the world twice / From knowledge born back to knowledge precise / Across the desert that's hot as the Arabian." He continues, "Reaching for the city of Mecca, visit Medina / Visions of Nefertiti then I seen her / Mind keeps traveling, I'll be back after I stop and think about the brothers and sisters in Africa." While these songs and almost any other of Rakim's songs are deeply lyrical and metaphysically abstract and rarely touch on overtly political ideas, his 1992 song "Casualties of War," from the *Don't Sweat the Technique* album, is a rare exception among his body of work.

Rakim's "Casualties of War" is an incredibly vivid narrative about race and belief, slavery and imperialism, national allegiance and international belonging, and individual redemption in the face of horror and war. Rapping from the perspective of a U.S. soldier in Iraq during the first Gulf War of 1990, Rakim not only potently links U.S. power and violence with the Muslim Third World of Iraq within the narrative of the song but also connects himself to this region through Islam, as the "Asiatic Black man."

In the first verse of the song, Rakim reveals the violent similarities between New York City and Iraq with his vivid descriptions of "sand that is hot as the city streets" and "bullets whistlin' over my head remind me," which suggest that Rakim is linking the violence of the war in Iraq with the violent, warlike circumstances that exist in impoverished neighborhoods in the United States. Rakim's linkage of these two social traumas, war abroad and violence at home, reveals the powerful political and economic forces in the United States that contribute to both of these violent conditions. While one is the product of centuries of institutional racism and structured neglect, the other is the result of a colonial legacy of pillage and plunder by the United States and Europe.

Whereas the first verse only suggests these linkages, the third verse of the song drives this point home, with Rakim prophetically suggesting the possibility that New York City may be under attack. Released in 1992, "Casualties of War" came out before the first bombing of the World Trade Center in 1993 and well before the September 11, 2001, attacks. As Rakim says, "The war is over, for now at least, / Just because they lost it don't mean it's peace," and he continues, saying, "Remember Pearl Harbor? New York could be over 'g,' / Kamikaze, strapped with bombs, / No peace in the East, they want revenge for Saddam."

In poetically connecting place and violence, Rakim's "Casualties of War" further proceeds to highlight the powerful forces at play in structuring the racial and economic basis for the war. But whereas Denzel Washington became the cinematic citizen–solider who mirrored Colin Powell in the post–Cold War 1990s, Rakim seeks to challenge this incorporation of Blackness into the national fabric. Washington's character in Edward Zwick's film *Courage under Fire* (1996) is the moral center responsible for righting the national ship after the first Gulf War in Iraq, imploring his commanding officers to "tell the whole truth" about what happened in Iraq. Rakim's redemption though comes not in his identification with and allegiance to the American nation-state but in his rejection of it.

Throughout "Casualties of War," Rakim defiantly expresses his rage against U.S. control and domination of the Muslim Third World. While at the end of the first verse Rakim critically elaborates on American bloodthirst and his own "training for torture" as a member of the U.S. military, the second verse forms the ideological basis for his critique of U.S. power. In the middle of the second verse Rakim comes to a self-realization of his own position regarding military service and national belonging when he raps, "But what are we here for? Who's on the other side of the wall? / Somebody give the president a call! But I hear warfare scream through the air, / Back to the battlegrounds, it's war they declare, / A Desert Storm, let's see who reigns supreme, / Something like monopoly, a government scheme." Rakim's questioning leads him to forge a historically nuanced critique of Black identity and belonging in relation to the Muslim Third World.

Rakim refuses to comply with dominant U.S. conceptions of individual achievement for Black men through military service when he says, "Go to the army, be all you can be / Another dead solider? Hell no not me." He then proceeds to forge a powerful critique of slavery and a nationally bounded conception of Black identity that is in dialogue with Malcolm X and the longer history of Black radicalism, internationalism, and the Muslim Third World that emerged after World War II. Instead of describing empowerment and self-actualization coming from military service and an embrace of U.S. nationalism, Rakim says:

> So I start letting off ammunition in every direction
> Allah is my only protection
> But wait a minute, Saddam Hussein prays the same
> And this is Asia, from where I came
> I'm on the wrong side, so change the target
> Shooting at the general, and where's the sergeant?
> Blame it on John Hardy Hawkins for bringing me to America
> Now it's mass hysteria.

In invoking Allah, not only does Rakim proceed to provide a powerful critique of modernity itself by linking the history of slavery with American imperial aggression in Iraq, but he also suggests an alternative vision of Black identity that expands the geographic referents of Black origins that emerged out of Black Islam and sought to connect Black peoples in the United States with those in the Third World of Africa and Asia.

In saying "this is Asia, from where I came," Rakim mobilizes a powerful trope within Black Islam regarding the expanded origins of Blackness, that of the "Asiatic Black man" (or the "Afro-Asiatic Black man"). In doing so, Rakim taps into Black Islam's rich legacy and resources, which have been used to connect Black peoples in the United States with those in Africa and Asia, specifically those in the Muslim Third World. Rakim's epiphany regarding his origins and community of belonging within the song's narrative specifically links him with the Iraqi people, who are seen as the victims of U.S. imperial aggression, and at the same time rejects any identification with the American national body. He rhetorically rejects Americanness and its racially coded whiteness, and he also begins to fire his weapon at the agents and symbols of Americanness and American aggression—namely, his general and the sergeant. What underscores the racial component of Rakim's embrace of his Asiatic roots, his rejection of America, and the shooting of U.S. military officers is his reference to John Hardy Hawkins, who bears the blame for "bringing me to America," for Hawkins is responsible for initiating British involvement in the slave trade in 1562, which was the year the institution of slavery was first established for the British empire.[48]

In linking slavery to his embrace of his Asiatic roots, Rakim's "Casualties of War" powerfully bears witness to the philosophical basis of Black Islam and its relationship to the larger Muslim Third World. Just as Malcolm X saw Islam as the bridge that connects Black peoples in the United States with those in Africa and Asia, Rakim embraces his Muslim identity to forge a vision of the Muslim International that powerfully and poetically combines the past and present, the local and the global, and slavery and contemporary imperialism into a grammar of resistance that critiques not only the U.S. nation-state but also any bounded sense of Black identity.

Black Star, Crescent Moon

Mos Def first came to prominence in the mid- to late 1990s through his collaborations with Da Bush Babees and also De La Soul. But it was through his collaboration with Talib Kweli that he emerged as a maverick for a new era in hip-hop. Mos Def and Kweli's landmark single "Fortified Live" signaled a new moment for hip-hop in 1997 and became the launching pad for their careers and the birth of their collaboration known as Black Star one year later. On "Fortified Live," they not only invoke the female revolutionary Assata Shakur, exiled in Cuba, but also create a visual narrative that culminates in the hook in which both Talib Kweli and Mos Def rap, "This once in a lifetime like a Halley's comet / Yo, we bring it to Medina like the Prophet Muhammad / Peace be upon he / and we MC's." Also, Mos Def and Talib Kweli invoke Islamic themes throughout their self-titled full-length collaboration *Black Star.* In the song "Astronomy (8th Light)," they signify on the Last Poets' song "Black Is Chant" by cleverly ruminating on the various meanings and possibilities of Blackness in contemporary society, rapping, "Black like the veil that the Muslimeena wear / Black like the planet that they fear, why they scared? / Black like the slave ship the day they brought us here." On his song "Beef," Mos Def invokes the Muslim Third World: "When a soldier ends his life with his own gun / Beef is tryin' to figure out what to tell his son / Beef is oil prices and geopolitics / Beef is Iraq, the West Bank, and Gaza Strip."

Beginning all of his albums (and some songs) with an Islamic prayer, Mos Def's body of work is full of Islamic ideas and a unique and gifted blend of poetry, politics, and Black internationalist sentiments. His most recent album, 2009's *The Ecstatic*, is a globe-trotting collection laden with Islamic references. Although the album cover is a still from one of the L.A. Rebellion's landmark films (Charles Burnett's brilliant film *Killer of Sheep*), Mos Def uses several Islamic references, including a photo of the Moorish Science Temple on the back of the album, a sampling of a Malcolm X speech that opens the album, Turkish protest singer Selda Bağcan's "İnce İnce," a scene spoken in Arabic from the *Battle of Algiers*, and also names one of the songs "Wahid," which is Arabic for "oneness." While this eclectic range and Pan-Islamic mash-up inform much of Mos Def's work, it was his first solo venture, 1999's *Black on Both Sides*, with which he solidified his place as one of hip-hop's most talented and gifted lyricists.

The opening song on *Black on Both Sides* is "Fear Not of Man," one of the most historically rich, culturally layered, and politically complex songs in recent times. Using the opening track as an opportunity to discuss and describe the state of the hip-hop union, Mos Def, rather than aiming his lyrical sights at other MCs who somehow dilute or damage the art form, meditates on hip-hop's possibilities and the power of self-realization. In doing so, he creatively and brilliantly taps into the rich history of Black Islam and Pan-Africanism that Malcolm X embodied, imagining Black peoples beyond the United States.

In beautifully expressing his position in "Fear Not of Man," Mos Def raps over a pulsating and insurgent beat that is sampled from a 1977 song titled "Fear Not *for* Man" (italics mine), from the legendary and incendiary king of Afro-beat, Fela Kuti. Fela, who was and is arguably one of the most radical cultural spokespersons from within the history of popular music, recorded numerous albums from the early 1970s until his death in 1997. Influenced by James Brown, Curtis Mayfield, Stevie Wonder, and the Black Power movement in the United States, Fela's music is a hypnotic blend of Nigerian rhythms, jazz, and funk, over which he sang some of the most politically charged anthems of anticolonial dissent and Pan-African hopes and dreams. In invoking the spirit and soul of Fela Kuti, Mos Def's "Fear Not *of* Man" (italics mine), is an ongoing dialogue with Fela's vision and a slight, but significant, recontextualization of the Fela original.

Fela Kuti's 1977 song "Fear Not for Man" begins with the words "The father of Pan-Africanism, Kwame Nkrumah, has said: 'The secret of life is to have no fear,'" and then Fela and his band, driven by the beautiful percussion of Tony Allen, proceed to unleash a beautifully intoxicating rhythm of resistance. In invoking the revolutionary Ghanaian leader Kwame Nkrumah, Fela admonishes Black peoples to continue the struggle of those who came before and to do so without fear. In the throes of the postcolonial misery that has viciously and violently characterized the postindependence moment for the decolonizing Third World, Fela's "Fear Not for Man" is meant as an inspiration for collective solidarity, suggesting that man, as the gendered representative of humanity, will prevail despite the men who create and perpetuate injustice and inequality. As an empowering ode to a utopian vision in dystopic times, Mos Def's sampling of the Fela original creates a compelling conversation between two revolutionary cultural movements: Afro-beat and hip-hop.

In sampling Fela's song and slightly modifying the title, Mos Def artfully places his piece in the context of a Pan-African ideal reminiscent of Malcolm X and a diasporic Black radical imagination. Through the art of sampling, hip-hop has been able to reclaim a sense of history stripped from Black peoples as a result of slavery, while also creating forms of communal memory, as songs and fragments of the past get recontextualized and the past is made present and relevant to charting a redemptive future. By invoking the memory of Fela Kuti (through the sample and song title) and in turn Kwame Nkrumah (whose quote informs the philosophical basis for Fela and therefore Mos Def's song), Mos Def creatively connects the contemporary struggles of Black peoples in the United States with the insurgent, anticolonial history of both Nkrumah and Fela Kuti. This kind of cultural history and critical archaeology not only reflect the transnational dimensions and ideological reach of Mos Def but also serve to reimagine Black identity both within and beyond the borders of the American nation-state, forging a diasporic consciousness that is rooted in a specific antiracist critique of American society.

But in addition to connecting racial and cultural struggles transnationally by invoking Fela Kuti and Kwame Nkrumah, the song also invokes the politics of the Black Nationalist struggle within the United States by referencing the legendary Last Poets of the Black Arts Movement. After describing a world dominated by technology and filled with satellites, cameras, and televisions—as he says, "societies and governments trying to be God and having the all-seeing eye"—Mos Def follows this with, "I guess the Last Poets wasn't too far off when they said that certain people got a God complex / I believe its true." By referencing the Last Poets' classic song "White Man's Got a God Complex," Mos Def expresses a scathing critique of whiteness, and he assents to the Last Poets' powerful assertion regarding the machinations of white supremacy, as his silence in not naming who these "certain people" are becomes a deafening critique of race, power, and surveillance.

In addition, being that the song is a meditation on the power of the divine or at least the relative powerlessness of man ("Fear Not of Man"), Mos Def's employment of the Last Poets' "White Man's Got a God Complex" also serves to mobilize the history of Black resistance to and understanding of the claims regarding the whiteness of God/Jesus/the divine, thereby also subverting the dominant racial logic and hierarchy of white supremacy in America. In addition to this critique of the intersection of race and belief, Mos Def's "Fear Not of Man," in invoking the Last Poets, also suggests the historical connection and political possibilities between contemporary hip-hop culture and the radical spoken word tradition of the Black Arts Movement, both of which have been deeply influenced not only by Malcolm X and his Muslim Internationalism but also by Islamic themes, symbols, and iconography.

In linking past and present, memory and place, culture and resistance, and ultimately hope and redemption, Mos Def's "Fear Not of Man" echoes and reflects many of the central concerns that have defined the political and cultural history of Black Islam in the postwar period, by creatively remapping Black identity transnationally and even invoking and drawing historical connections to the legendary Last Poets and the Islamically influenced Black Arts Movement. Similar to Malcolm X modeling his Organization of Afro-American Unity on Kwame Nkrumah's Organization of African Unity, Mos Def, by implicitly invoking Nkrumah's memory, creates the hip-hop equivalent of Malcolm X's unfulfilled yet radical political ideal. As part of the broader iconography and history of the Muslim International, Mos Def uses hip-hop culture to explore the overlapping influences of Islam, Black internationalism, and Pan-Africanism within the realms of art and politics. By weaving together a powerful and poignant narrative that links Afro-Beat, hip-hop, and the Black Arts Movement, Mos Def, like many before him and since, continues to extend a radical tradition of resistance by powerfully envisioning himself and the Black liberation struggle beyond the borders of America.

After the Crescent

By conjuring the history of Malcolm X and the radical redemptive vision that he outlined throughout his life, hip-hop culture became a powerful space for expressing and extending Malcolm X's internationalist vision in the post–Civil Rights era. By reclaiming the terrain of Black Islam and internationalism during a period in U.S. history in which the "Black criminal" and the "Muslim terrorist" structured the logic of U.S. power domestically and globally, hip-hop's Golden Age and artists such as Gang Starr, Rakim, Public Enemy, and Ice Cube, among numerous others, challenged the limits of U.S. power to determine Black destiny. By imagining Black freedom beyond America and in Africa and elsewhere in the Muslim Third World, the history of Malcolm X and Black Islam provided a grammar of resistance and a language of revolt for these artists to use in crafting powerful platforms of rhetorical rebellion against white supremacy, militarism, and U.S. state power, as hip-hop culture became a powerful site for exploring how poetry, aesthetics, and the Black political imagination sought to shape the contours of the Muslim International in late twentieth-century America.

But when the Cold War was ending and the power and resonance of hip-hop were increasing in the late 1980s and early 1990s, the embrace of Muhammad Ali as a national hero sought to undermine the terrain of Black internationalism and Black Islam that hip-hop culture had struggled so hard to rekindle and reinvigorate. And when the "Green Menace" of Islam and Samuel Huntington's "Clash of Civilizations" thesis were becoming the defining paradigm for U.S. power in the 1990s, the domestic "culture wars" sought to contain the antiracist impulses that had powerfully emerged throughout U.S. society through a rhetoric of "diversity" and multiculturalism. As a result, the twin figures of "Blackness" and "the Muslim" that had haunted post–Civil Rights America now became celebrated as quintessentially American through a figure like Muhammad Ali. For the radical internationalism of Malcolm X was now being challenged by the silent ghost of Muhammad Ali, as the United States sought not only to domesticate Black Islam and fracture it from the Muslim Third World, but also to create new imperial citizens.

4

"GHOST IN THE HOUSE"
Muhammad Ali and the
Rise of the "Green Menace"

Boxing is nothing, just satisfying some blood thirsty people. I'm
no longer Cassius Clay, a Negro from Kentucky. I belong to the
world, the black world. I'll always have a home in Pakistan, in
Algeria, in Ethiopia.

— Muhammad Ali, in Marqusee, *Redemption Song*

IN OCTOBER 1970, in his first fight back after his ban from boxing for
refusing to fight in the Vietnam War, Muhammad Ali walked out of the
dressing room and toward the ring to fight Jerry Quarry, with Ali's
charismatic cornerman, Bundini Brown, shouting, "Ghost in the house!
Ghost in the house!" That Ali was fighting a white boxer in his first
comeback fight made this, like almost all of Ali's fights, a race war in the
squared circle. Many people in America—boxing fans or not—wanted
to see Quarry silence Ali for his strident and defiant political stance and
outspoken criticism of American imperialism and white supremacy. For
Bundini Brown, who relished this theater of war, the "ghost" he was referring to was that of Jack Johnson, the first Black Heavyweight Champion, who in the early twentieth century beat all white fighters in front
of him and flaunted his relationships with white women at a time when
lynching was seemingly a national sport. That all of Johnson's opponents
were deemed the "Great White Hope" (a term that has come to define
the racially determined world of sport) reflected the longings of white
America to restore the title to its "rightful" white place. Bundini Brown's
chants of "Ghost in the house" served not only to summon the past in
the spirit of Jack Johnson but also to reveal, in true Bundini style, that
the past is present or even prologue—and that the white anger, angst,

and rage directed at Ali were really a deeper-seated anxiety about the rise of Black Power and the trauma of Vietnam that threatened America as they knew it.

Earlier in that same year, Curtis Mayfield had claimed that "top billing now is killing" in his appropriately titled 1970 anthem "(Don't Worry) If There's a Hell Below, We're All Gonna Go," and Bundini's signifying on America's bloodthirst for Blackness, its racial quagmire, its imperial arrogance, and Ali's challenges to them revealed that ghosts are an appropriate metaphor with which to understand Muhammad Ali and his relationship to American political culture beginning in the Cold War 1960s and extending into the post–Cold War 1990s and the post-9/11 era. It is through the resurrection of Ali within the American imagination that ghosts and phantom pasts have been summoned and exorcised. Ghosts are the specter of the 1960s, the decade that continues to haunt the American present. Ghosts are the phantom dead in America's Cold War against the Third World. Ghosts are Patrice Lumumba, who was assassinated, and the countless others who have died and gone nameless. Ghosts are the history of Malcolm X, the specter of Black Islam and the Muslim Third World. And ghosts are the visage of Ali, muted and tamed but still a haunting reminder of what was.

For it is through Ali that we can not only understand the history of Blackness to the Muslim Third World but also the figure of the Muslim to American national identity. His legacy is a lens through which to view the shifting ideological currents of American national identity from the Black Power era and the Vietnam War through the post–Cold War 1990s and into the post-9/11 moment. Through Ali's legacy we can see how he became a figure who healed the domestic tensions of the "culture wars" around race and helped forge an imperial multiculturalism, a color-blind logic that served to redefine U.S. national identity and position America as the leader of the free world in its struggle against the new enemy of Islam, embodied by Samuel Huntington's influential "Clash of Civilization" thesis.

By placing Ali's initial conversion to Islam, his strident critiques of white supremacy, and his defiant stand against the Vietnam War within the context of Cold War liberalism, the rising tide of Black internationalism, and the influence of Malcolm X and the Muslim Third World on Black Power of the 1960s, this chapter will explore how Ali's recuperation

as national hero in the 1990s and into the twenty-first century has sig-
nified a great deal about America's redefinition of itself. For the United
States the fears of Black Islam and the influence of the Muslim Third
World on Black political culture have forced a shift from the ideals of
Cold War liberalism and the "Red Scare" of communism to the post–
Cold War imperial multiculturalism and the "Green Menace" of Islam,
which now defines U.S. nationalism.

The recuperation and resurrection of Ali are nothing less than an
attempt to celebrate and sanctify as national hero the most polarizing figure of the 1960s. And if Ali can be transformed into an American hero,
then maybe the threat of Black Islam, the bitterness of Black Power, and
the fears of Black internationalism can be assuaged so that the wounds
of the past can be healed and American redemption can be the moral
imperative for global dominance in the new American century as Islam
became the preeminent threat to U.S. national security. Ali's transformation from racial pariah to "national treasure" coincides with the shifting
terrain of late twentieth-century America, when the fall of the Berlin
Wall ushered in a high moment of triumphalism about America's past
and its possibilities for the future. How was the Cold War liberalism and
its domestic racial complement of "Civil Rights" going to be remembered and reframed? And how would this post–Cold War moment seek
to fracture the Muslim International by domesticating Black Islam and
reframing America's foreign policy toward the Muslim Third World?

Ali was the perfect vessel through which to reimagine America's past
and its future during the post–Cold War 1990s, because his redemption
as a national hero has not only served to contain the internationalist
impulses of Black Islam that he embodies but has also suggested that,
because of his "courage," the racism and imperialism that he fought
against no longer exist. As both icon of 1960s radicalism and the embodiment of Black Islam in the post-Malcolm period, Ali is a potent vessel through which to do tremendous ideological work: to solidify simultaneously New Right discourses on race by rewriting the 1960s vis-à-vis
the culture wars of the 1990s and an embrace of imperial multiculturalism; to domesticate and contain the internationalist impulses of Black
Islam and its historical relationship to the Muslim Third World during
a time when, through Huntington's "Clash of Civilizations" thesis and
the rise of the "Green Menace," Islam and the Muslim Third World have

been viewed as the predominant threats to U.S. national security and the post–Cold War order; to cement a unipolar American triumphalism that positions America as benevolent by sanitizing U.S. foreign policy in regard to the Muslim Third World; and finally to contain America's anti-Muslim image in the post–Cold War and post-9/11 eras.

Cash Rules Everything around Me

As an emblem of the Black liberation struggles of the 1960s, Ali embodied the combination of domestic antiracism in the United States and global anti-imperialism, particularly in light of his critiques of American imperial aggression in Vietnam. Since the mid-1990s though, Muhammad Ali has experienced an unprecedented resurgence in his visibility in contemporary culture. Having signed a licensing deal with CKX, which paid Ali fifty million dollars for an 80 percent interest in his name, image, and likeness (and which also owns the rights to the name, image, and likeness of Elvis Presley), Ali has become one of the most visible and beloved figures within the American popular landscape. Arguably the most iconic figure within all of sports anywhere in the world, Ali lit the torch at the 1996 Olympic Games in Atlanta, has been named "Athlete of the Century" by *Gentleman's Quarterly, Sports Illustrated*, the British Broadcasting Company (BBC), and *USA Today*, has been the subject of numerous television documentaries, had his sixtieth birthday nationally televised in January 2002 in the aftermath of 9/11, was called a "national treasure" by former president Clinton, was awarded the Presidential Medal of Freedom by George W. Bush in 2005, and was a guest of honor at an inauguration party for Barack Obama in 2009. In addition to these appearances and honors, he is also the subject of both the 1996 Academy Award–winning documentary *When We Were Kings* and the 2001 feature-length film *Ali*, the latter by Michael Mann and starring Will Smith.

But why has there been such a sudden and immense interest in Muhammad Ali? Why has America been so celebratory of a figure that it so reviled in the 1960s and '70s? Why was Ali, who has represented and embodied the Other like no other within the American imagination, asked to light the 1996 Olympic torch after he threw his own 1960 Gold Medal into the Ohio River because legal segregation barred him from eating in a restaurant in his own hometown of Louisville, Kentucky?

Why has he graced the cover of numerous magazines in the last few years, as "Athlete of the Century," after his conversion to the Nation of Islam and his incisive critiques of American racism?

Clearly, Ali's inability to speak now stands in stark contrast to his reputation for eloquence, a quick wit, and a sharp tongue in the 1960s and 1970s. And it begs the question: Would Ali be as revered as he is today if he were still able to articulate his thoughts and feelings the way that only Ali knew how? Is he less threatening now because of his silence? And has he become a signifier, an empty vessel that America can fill with its own desires and myths—a tabula rasa on which America can not only rewrite its own history, particularly of the highly contested 1960s, but also imagine its triumphalist future?

Clearly, it is important to understand the encroaching role that commodity capitalism has increasingly played, particularly in the post–Cold War era, in which market dictates have colonized and commodified dissent, stripping rebellion and resistance of their oppositional possibilities and making "revolution" a target demographic in and of itself. Ali himself has become a commodity in late-capitalist America—a cottage industry in which popular culture, Black radical chic, and opposition have converged.

Cultural critic bell hooks, in her essay titled "Eating the Other," explores the ways in which racial difference is circulated within the mainstream media and the implications of this. According to hooks,

> The commodification of difference promotes paradigms of consumption wherein whatever difference the Other inhabits is eradicated, via exchange, by a consumer cannibalism that not only displaces the Other but denies the significance of that Other's history through a process of decontextualization.[1]

Hooks's insightful comments on the commodification of difference underscore the power of commodity capitalism. But more important, in highlighting the importance of history, hooks opens up a space of interpretation to understand the contemporary manifestations of the resurgence of Black liberation struggles in general and Muhammad Ali in particular.

In building upon hooks's evocative arguments regarding capitalism and decontextualization, we should consider Michael Eric Dyson's discussions of memory for a more nuanced understanding of Ali's recent recuperation. In his work on Malcolm X, Dyson differentiates between "collective memory" and "selective memory" in his exploration of the role of historical consciousness. In doing so, he asserts that collective memory for Black peoples has been an "instrument for survival," because it has continually stimulated and preserved Black cultural and political achievement in order to fight "against the detrimental consequences of racial amnesia represented in the selective memory of the recent past in white America." For Dyson, selective memory (often the product of white America) "expresses the desire for reconciliation—through strategies of depoliticization and amnesia—by dominant traditions that obscure or distort the collective memory of minority traditions."[2] These processes of depoliticization and amnesia are central to an understanding of Muhammad Ali and his recent embrace in contemporary culture.

Dyson's examination of selective memory is echoed and inflected by Herman Gray, who, in his essay titled "Remembering Civil Rights," argues that for an entire generation "feature films, fictional television, documentaries and popular representations of blacks in contemporary visual culture are the chief means by which memory, history, and experience of the past become part of the common sense understanding of the present." Gray suggests that contemporary television is engaged in a kind of recuperative work in which historical subjects are forced to fit the requirements of contemporary circumstance. Gray supports this view by examining contemporary television's representations of the Civil Rights subject—what he defines as the Black, largely middle class who gained the most visibility as well as the most material and status rewards from the struggle of the Civil Rights movement—and suggests that such representations serve to "construct the mythic terms through which many Americans can believe that our nation has now transcended racism."[3]

Gray's critique of televisual history is a compelling one, and it resonates with Dyson's idea of selective memory, both of which inform much of the complexity of Ali's relatively recent assimilation into the American narrative. But "the Civil Rights subject," emphasized by Gray, differs from Ali, who, in contrast, was not only part of the Black Power movement but also a Black *Muslim* and ideologically opposed to Civil Rights as well as the Cold War liberalism that defined the era. As a result, the meanings surrounding Ali's contemporary reception are different. Because Ali is a Black Muslim, his recuperation as a national hero has occurred at a time when the meaning of race began to shift, as the New Right forged an imperial multiculturalism and altered the memory of the 1960s and America's Cold War past and its post–Civil Rights present. But in addition, Ali's recuperation is also informed by the national memory and fear around the role of Black Islam and its internationalist impulse toward the Third World more broadly and the Muslim Third World specifically, as it has challenged the containment of Black freedom within a narrative of U.S. nationalism.

Behind Enemy Lines

The day after winning the heavyweight championship from Sonny Liston, Ali announced that he had converted to Islam. The furor of a heavyweight champion converting to Islam and openly critiquing American racism was immense, particularly in light of how the Nation of Islam was seen by mainstream America at that time. With Mike Wallace's televised documentary *The Hate That Hate Produced* still resonating with the American public, and with Malcolm X still a highly visible figure, the announcement of Ali's conversion and name change created a visceral response from every corner of American society that could only be characterized as shock and awe. Endorsements and television appearances were canceled, attempts were made to strip him of his title, and prominent figures in all walks of life spoke out vehemently against him, creating a firestorm of criticism that ultimately turned the public against Ali. Numerous journalists and newscasters refused to call Ali by his new name and continued to call him Clay while disparaging him at every turn. Jimmy Cannon, a respected boxing journalist, said that prior to this, boxing had never "been turned into an instrument of hate" and that "Clay is using it as a weapon of wickedness."[4] The NAACP's Roy Wilkins said, "Cassius may not know it but he is now an honorary member of the White Citizen's Councils. . . . He speaks their piece better than they do,"[5] and he held up the Nation of Islam as the mirror image of the Ku Klux Klan. Thurgood Marshall called Ali the "ugly American," and revered former heavyweight champion Joe Louis also spoke out against him, saying that Ali would "earn the public's hatred" because what the Nation of Islam "preach[es] is the opposite of what we believe."[6] Floyd Patterson, the former Heavyweight Champion and a staunch integrationist, said that the "image of a Black Muslim as Heavyweight Champion disgraces the sport and the nation," and he wanted to personally return the championship to America and Christianity, adding that "Clay needed to be beaten and the Black Muslim scourge removed from boxing."[7] Unfortunately for Patterson and his backers, Ali mocked and humiliated Patterson in their fight, battering him into submission.

While Ali's conversion to Islam once again stoked the fears of Black Islam in the aftermath of Malcolm, public outcry against him reached its ultimate fever pitch in 1967, when he refused to fight in Vietnam. Though somehow he went from the lowest priority for being drafted to becoming classified by the U.S. government as 1A—the highest priority—after winning the title, Ali's refusal to fight in Vietnam and his critique of an imperialist war sent shock waves through American political culture. With Malcolm X's influence still resonating and his Muslim Internationalism defining the shape of SNCC, the Black Arts Movement, and the emerging Black Panther Party, Ali's refusal to fight in Vietnam and his denunciation of white America and its imperialist impulses brought front and center a resurgent Muslim internationalist who rejected America's Cold War liberalism and the Civil Rights movement's claims on Black freedom dreams. In the view of the American mainstream, if Ali were given a platform and were allowed to escape the draft, not only would many other Black youth follow his lead, but they might also become Muslims or members of other radical organizations such as RAM, SNCC, and the Black Panther Party. And though he was ultimately stripped of his title, had his passport revoked, was unable to fight and generate income, and was facing a five-year prison sentence, Ali continued to be a lightning rod for both controversy and mobilization, for he arguably became the defining figure within popular and political culture to capture the internationalist zeitgeist.

Like Malcolm before him, Ali challenged the idea that Black freedom should be limited to and contained within the context of the United States. Ali boxed several times throughout the world, and his fights, in combination with his stand on Vietnam and his burgeoning relationships with the Third World, can be seen as stages upon which the drama of the Muslim International unfolded, as the global theater that was his fights in Munich, London, Kuala Lumpur, Manila, Kinshasa, Jakarta, and other places made Ali a figure who not only transcended America but also rallied support for himself and his cause throughout the Third World. When he made his famous remark "I don't have to be what you want me to be," he was directing it as much at a racist America as at Black Cold War liberals of the Civil Rights movement and mainstream Black communities. Ali embodied the rebel spirit that had also become style in the late 1960s, and in many ways he was the popular incarnation and even genesis of the "Black is beautiful" mantra, which emerged during this time.

The emergence also of a distinctly Third World Left within U.S.-based Black communities during the mid- to late 1960s and early 1970s was undeniable, especially in light of the vocabulary that Robert Williams, Harold Cruse, and numerous others crafted in the 1950s and '60s, situating Black struggles in the United States alongside and in solidarity with the struggles of the peoples of the Third World against white supremacy. With the Black Panthers vocally supporting the National Liberation Front of Vietnam and even offering up Black men to fight as soldiers in the NLF against the U.S. military and with the influence of Che Guevara, Mao Tse-tung, Frantz Fanon, Patrice Lumumba, the Mau Mau of Kenya, and the Third World anticolonialism of Cuba, Algeria, and China, the militancy of the moment saw kindred souls in the national liberation struggles taking place throughout Africa and Asia. The "revolutionary violence" of Che, Fanon, and others captured the hearts and minds of young Black radicals in the streets, as RAM, the Black Panthers, and other radical youth within Puerto Rican, Native American, Chicano, and Asian communities formed groups such as the Young Lords Party, the American Indian Movement, the Brown Berets, and I Wor Kuen. The spirit of internationalism was endemic and widespread in the United States through the use of the Third World and colonialism as lenses to frame and understand the conditions of Black peoples in the United States. As Stokely Carmichael said, "Black Power means that we see ourselves as part of the Third World; that we see our struggle as closely related to liberation struggle around the world."[8]

But more than any other figure, it was Malcolm X whose linking of the Muslim Third World of Mecca, Egypt, Bandung, and Palestine to the freedom struggles of Black people in the United States who clearly influenced the shape and tenor of Black radical political culture in the mid- to late 1960s and on through the emergence of Black Power. Ali, who was a central figure within the unfolding drama of Black internationalism and who continued to shape and be shaped by the Muslim International, became the most visible and powerful figure after Malcolm to connect Black Islam in the United States with the larger worlds of Africa, Asia, and the Muslim Third World. Soon after winning the heavyweight championship and converting to Islam, Ali claimed that he was the champion of the whole world, and when he went with Malcolm X to visit the United Nations, he said, "I want to meet the people I am champion of."[9] Upon winning the heavyweight title, Ali went on a trip to Africa, traveling to Ghana, Nigeria, and Egypt and meeting with Kwame Nkrumah and Gamal Abdel Nasser as he solidified his place within the African and Muslim Third World, linking Black radical politics to the broader Muslim International. Because his religious conversion was the means through which he identified with the broader Third World of Africa and Asia, he would say, "Islam is a religion of 750 million people all over the world who believe in it and I'm one of them," tapping into the same internationalist vein that Malcolm had tapped into in connecting Black peoples in the United States to the Muslim Third World of Africa and Asia.[10]

Mobilizing the Nation of Islam's expanded understanding of "Black" to include anyone who is not white, Ali would later say, "Boxing is nothing, just satisfying some blood thirsty people. I'm no longer Cassius Clay, a Negro from Kentucky. I belong to the world, the black world. I'll always have a home in Pakistan, in Algeria, in Ethiopia."[11] Not only did Ali's ability to imagine Black belonging and freedom beyond America make him a global icon, it also brought a new dimension to the Muslim International in which performance and sport became another site to explore the possibilities of the political. For Ali was a new aesthetic of athlete, and he also represented a new aesthetic of what could be political. He redefined, or better yet broke, the mold of athletic identity, particularly for Black athletes. And he also embodied a new spirit of rebellion, one that linked new forms of self-identity with a global politics that simultaneously took shape and shaped the contours of the Muslim International and the revolutionary currents coursing throughout the globe as newly formed nation-states fought to break out of the yoke of centuries of colonialism. When he said his infamous line "I ain't got no problem with them Vietcong, ain't none of them called me nigger," Ali exposed the fundamental hypocrisy of American exceptionalism and within U.S. imperial culture.[12] He would poetically and poignantly expand upon this in a speech made in his hometown, Louisville, in 1967:

> Why should they ask me to put on a uniform and go ten thousand miles from home and drop bombs and bullets on brown people in Vietnam while so-called Negro people in Louisville are treated like dogs and denied simple human rights? No, I'm not going ten thousand miles from home to help murder and burn another poor nation simply to continue the domination of white slavemasters of the darker people the world over. This is the day when such evils must come to an end. I have been warned that to take such a stand would put my prestige in jeopardy and could cause me to lose millions of dollars which should accrue to me as the champion. But I have said it once and I will say it again. The real enemy of my people is right here. I will not disgrace my religion, my people or myself by becoming a tool to enslave those who are fighting for their own justice, freedom and equality. . . . If I thought the war was going to bring freedom and equality to twenty-two million of my people, they wouldn't have to draft me, I'd join tomorrow. But I either have to obey the laws of the land or the laws of Allah. I have nothing to lose by standing up for my beliefs. So I'll go to jail. We've been in jail for four hundred years.[13]

For Ali, despite his ban from boxing for three and a half years, the Muslim International and Black radical politics became the sites of his new struggles outside the ring, bearing witness to the truth that the battleground, as Fanon would say, is in fact everywhere. And though Ali was ultimately able to return to the ring after refusing the military draft, he lost the prime years of his boxing life. Though he had incredible moments and victories, one can only wonder what might have been as far as the ring was concerned. But his ban may have been a blessing in disguise, for he was at the frontline of a very different battle—a battle over the limits of white power and the possibilities of freedom for Black and Third World peoples worldwide. All of which continues to beg the question, what does it mean that he is so revered today, after taking the positions he took?

(Re)Birth of a Nation

Ali's resurrection in the 1990s coincided with the emergence of a broader set of ideological forces that erupted after decades of white backlash and state repression during the post–Civil Rights era and the expansion of U.S. empire. As a result, a resurgent American nationalism emerged that was predicated upon the creation of both domestic and foreign enemies of the state, which the "Black criminal" and the "Muslim terrorist" came to embody. On the domestic front, beginning in the late 1960s with Nixon and his "law and order" campaign and continuing into the Reagan–Bush years of the "War on Crime," a national consensus was created that sought to link the idea of America to an implicit idea of whiteness that leaned heavily upon ideas of tradition, family, responsibility, work ethic, and character, ideas that were then molded into a larger conception of citizenship. Against this backdrop, Reagan made very coded appeals to whites by distinguishing them from and contrasting them to the inhabitants of urban America and the sensationalized fears and assumptions that were created about "Black criminality," "welfare queens," drug dealers, and the supposed pathologies of the inner city. In the calculus of the New Right, post–Civil Rights America had transcended race, suggesting that overt expressions or explicit appeals to race were themselves viewed as racist, ultimately nullifying and silencing those who sought to challenge the persistence of systemic forms of racism in housing, education, and the like. This had the desired effect of positioning whites as victims of policies such as affirmative action, welfare, and other social programs, a strategy that was central to the New Right and their allies who sought to continue to protect white privilege by tapping into the decades-long white anger and resentment over Civil Rights and Black Power.

On the international front, the hypernationalism of the post–Civil Rights era and the desire to restore "greatness" to America were predicated upon the fears stoked by the "Muslim terrorist." The fear of the threat of Islam and "terrorism" to U.S. national security was fueled by the oil embargo, the Palestinian–Israeli conflict, the Iranian hostage crisis, and a deepening U.S. involvement in the Muslim Third World of Lebanon, Libya, Iran, Iraq, Afghanistan, Pakistan, Egypt, and numerous other countries. With anticommunist battles being pitched in Central

America and covert wars being fought everywhere, the Muslim Third World was imagined as a region of threat, if not a proxy for Soviet influence, so it witnessed a deepening U.S. military and political presence.

But with the end of the Cold War in 1989 and in light of the domestic consensus around race that had supported the Cold War liberalism of the previous four decades, a great deal of discussion and debate occurred over who and what were going to define United States nationalism in a post–Cold War world. On the international front, the fall of the Berlin Wall and the end of the Cold War were the cause of both a euphoric triumphalism and a tremendous anxiety that gripped the architects of American power. What would America's role be in this new world? And if the country assumed the position of lone superpower, now that democracy and capitalism had "won," what were the new "threats" to American power going to be? If the Cold War liberalism had assumed that communism was more of a threat to the Third World than colonialism was, thereby justifying European and American control of the Third World, what now for America's relationship to the countries in Africa, Asia, and Latin America?

What was clear, despite the ambiguity and unease, was the sense of collective triumphalism that gripped the nation. The Cold War was won as a result of what many viewed as successful American policies and interventions, and a moral flair and imperial arrogance suffused the rhetoric of triumphalism, which seemed to justify and legitimize the violence and havoc created in Africa, Asia, and Latin America. This triumphalism was reflected on the international front, with the United States' assumption of lone superpower status, its swift victory in the Persian Gulf War, and the vanquishing of the "Vietnam Syndrome," all of which situated America as poised to dominate the new global landscape.[14] While the end of the Cold War seemed like a radical rupture from the past, a breaking point, and a clean slate, that was far from the truth, because Cold War alliances, policies, and legacies continued to play out. But as the celebrations continued, the smoke began to settle, and the fractures and fissures around the American nation began to reveal themselves.

Just as the Soviet Union and communism had created the ideological blueprint for both U.S. domestic and foreign policy during the Cold War, the singular rise of the "Green Menace" of Islam replaced the Red Scare, providing policy makers and think tanks with the ideological impetus, contour, and purpose for reinvigorating American domestic and foreign policy. Edified and crystallized by Samuel Huntington's influential "Clash of Civilizations" thesis, which sees Islam and the West on a collision course, as well as by the viewpoints of Bernard Lewis, Martin Kramer, and others, the American perspective came to view Islam and Muslims as the predominant threat to the post–Cold War world. For just as communism was viewed as a bigger threat to the Third World than colonialism in the aftermath of World War II, Islam has been viewed in the post–Cold War era as the biggest threat to global security and the hard-fought "gains" of the United States in the Cold War, a view that has served to justify not only the United States' position as a unipolar leader in the world but also its continuing presence in the Third World as a bulwark against "Islamic terrorism."

As the "Muslim terrorist" came to be seen as a foreign threat to U.S. power and the West in the post–Cold War moment, so were racial minorities, feminists, and queer communities seen as domestic threats—"radicals" threatening the coherence and cohesiveness of America and the West. In response, the New Right agenda asserted its ideological footprint with the "culture wars," which involved attacking the legacies and gains of the 1960s by targeting multiculturalism, identity politics, and other race-, class-, gender-, and sexuality-based remedies, viewing these as threatening to national unity and "common culture." In defending the West and seeking to redefine America, the New Right agenda cemented the triumphalism of Cold War liberalism by vanquishing America's racist past and celebrating an idealized present through the valorization of Civil Rights and "color blindness."

Referred to as the "culture wars," the battle over multiculturalism and "political correctness" picked up steam in the late 1980s and was raging by the early 1990s. The tensions between a "common culture" and the "disuniting of America" through minority voices—which was called multiculturalism—became common refrains and tropes that appeared in numerous media, including television, major newspapers such as the *New York Times* and the *Los Angeles Times*, and magazines such as *Time* and *Newsweek*, as well as in scholarly treaties, including Dinesh D'souza's *Illiberal Education*, Allan Bloom's *The Closing of the American Mind*, and Todd Gitlin's *Twilight of Our Common Dreams: Why America Is Wracked by Culture Wars*, to name just a few. Numerous politicians and senior cabinet members, such as Secretary of Education William Bennett and even President George H. W. Bush, weighed in on the topic, marking the impact and sense of furor that these issues raised.

George Will, a leading conservative columnist, wrote in *Newsweek* magazine immediately after the conclusion of the Persian Gulf War that Lynne Cheney, who was head of the National Endowment for the Humanities (NEH), would have a more difficult battle to fight than the one her husband, Dick Cheney, had as secretary of defense. According to Will, "In this low-visibility high intensity war, Lynne Cheney is secretary of domestic defense. The foreign adversaries her husband, Dick, must keep at bay are less dangerous, in the long run, than the domestic forces with which she must deal."[15] Emblematic of the volatility and fluidity of the post–Cold War moment, the rhetorical frameworks of newly emerging threats, both foreign and domestic, began to mirror and complement each other. On the international front, the threats to the post–Cold War order might take the shape of breakaway republics, rogue nations, and demagogic leaders, and on the home front, an unofficial civil war was being fought in the eyes of the New Right to maintain the unity of the United States and, by extension, the West. As a result, the debates around multiculturalism, feminism, and other racial and ethnic minorities were seen through the lens of global threats, as domestic complements to the fracturing and Balkanization that was perceived to be taking place throughout the world. In this way, these domestic "identity" movements were a threat to American unity and "common culture," much like "Islamic terrorists," the former Yugoslavia, the former Soviet republics, and other nations fracturing were a threat to the new global order being led by the United States. As a result, this American motley crew was seen as the domestic versions of breakaway racial republics, feminist rogue nations, and demagogic radicals in universities threatening the unity and hard-fought cohesion of the nation that was gained by the Cold War. In the eyes of the Right and even many liberals, such as Gitlin, Hollinger, and others, the domestic war was on—and there was a great deal at stake—nothing less than the very idea of America.

The perceived threat of multiculturalism, feminism, and queer politics—as problematic as any and all of these were in arguing ultimately for inclusion instead of fundamentally challenging the forces that led to their exclusion in the first place—stemmed from a deep-seated white fear that these "movements" would undo the work of the New Right and fracture the social cement that has made America what it is. The calls for the inclusion of minority writers, voices, and ideas within school curricula were seen as an attack on the established literary canons and historical "truths" of the West, as minority writers such as James Baldwin, Toni Morrison, and Maxine Hong Kingston, among numerous others, were perceived as having politicized literature and history by pushing out the "greats," such as Dickens, Shakespeare, and so forth, and attacking the very idea of truth and objectivity. In the minds of the New Right and their liberal accomplices, to emphasize or recenter discussions of power around gender, race, and sexuality was to privilege these other identities over and above being "American." For, according to the New Right, who had hijacked the rhetoric of race in the post–Civil Rights era, to speak about race was itself racist, an ideology that undermined race-conscious social remedies and silenced the challenges brought forward by Blacks, Latinos, women, and others, deeming these minorities un-American and their approaches antithetical to the post–Civil Rights consensus.

The teaching of eternal values and truths was thought to be the hallmark of the West, and to include other voices and perspectives that might challenge or destabilize the master narratives of the West was seen as an attack on those values, which only served to "politicize" literature and history, and relativized "truth." But the New Right critics of these challenges to the canons of the West (often referred to as "revisionist" by the new Right) overlooked how Blacks, Latinos, women, and other minorities sought to place literature, history, and the notion of truth within a historical and political context. Challenging the five-hundred-year celebration of Columbus's "discovery" of the New World and critically engaging minority voices and perspectives in the discussion of literature and history were about foregrounding how power, authority, and ultimately historical "truth" were created and also about the implications this had for understanding contemporary forms of inequality. But more poignantly, these movements, at their best, sought to challenge the established canons by revealing how the universal "truths" espoused by the West are themselves marked by what critic Richard Dyer has called the "invisibility of whiteness."[16] Ironically and quite hypocritically, the

New Right claimed that these minority voices were tainted by the peculiarities of race and gender and therefore "biased." But what the New Right critics overlooked was how the very idea of the "West" and its notions of "truth" and "objectivity" were themselves imbued with particular race and gender politics, specifically the privileging of white male perspectives, which have historically masked themselves as universal and transcendent. For what ultimately was at stake in the New Right's calls for a "common culture" and a preservation of the West was an unspoken and deep-seated anxiety about the role of Eurocentrism in historically coding and privileging the voices of straight white males as truth telling and authoritative. These challenges, then, to the canons of literature, the notion of truth, and the force of history were framed by the New Right as an attack on not only the "dead white men" who created the West, but also on the living white men whom the New Right constructed as the victims in the Reagan era backlash against Civil Rights. In fact, much of the New Right's condemnation of these movements was a not-so-coded criticism of the 1960s as the origin of these struggles with minorities, as that decade was consistently characterized as not only naïve and permissive but also responsible for dangerously fracturing the very fabric of the nation, which then led to the current struggles over "identity" politics that undermined the post–Civil Rights consensus that the New Right had ushered in. The criticism coming from the New Right and from many liberals was then ultimately about recentering whiteness and its invisibility, through appeals to "common culture" and "the West," without understanding the powerful forces of slavery, genocide, and colonialism that were unleashed in the name of the West and that ultimately led to these challenges in the first place.[17]

Premillennium Tension

During this moment of seeming transition after the fall of the Berlin Wall, the United States sought to redefine its global military posture to reflect what it saw as a very different political order around the world. While some argued for a multipolar world, political columnist Charles Krauthammer wrote an influential article titled "The Unipolar Moment," which had widespread support across the American political spectrum, ultimately arguing that the United States should seize the moment and assume the role of leader in the new global environment. And with the threat vacuum created by the fall of the Soviet Union, questions arose as to who or what would begin to define this new U.S. military posture.[18] Would it be a series of rogue leaders, so-called teacup dictators? Individual outlaw states? Or would there be a coherent threat, similar to the threat of communism? While debate raged, a consensus began to develop that later emerged from the buildup to Gulf War I, as the one-time U.S. ally Saddam Hussein was being compared to Hitler. Numerous influential columnists, think tanks, and policy makers began to make the argument that Islam, as the "Green Menace," would replace the Red Scare of the Soviet Union as the new and emerging threat not only to U.S. interests but also to the ambiguous idea of "Western" values.

Like the threat of communism, this new Islamic threat was seen as spreading throughout the world and undermining Western political interests and values. Much as communism was seen as a bigger threat than colonialism to the post–World War II order that justified the European and U.S. extension of colonial rule wherever democracy and freedom were "protected," the Islamic threat was seen as the biggest threat to the post–Cold War global order and viewed as potentially undoing all that had been gained by and for Western political interests during the Cold War. This emerging threat demanded that the United States assume a singular role in the New World Order and create new alliances, strengthen existing ones, and develop new long-term political, economic, and diplomatic strategies to "protect" the world.

As a result, think tank papers, policy conferences, op-ed pieces, and congressional hearings exploded around the idea of a new "Islamic threat," and this, coupled with the buildup that led to Gulf War I around Saddam Hussein, signaled a turning point in U.S. post–Cold War orientations in the early 1990s. In addition to Iraq, Iran was also singled out as an emerging threat, as were the Central Asian countries of the former Soviet republics, several Arab countries, Afghanistan, Algeria, Pakistan, Sudan, Somalia, Egypt, and other so-called hot spots around the globe.

Influential policy wonks and scholars began to produce the rhetorical frameworks for the new "Islamic threat." In 1990, an influential article titled "The Roots of Muslim Rage," written by the veteran historian Bernard Lewis and given book-length treatment in his influential *Islam and the West*, stated, the West is "facing a mood and a movement far transcending the level of issues and policies and the governments that pursue them. This is no less than a clash of civilizations—the perhaps irrational but surely historic reaction of an ancient rival against our Judeo-Christian heritage, our secular present, and the worldwide expansion of both."[19] In addition, Charles Krauthammer's 1993 piece in the *Washington Post* titled "The New Crescent of Crisis: Global Intifada" increased the alarmist tone that was part and parcel of the moment. More telling is a 1992 *Washington Post* article that argues that Islam "spreads across vast swaths of the globe that can be colored green on the television maps in the same way that communist countries used to be colored red."[20] And Douglas E. Streusand, who was then at the Heritage Foundation, wrote, "A new specter is haunting America, one that some Americans consider more sinister than Marxism-Leninism. . . . That specter is Islam."[21]

But it is Samuel Huntington's famous article in 1993, "The Clash of Civilizations," published in *Foreign Affairs*, and then his full-length book published three years later, titled *The Clash of Civilizations and the Remaking of the World Order*, that ideologically codified and gave power and sanction to the post–Cold War consensus around the "threat" posed by Islam and the Muslim Third World. Huntington's thesis resonated with the broader political culture. In fact, it is a thesis that not only echoes but also replicates Cold War ideologies, more so than many have realized. Huntington's "Clash of Civilizations" thesis (a phrase taken from Bernard Lewis's "The Roots of Muslim Rage") resonates with the work of George Kennan, who is often referred to as the "father of the containment policy" for America's Cold War and whose famous anonymous piece "The Sources of Soviet Conduct," in the 1947 issue of *Foreign Affairs*, heavily influenced Truman, Eisenhower, and the architects of American anticommunist policy in the Third World. Kennan argued that there is an "innate antagonism between capitalism and socialism,"[22] a framework that ultimately became the ideological blueprint for the Truman Doctrine and Cold War policy, and his argument included the idea of "the West versus the rest," as did Huntington's, revealing not only the rhetorical and ideological links between the creation of the "Red Scare" and the "Green Menace" but also the deeply held existential need and desire for a narrative of threat that could give coherence to U.S. national identity and the West.

In his work, Huntington argued that nations, economies, and ideologies would be less important in the new post–Cold War world than civilizations, and in particular "civilizational identities." In the euphoria that was raging around globalization, free markets, and the decline of the nation-state in the new "global village," Huntington's thesis strongly suggests that the belief in a global community is a fiction and that the "West" should aggressively work to protect its interests. While Huntington discussed seven or eight civilizations, he highlighted "Islamic" civilization as the biggest threat to the West, arguing, "The underlying problem for the West is not Islamic fundamentalism. It is Islam, a different civilization whose people are convinced of the superiority of their culture and are obsessed with the inferiority of their power."[23] Huntington's deeply Orientalist framework echoes other undercurrents within American's post–Cold War political culture. And his rhetorical flourishes about the West no doubt give pause for their sheer sweep. Whereas the idea of "the West" during the Cold War was slightly ambiguous—including as it did the United States, its NATO allies, and the colonial powers in western Europe—after the Cold War, in a unipolar world, the idea of who the West is has clearly rested more squarely on the shoulders of the United States. So Huntington's thesis, while privileging civilizations over nations—in this case "the West" over Islamic or Sinitic (Chinese) nations—ultimately suggests that the United States, though a nation, should stand in as the embodiment of the West to protect not only its own ideals and interests but also those of the countries of Europe and their allies the world over:

> [The world] is a dangerous place, in which large numbers of people resent our wealth, power, and culture, and vigorously oppose our efforts to persuade or coerce them to accept our values of human rights, democracy, and capitalism. In this world America must learn to distinguish among our true friends who will be with us and we with them through thick and thin . . . and unrelenting enemies who will try to destroy us unless we destroy them first.[24]

Clearly this line of alarmist, triumphalist, and hegemonic thinking has echoed and supported the views of many within U.S. policy circles, military agencies, and security apparatuses about the United States' lead role in the post–Cold War world. But ultimately, Huntington's ideas have gained credence and legitimacy because they absolve the West (i.e., the United States and its allies) of any responsibility in creating a current geopolitical order in which massive inequality, wars, and poverty exist. Consistent with the post–Cold War triumphalism that sought to reinscribe American exceptionalism, Huntington saw poverty, war, and massive inequality as the result of intrinsically different—and even deficient—civilizations and their values. His ideas have ultimately become an uncritical endorsement of power and the status quo, because he refused to see the heterogeneity within and among groups and completely discounted what Edward Said argued is "the bewildering interdependence" of humans, ideas, and the march of history.[25]

In addition, what is interesting and often overlooked in Huntington's work is his argument that uniform and cohesive states are stronger than those that are composed of different civilizations. In arguing this, Huntington warned America that the influx of immigrants and the various debates around multiculturalism challenge the uniformity of what it means to be American, which echoed and underscored many of the New Right "culture warriors." He asked, "Are we a *Western* people or are we something else?" And he continued, "The futures of the U.S. and of the West depend upon Americans reaffirming their commitment to American civilization."[26] Clearly Huntington viewed the success of American hegemony—in particular over its archrival the "Islamic world"—as deeply intertwined with domestic questions about America's own sense of itself and its ability to maintain a coherent "civilizational identity" amid the battles raging around race, gender, and sexuality, which have challenged the post–Cold War consensus.

In fact, as the new national Other of Islam and the Muslim Third World began to crystallize in the post–Cold War moment, U.S. nationalism, instead of seeking to subsume its racial differences within a national framework, sought to celebrate and fetishize difference as the basis of a reinvigorated U.S. expansionist posture in the post–Cold War era. This new imperial multiculturalism ultimately maintained the traditional relations of power, with whiteness still being the invisible norm (and what Huntington might have meant by a "civilizational identity"), as the celebration of a multicultural United States gave moral sanction and ethical legitimacy to the country as a global superpower. In very specific ways, imperial multiculturalism reinvigorated in a new era the older arguments of American benevolence that arose in the post–World War II moment. But instead of the racial liberalism that defined U.S. Cold War policy against the communist "menace," the new imperial multiculturalism assumed the logic of Huntington's "Clash of Civilizations" thesis and projected a multicultural America as an entity against the panracial enemy and threat of Islam.

With the United States embodying the West, its renewed and redefined multicultural identity has echoed and edified American exceptionalist ideas about the country's role and position in the world. As the United States has sought to protect the world from the supposed threat of Islam and the Muslim Third World, the new multicultural and cosmopolitan nationalism has positioned the United States as a representative embodiment of the world, giving it an implicit mandate to lead and dominate in the post–Cold War moment. Imperial multiculturalism could then disarm critics of U.S. foreign policy, intervention, and war by appealing to the democratic and pluralistic image of the United States, thereby suffusing U.S. policy with a moral righteousness and a benevolent flair.

But with the country's peculiar history of slavery, which continues to haunt any semblance of U.S. triumphalism, Blackness continued quite predictably to play a central role in the reconstitution of the United States in the 1990s. The use of Blackness as an imagined symbol of democracy has its roots in the U.S. Information Agency's Cold War propaganda campaigns and the widespread belief that Jim Crow and segregation were America's Achilles' heel in the Cold War, as racial violence on Black peoples was seized upon by a skeptical Third World. As a result, Black faces were strategically placed in positions of visibility, for as Adam Clayton Powell told Eisenhower, "One dark face from the US is of as much value as millions of dollars in economic aid."[27] As the United States worked to frame itself as a racially harmonious place during the era of decolonization, the racial liberalism of the Cold War placed Blackness front and center, and so did the imperial multiculturalism of the post–Cold War era.

Whether it was the meteoric rise of Colin Powell as chairman of the Joint Chiefs of Staff under President George H. W. Bush or the emergence of Denzel Washington in the 1990s as the paradigmatic cinematic citizen–soldier (*Glory, Courage under Fire, Crimson Tide,* and *The Siege*) that paralleled Sidney Poitier's appeal during the Civil Rights era, the embrace of Blackness signaled a shift in the politics of race in the post–Cold War moment. But it was the embrace of the Black Muslim Muhammad Ali as national hero that arguably did the most penetrating ideological work. As the United States redefined its national identity through the idea of multiculturalism and against the new threat of Islam and the Muslim Third World, the embrace of Ali sought to domesticate Black Islam, as he became a central component in the drive and desire for consensus. And in the highly celebrated 1996 film *When We Were Kings*, Ali became the proxy for reconstituting America in this troubling and telling moment.

When Were We Kings?

Winner of the 1996 Academy Award for Best Documentary, *When We Were Kings* captured the famous 1974 "Rumble in the Jungle" fight in Kinshasa, Zaire (now the Democratic Republic of the Congo), between champion George Foreman and challenger Muhammad Ali. As suggested by its title, the film is framed as both a triumphalist "Back to Africa" narrative and a celebratory "Black Power" spectacle of the 1970s, as it carries a nostalgic impulse behind it, suggesting an idealized pre-slavery Africa that attempts to tap into and unites the anticolonial nationalisms of Africa and the Black Power movement in the United States. Even though both movements had for the most part been destroyed and their utopian possibilities undermined by the CIA and FBI, respectively, as well as by U.S. Cold War policies, *When We Were Kings* nostalgically and awkwardly tries to rekindle that spirit of those movements with its pastoral, exoticizing, and even romanticizing images of Zaire/Congo. Including an all-star concert of Black performers from throughout the diaspora, such as James Brown, B. B. King, Miriam Makeba, Celia Cruz, Bill Withers, and the Spinners, the narrative arc of *When We Were Kings* follows the charismatic Muhammad Ali as he tries to regain the heavyweight championship for the first time since it was stripped from him for his refusal to fight in Vietnam in 1967.

Throughout *When We Were Kings*, the fight as event is played as a Black Power spectacle back in the motherland of Africa. There is footage of Ali on the plane to Zaire/Congo marveling at Black pilots on a Black airline, the reception of Ali at the airport, the support of the people during his stay in Africa, and various talking heads, including Don King, George Plimpton, Norman Mailer, James Brown, and others who consistently reference and talk about the significance of the fight in racial terms. But in the end, the Pan-African and Black Power veneer is just that, for Ali and the rest of the players in the film are deafeningly silent on the political history of the U.S. involvement in Zaire/Congo. By the time of the film's release in 1996, it ultimately plays as imperial cinematic wish fulfillment, celebrating America's Cold War liberalism not through the typical narrative of Martin Luther King and his "I Have a Dream Speech" but instead through Muhammad Ali, who came to embody the ideal of Black Islam after Malcolm. As a result, *When We Were Kings* resonates deeply with a sense of post–Cold War U.S. triumphalism, as the country was reflecting on its past in order to define itself for its future as the lone superpower in a unipolar world.

In fact, the film's Pan-African veneer serves as a substitute for any substantive engagement with the political and cultural context of the fight, sidelining any real engagement with larger political concerns. And even though the film centers on Ali, a purportedly politicized figure, there is very little engagement with him and his political voice. Yes, Ali is shown speaking, with his monologues and soliloquies meant to convey his wit and his outspoken persona. And though fragments of Ali speaking about race fall into thematic line with the film's celebratory Black spectacle, they are substituted for any real engagement with the setting and context of the time period of the fight—namely, 1970s Africa and the immediate post–Black Power period in the United States. Without placing Ali's few and brief comments about Africa or Black peoples in the United States within this larger framework, the film ultimately relegates those comments to the status of Ali's other rants in the film, from his joking with Howard Cosell to his mocking of George Foreman and even his monologue about the importance of dental care for young children. In keeping with the general apolitical nature of the film despite its Pan-African veneer, the presentation of Ali is as a character, not as a figure of tremendous ideological import who fundamentally altered the political landscape in the mid- to late 1960s.

In addition, the political history of Zaire/Congo is never dealt with. And when we consider the central place that the anticolonial movement played in freeing the Congo, not only within the Afro-diasporic imagination, but also within American Cold War designs, this silence is all the more troubling. As the first democratically elected prime minister in the newly "independent" Congo of 1960, Patrice Lumumba was a hero not only to the African continent but to the whole Third World. He represented the defiant utopian possibilities of anticolonial nationalism and the spirit of Bandung. But the Congo was the richest country in natural resources on the continent of Africa and perhaps in the world, making Lumumba a man with many enemies. Viewed by the U.S. security establishment, namely, former CIA director Alan Dulles, as "Castro or worse" in 1960,[28] Lumumba would write in his last letter from his prison cell, "We are not alone. Africa, Asia, and free and liberated peoples in every corner of the globe will ever remain at the side of the millions of Congolese."[29] Within ten weeks of being elected as prime minister, Lumumba was kidnapped, after which he was kept in hiding and, following a brief escape, brutally assassinated at the behest of the American CIA.

The worldwide reaction from the nonwhite world was stunning. Not only did Black peoples in the United States storm the United Nations building in New York, with street clashes breaking out, but also Third World communities in Europe, as well as Asia, Africa, and Latin America, vehemently protested and challenged their leaders to raise the question of Lumumba's ouster and assassination in international forums. In fact, Malcolm X continued to raise the issue of the Congo even after Lumumba's assassination, calling out the CIA and their support of Moise Tshombe and Joseph Mobutu (who was head of the military at the time) several times in the context of American imperial aggression in the Third World. Malcolm X said, "Lumumba [is] the greatest Black man who ever walked the African continent."[30]

With American and European leaders bombing the Congo in the years after Lumumba's assassination, Joseph Mobutu seized power there in 1965 with the backing and support of the United States and was viewed as "the most important piece in the jigsaw of U.S. Cold War strategy."[31] Known as "America's tyrant," Mobutu began to "Africanize" the country in the late 1960s and early 1970s, changing the country's name to Zaire in 1972 and the capital from Leopoldville (after the former colonial Belgian king) to Kinshasa. Mobutu also changed his own name to Mobutu Sese Seko Kuku Ngbendu Wu Za Banga, a symbolic rebirth that linked him to the newly born nation-state of Zaire. As leader, Mobutu was immensely corrupt and brutal, as he and his backers raped the country, making him one of the seven wealthiest men in the world. And at the time of the "Rumble in the Jungle," in 1974, the United States was still providing Mobutu with bodyguards.[32]

But *When We Were Kings* contains very little regarding any part of this history. Except for a quick montage that links Black protestors in the United States during the Civil Rights movement with a brief history of the Congo and a brief but telling glimpse of Lumumba in handcuffs when he was arrested by the coup leaders and described as a "Red," *When We Were Kings* ultimately reveals its ideological orientations by implicitly endorsing the United States as a moral force of good around the world. That the iconic Civil Rights moment had passed (both in 1974 when the fight took place and in 1996 when the film was released) *When We Were Kings* positions the United States and its Cold War involvement in the Congo as just. By linking the overthrow of Lumumba as a "Red" with the images of Civil Rights protesters in the United States, not only does the film endorse the logic of Cold War liberalism, which thwarted Third World decolonization and Black internationalist impulses by tying Civil Rights to anticommunism, but it also positions the United States as a benevolent beacon of democracy and human rights by suggesting that the overthrow of Lumumba and the installation of Mobutu were justified.

So despite the blind euphoria about a Black Power celebration in Zaire at the time of 1974's "Rumble in the Jungle," Ali's refusal in the film to speak out about this history and the United States' role within the Congo seems incredible. Why would he remain so silent about all that was happening? Considering the climate of the 1990s and the post–Cold War ideological battles that were raging around America's Cold War past and its role in the future, we get a better sense of why this film was so celebrated and perhaps how to better understand Ali's silence. As the cultural critic Grant Farred points out, Ali "prais[ed] the post-colonial world fulsomely. His endorsement of Africa was not only a demonstration of loyalty to the Third world, but it was also an articulation of his opposition to the American mainstream." Farred continues by saying, "Ali understood how his critiques would resonate for mainstream America—it would confirm their Orientalist perceptions and implicitly make him a traitor to the Third World nation-state."[33]

If Farred is correct that Ali was silent because he did not want to confirm the "Orientalist" stereotypes that the American mainstream held of the Third World, then in 1990s America—let alone 1974 America—this silence is profoundly problematic, because it actually *confirms* what the American mainstream believes about American exceptionalism and the United States' relationship to the rest of the world. That is, to a triumphalist American nation, *When We Were Kings* confirms that if there was a relationship between the United States and Zaire, then it was a benign and benevolent one—a political, economic, and diplomatic relationship that benefited both countries and spread democratic rule in Zaire. And if Mobutu was ruthless, it was not because of America's involvement in the overthrow and murder of Patrice Lumumba and the United States' central role in installing and backing Mobutu when he seized power, but rather because of the political immaturity of Zaireans in particular and Africans in general. In this way, *When We Were Kings* absolves America and also Europe of any complicity or responsibility in the Congo's affairs, suggesting that Mobutu's style of leadership was a result of a "backward," "violent" country, confirming to a post–Cold War American audience what they are already inclined to believe about the Third World in general and African states in particular.

Almost more troubling is that American Cold War policy had a logic of its own. That is, if in fact there was a deep and violent relationship between the United States and the Congo (which there was), then it was a price worth paying, because it was the lesser of two evils—either support a dictator or endure "communism" and Lumumba in the Congo. This was classic Cold War logic in the era of decolonization, a logic that argued that communism was a bigger threat to the Third World than colonialism and ultimately that true democracy, decolonization, and Third World sovereignty had to be sacrificed in the interests of global capitalism and the spread of American-style rule.

When We Were Kings uses Mobutu's treatment of "criminals" to try to show him as a feared and repressive leader. But for an American populace weaned on the fears of "Black criminality" in the "War on Crime" sagas of the Reagan–Bush–Clinton 1980s and 1990s, that characterization of Mobutu wouldn't necessarily position him as repressive but rather as rational and right. The documentary doesn't tell us who these so-called criminals were, nor does it give us any idea about the dissidents, political opponents, critics, and activists who were being silenced, imprisoned, tortured, and killed by Mobutu in order to maintain power and order for his international backers. In fact, it is the figure of Mobutu—"America's tyrant"—who literally and ideologically contains everyone in the film because of the fear he inspired. In this way, Mobutu, as proxy, is the conduit for American imperial power and the simultaneous erasure of America's role in the Congo.

Farred also astutely points out that Ali's radical outspokenness made him a hero of the Third World. And when he went to Africa and Asia, he was not only embraced by the people but also inadvertently gave legitimacy to dictators such as Mobutu, Suharto, and Marcos and deflected their actual relationships with the United States. Farred argues that Ali gave Third World nations "an artificial unity,"[34] which in turn silenced dissent and political opposition in the period leading up to the fights in Zaire, Indonesia, and the Philippines.

When seen through the lens of *When We Were Kings*, Ali's refusal to speak is disheartening, in the 1970s, the 1990s, and even now. Ali had always spoken truth to power, sifting through the ideological rubble and galvanizing the antiwar and Black Power movements in the post-Malcolm phase of the mid- to late 1960s. He had made some of the most astute and insightful political observations of the Johnson and Nixon regimes, yet in Zaire, Indonesia, and the Philippines, he couldn't—or wouldn't—craft a critical political vocabulary that simultaneously positioned him as a Third World populist and also critiqued dictatorial rule and puppeteering for U.S. Cold War interests. Instead in *When We Were Kings*, Ali is the rebel without a cause—silent and muted, a posture that anticipated his place in post–Cold War and post-9/11 America.

In *When We Were Kings*, Ali says, "Look at George—he's an American." But in 1990s America, so too was Ali. In 1974 though, the distinction Ali created between himself and Foreman was part and parcel of his strategy for almost all of his fights, particularly when it came to Black fighters. *They* were the establishment; Ali the rebel. *They* were Americans; Ali was Black Power. *They* were Toms; Ali was the Field Negro. But in the 1990s, through America's embrace of Ali and the lens of color blindness, that moment of *When We Were Kings* seems so anachronistic, so out of place. For both Ali and Foreman seem like Black men from America going into that Heart of Darkness—and like Conrad's Kurtz, Ali was supposedly the skeptic. But in the 1990s, the film positions Ali as unaware of the history of the Congo, about Lumumba, America's Cold War designs there—or even the worldwide uproar over Lumumba's forced and violent removal from power and his brutal and ghastly murder with the backing of the CIA.

Ultimately *When We Were Kings* is celebrated because Ali is seen through the lens of color blindness and the prism of the neoconservative thought that reframed the 1960s and Black Power as a failure and Civil Rights as the pinnacle and endpoint of race in the post–Cold War moment. And when the challenges to white privilege and historical truth erupted in the early 1990s through the "culture wars," history—we were told—*is* told from the perspective of the victors, and we should all accept it. Not simply a history told about "dead white men," but a history and a present told through living white men about everyone else.[35]

The End of History?

In many ways, through his embrace as a national hero, Muhammad Ali has come to embody the reinvigorated ideal of U.S. national identity in the post–Cold War era. By suturing the gap between 1960s racial discontent and 1990s multicultural consensus, Ali became the rallying point and the redemptive figure who healed the open wounds of the 1960s and their ideological legacies that erupted in the 1990s around "identity politics," multiculturalism, and the challenges to the white power that America is predicated upon.

In this way, the embrace of Ali stood as a national rejection of Black Power politics and an uncritical endorsement of Civil Rights, because Ali came to embody a redefined U.S. nationalism, healing the wounds of the nation's troubled past while being the redemptive figure who has helped America transcend its racist legacy. That Blackness, and in particular Ali's radical past, would become a unifying force in the era of imperial multiculturalism in many ways anticipated the Obama presidency by presenting America as an inclusive and enlightened place, on a linear and evolutionary trajectory toward national self-realization. In this way, nostalgia and America's collective memory of Ali have made him an icon for an era when America was coming to terms with its racial politics, and because of *his* courage, America is now a better place, able to transcend the limits that its own racism once imposed upon it. Ali is therefore lionized as a hero, someone who represents both a bygone era and the possibilities for a progressive future one.

Ali's recuperation as national hero in many ways paved the way and became the symbol for a broader redefinition of U.S. national identity around this new imperial multiculturalism, reemboldening and reinvigorating U.S. foreign policy in the post–Cold War moment when the U.S. security state declared that the "Green Menace" of Islam and the Muslim Third World are the new enemy that would define U.S. national identity even *before* 9/11. But in this new global order that the United States claims to defend, Ali's embrace as a national hero reveals troubling issues around the history and legacy of Black Islam and Black internationalism. For it is through Ali that the United States sought to domesticate Black Islam and strip it of its internationalist impulses, and fracture it from the larger Third World of Africa and Asia. For just as Cold War liberalism fractured the Black Left and its internationalist impulses from the Third World by imagining "Negroes as Americans" and tying Black destiny to the American national project through an embrace of anticommunism and Civil Rights, the embrace of Ali as a national hero suggests something similar in regard to the history of Black Islam and its relationship to the Muslim Third World in the post–Cold War era.

Despite the repression of the Black Left brought on by the Cold War and its racial liberalism, Malcolm X and Black Islam continued the tradition of linking Black liberation in the United States with the Third World and providing a trenchant critique of U.S. domestic racism and its imperial foreign policy, viewing that policy as an extension of European colonialism. Ali was an extension of this tradition that Malcolm established as part of the Muslim International, a tradition in which Black Islam saw the Muslim Third World of Mecca, Bandung, Egypt, Algeria, Iraq, and Palestine and their political orientations and anticolonial struggles as deeply informing Black liberation struggles in the United States. By viewing Islam as the link between Africa and Asia and between Black peoples in the United States and peoples in the broader Third World, Ali, like Malcolm and the history of Black Islam, tied

Black political fate not to the U.S. nation-state but to the fate of the peoples in the Third World.

The embrace and recuperation of Ali as a national hero in the 1990s, then, sought to domesticate and contain Black Islam within a U.S. nationalist framework and to fracture Black Islam from the larger Muslim Third World, undermining and weakening the possibilities of the Muslim International. In many ways, embracing Ali and domesticating Black Islam were direct responses to the deep imprint and influence that Black Islam has left on Black political culture in the post–World War II era, whether it be through Malcolm X and his Muslim Internationalism, through its influence on RAM, SNCC, and the Black Panther Party, or through figures and movements such as Fanon, Gamal Abdel Nasser, the Bandung Conference, the poets and writers of the Black Arts Movement and more recently of hip-hop culture, in which Black artists defiantly challenged U.S. racial domination, militarism, and imperial power. For Black Islam became a significant vehicle toward an expansive Black internationalism that not only challenged the containment of Black freedom within United States institutions and frameworks but also refused and resisted Black underwriting and sanctioning of U.S. foreign policies and empire building.

By embracing Ali as a national hero, domesticating Black Islam, and undermining its desire to imagine Black freedom outside the United States, the post–Cold War consensus sought to destroy a historical legacy in which Black Islam provided a framework for Black redress, such as when Malcolm X made a call for "human rights" over "civil rights." Equally important, the embrace of Ali and the containment of Black Islam fractured it from the politics of the Muslim Third World, betraying a whole legacy in which Black political culture and the Muslim Third World were deeply intertwined. The post–Cold War moment sought to create a context in which Black political culture in general and Black Islam specifically viewed the Muslim Third World as not only having no bearing on Black freedom but as antithetical to it. By stripping Black Islam of its internationalist legacy and seeking to contain the imagining of Black freedom beyond the United States and in solidarity with Africa and the Muslim Third World, the new post–Cold War consensus sought to tie Black Muslim freedom to the project of U.S. nationalism at a time when the United States has been at war with the

Muslim Third World, fracturing and undermining the possibilities of the Muslim International.

While Black Islam has long been held captive within a U.S. nationalist framework, a prisoner to the larger edifice of post–Cold War empire building, the post-9/11 moment has only served to intensify the U.S. security state's containment of it. As the post-9/11 climate sought Black sanctioning and underwriting of U.S. imperial policy and empire building in the Muslim Third World under the guise of the "War on Terror," the fears of Black Islam and Black internationalist postures toward the Muslim Third World have sparked tremendous national anxiety. For just as the United States sought to contain Black radicalism through mass incarceration in the post–Civil Rights era, so has it reanimated its carceral imagination in the post-9/11 era and returned to the prison as the site within which to crack down on and destroy the historical legacy and interpretive possibility of Black Islam.

5

PROTECT YA NECK

Global Incarceration, Islam, and the
Black Radical Imagination

I ain't never been nowhere near Angola, Louisiana
Down in St. Charles Parish
Where the sun won't go alone
But injustice is not confined to Angola, Louisiana
It can walk in your living room
As long as it's around your home
          —Gil Scott-Heron, "Angola, Louisiana"

IN MAY 2001, a hip-hop benefit concert was held in Watts, California, for Jamil Al-Amin (formerly known as H. Rap Brown), who had recently been arrested and charged with killing a police officer in Georgia. Using hip-hop as a vehicle, artists such as Mos Def, Talib Kweli, Jurassic 5, Dilated Peoples, and Zion I, along with numerous others, sought to raise awareness about the man formerly known as "Rap" for his powerful ability to captivate audiences with his fiery political rhetoric as a member of the Student Non-Violent Coordinating Committee (SNCC) and the Black Panther Party during the mid- to late 1960s. As arguably the most charismatic figure within the Black Power era of the mid- to late 1960s, H. Rap Brown was a lightning rod for controversy during that time, picking up the baton where Malcolm X had left off as he dissected U.S. racism and militarism with a biting wit and a sharp tongue that often landed him in trouble with the authorities. Brown ultimately converted to Islam in the early 1970s, and despite the support from the hip-hop community and other activists in 2001, Al-Amin was put on trial in 2002 amid the hysteria of 9/11, in which he was framed as a "homegrown terrorist," convicted of murder, and sentenced to life in prison, only to get transferred to the federal Supermax prison in Colorado in 2007, a place that has been called the "domestic Guantánamo" and what *60 Minutes* in October 2007 referred to as "a cleaner version of hell."

Jamil Al-Amin was a central figure in Black radical politics in the late 1960s whose gift of gab earned him the nickname "Rap," so it was more than fitting that the hip-hop generation sought to raise awareness about Al-Amin's case, seeing him and the history he represented as deeply connected to hip-hop's own, and continue it. Many of the artists performing at the hip-hop benefit concert in Watts were Muslim rappers, including Mos Def, Jurassic 5, Masspyke, and others, and they tapped into a deep history in which Black art, Islam, and politics intertwined with Black creative impulses, from jazz through the Black Arts Movement to hip-hop.

Al-Amin was seen as part of a longer history of Black Islam and its internationalist spirit, which Malcolm X had so powerfully crafted in the post–World War II era by connecting the struggles of Black liberation in the United States with those of decolonization in the Third World. The personal and political trajectory of Al-Amin, who was the last remaining link between SNCC, Black Power, and Black Islam, served as a microcosm for understanding the history of Black Islam and its penetrating relationship not only to internationalism and domestic antiracism but also to Black Islam's current place within the post-9/11 climate.

In many ways Al-Amin has become a symbol and icon of Black Islam, especially for incarcerated Black Muslims in the U.S. prison system, a group that since 9/11 has come under intensified surveillance as a potential fifth column of "radicalization" within the United States. For in seeking to silence and destroy the internationalist dimensions of Black Islam and its enduring critique of U.S. racism, militarism, and imperialism, the United States in the post-9/11 era has combined its current "War on Terror" rhetoric with the already existing "War on Crime" rhetoric that was used to silence and police Black communities in the post–Civil Rights era.

As the threat of the "Black criminal" and the "Muslim terrorist" shaped U.S. national identity in the post–Civil Rights era, it was through the mass incarceration of Black bodies that the prison became the primary site for the containment and silencing of Black political possibility. This massive prison architecture that radically redefined U.S. state building is now being exported abroad to the Muslim Third World in the post-9/11 era in order to contain Muslim bodies and their challenges to U.S. imperial power and its proxies, whether it be Abu Ghraib, Guantánamo Bay, Bagram, or other secret detention centers throughout the world. In exploring the prison as a form of transnational power and empire state building of Pax Americana, the lines between the domestic and the foreign are becoming increasingly blurred, a process that, according to Amy Kaplan, occurs because the "dynamics of imperial expansion cast them into jarring proximity."[1] What U.S. imperial imprisonment abroad has revealed is that this global archipelago of prisons is really the logical extension of the dirty war that has been fought in the United States through the containment, incarceration, and torture of Black bodies. Whether it was a war on "drugs," "crime," and now "terror," the Bush-era policies of preemptive war, racial panic, and aggressive state violence were not departures from American ideals—as many liberals have claimed—but rather the fulfillment of them. Through the figure of the Muslim, the post-9/11 security state has revitalized a form of governance under the rubric of "terrorism" that marks racial others as unruly populations that demand detention, deportation, and even death. The linking of American imperial reach today through the space of the prison becomes a way of exploring and exposing the lie that is American exceptionalism—a brutal charade about a mythic American universalism that not only fractures America's historical complicity with European empire building but also masks America's own violent history as an expansionist power through slavery, Native American genocide, and the country's continuing imperial ambition throughout the globe.

While the post–Cold War era sought to strip Black Islam of its legacy of internationalism and contain it within the framework of U.S. nationalism through the embrace of multiculturalism and the figure of Muhammad Ali, the post-9/11 era has intensified this assault on Black Islam and has viewed the prison as the site of violent containment and even erasure. For just as the post–Civil Rights era defined domestic and foreign threats to U.S. national security using the figures of the "Black criminal" and the "Muslim terrorist," respectively, the post-9/11 era has witnessed the collapse of these categories and logics into the figure of the Black Muslim, who is now viewed as the "homegrown terrorist," with federal and state authorities viewing Black Muslims through the lens of "criminality," "prison Islam," and "gang Islam."

The collapse of the categories of the "Black criminal" and "Muslim terrorist" reveals the ways in which the post-9/11 security state has blended and blurred the domestic and foreign realms of American power, and it allows us to trace the intimacies between the emergence of imperial imprisonment in the Muslim Third World of Iraq, Afghanistan, and Guantánamo Bay and the explosion of the domestic U.S. prison apparatus in the post–Civil Rights era. For the prison, through a global carceral imagination, is another space within which to contain, and wage war against, the Muslim International. While the Muslim Third World is enveloped within the prison regime through the export of American carceral power vis-à-vis Abu Ghraib, Guantánamo, Bagram, and secret detention centers, the specter of the Black Muslim, as the "enemy within," continues to haunt the domestic homeland and U.S. imperial culture in the post-9/11 landscape. The relationships between domestic and imperial imprisonment, as well as published reports of the Departments of Justice and Homeland Security and congressional committee testimonies, expose a troubling and haunting picture that provides a historical context to the heightened surveillance and repression Black Islam through the United States' legal, political, and security apparatuses. But while the prison regime reveals itself as a site of repression of both Black Islam and the Muslim International, the prison writings of Jamil Al-Amin reveal that the state must also contend with the persistent reality that the prison itself is the site of resistance and witness to the enduring spirit of the Muslim International.

Black Steel in the Hour of Chaos

In the post-9/11 era, the rhetoric of "terrorism" has become a proxy for race, generating tremendous political and ideological capital for U.S. nationalism and the implementation of a whole infrastructure and apparatus of control through the "War on Terror." The embodiment of "terrorism" has been the Muslim, a highly racialized figure that has been mobilized to reinforce American hegemony abroad and also to contain anti-racist and economic justice movements domestically. This threat of "terrorism" to American interests abroad has justified a violent reassertion of American power and militarism to extend Cold War alliances, further American geopolitical dominance, and refashion the United States as the sole power in a unipolar world through "preemptive war," covert intervention, aggressive militarism, and unilateralism. Domestically, the threat of "terror" from the *immigrant* Muslim has justified a highly racialized crackdown on immigrants in the United States, resulting in the normalization of deportations, detentions, and disappearance. Muslims now occupy a space where the rule of law has determined that the rule of law does not apply, and they embody a condition in which they do not have the right to have rights.

The racial anxieties concerning the threats posed by Muslim "terrorists" abroad have been projected onto the country's racial analog, the Black Muslim, who is being coded and understood through the lens of "Black criminality" and the deep-seated anxieties that this causes within white America and U.S. political culture in the age of mass incarceration and the "War on Terror." A November 2007 episode of the PBS series *America at a Crossroads*, titled "Homegrown: Islam in Prison" and focusing on Black Muslims, revealed that these fears are alive and well, as the documentary's alarmist tone echoes that of the U.S. security establishment in regard to Black Muslim communities. As an "enemy within," Black Islam resurrects deeply held fears in the United States, because it has historically been a site of resistance to U.S. state power in both its domestic and global forms. The specter of threat is deeply rooted within fears of Black conversion to Islam, what Richard Brent Turner calls "signification,"[2] since this conversion involves a radical redefinition of the self that signifies a meaningful attempt to resist the legacy of chattel slavery and the racist history of U.S. state building that gave slavery birth. By reclaiming agency and self-determination, Black conversion subtly but poignantly has sought to redefine Black peoples not as property but as person and not as slave but as human. As Chuck D of Public Enemy argues, "If people with African roots are connected to Islam, then you got a problem of taking your slaves away: 'We've lost our slaves—our slaves are international now!'"[3] As Chuck D's poignant argument suggests, this *loss* demands that Black Muslims be monitored, policed, and disciplined as fundamental threats to America's racial logic and its manic desire for control over Black bodies and destinies, for the history of Black Islam reveals a remapping of Black identity that Amiri Baraka referred to as "post-American."[4]

The collapsing then of the twin towers of U.S. state building in the post–Civil Rights era has revealed a post-9/11 national anxiety, as the fears of the "Muslim terrorist" are being conflated with "Black criminality" so that Black Islam is being understood and coded through "gangs," prison culture, and urban violence, forging and mobilizing a carceral imagination that brings together the rationales and ideologies of imperial imprisonment in Iraq, Afghanistan, and Guantánamo and conflates them with the post–Civil Rights logics of mass incarceration. This geography of violence has resulted in the crackdown on Black Muslims in U.S. prisons as a response to the redemptive forms of resistance that Black Islam and Black conversion to Islam reveal within the prison itself, for it has become the site for transformations in selfhood of all types, where a whole new aesthetics of being erupts. For Muslims like Malcolm Little, who got his "X" inside, or H. Rap Brown, who in the 1970s became Jamil Abdullah Al-Amin, the prison becomes the crucible for a rejection of that imposed master narrative of nonbeing and the subjection of Blackness—through chattel slavery, disenfranchisement, and social death—upon which America ultimately rests. For if prison is about disappearance and erasure, silence and violence, then epiphany, conversion, or politicization is a kind of ontological resurrection against social and civic death, redefining one's existence and challenging the panoptic power of the state.

For what the fears of Black Islam as an "enemy within" and as "homegrown terrorism" reveal is a deeper anxiety about the history and legacy of Black Islam, one that has continually challenged domestic racial control and imagined Black freedom beyond the United States and into Africa and other parts of the Muslim Third World. The history of Black Islam and its deep influence on Black political culture has been profound, including the history of Malcolm X and his effect on Black radicalism in the 1960s, including the Black Arts Movement, SNCC, RAM, and the Black Panther Party, as well as most recently on hip-hop culture, which in many instances continues to embrace Islam and see Malcolm as its prophetic voice.

With Islam and the Muslim Third World under rabid assault in the post-9/11 era, the attacks on Black Islam are really a broader assault on

Black political culture and its history of internationalism. For in this moment of heightened nationalism and empire building, the fears of Black Islam and its penetrating history of internationalism, especially in relation to the Muslim Third World, could fundamentally alter the landscape of Black political culture. For it is this very history and possibility of the Muslim International that Malcolm, Black Power, hip-hop, and so many others shaped and sharpened that explain the vast carceral regime being mobilized around the world to combat and undermine it. The emergence of imperial imprisonment in Iraq, Guantánamo, Afghanistan, and elsewhere, combined with the domestic architecture of mass incarceration and the assault on Black Islam in the United States, forms an archipelago of power and a geography of violence in response to the possibilities of the Muslim International, as the prison seeks to contain and prevent its power and possibility. But the state does not recognize that it is not only in the prisons where the Muslim International emerges but also through the very *possibility* of incarceration itself. Whether we consider Black conversions in prisons (such as Malcolm X, Jamil Al-Amin, and thousands of others) or Muslims in Abu Ghraib, Guantánamo, Bagram, and other "Black sites," the Muslim International is constituted within the context of incarceration and even despite it. For it also sees the world as a prison, with national boundaries, global capital, slavery, and wars of colonization as part of an earthly inheritance.

From Abner Louima to Abu Ghraib

In *Discipline and Punish*, Michel Foucault argues that prior to the prison, violence inflicted upon the prisoner, or the executed, brought pleasure to the crowd as a parade of body parts became central to popular violence and the imagination that fueled it, and so the prison transformed punishment and its relationship to power. With the "birth of the prison" in the nineteenth century, "the great spectacle of physical punishment disappeared; the tortured body was avoided; the theatrical representation of pain was excluded from punishment. The age of sobriety in punishment had begun."[5] For Foucault and others, the prison ushered in an "age of sobriety" around punishment, and it seems that in the post-9/11 imperial state, the public display of the body and the "imagination" that it fuels in the Age of Abu Ghraib and the Birth of Guantánamo have revealed a new "age of excess" encompassing torture, display, and penal power involving the Muslim body.

This age of excess is central to the globalization of imprisonment and the carceral logic of America's "War on Terror." In exploring the transnational logic of incarceration and the institutional links between the prison regimes around Black Muslims in the United States and the emergence of military prisons in Iraq, Afghanistan, and Guantánamo, history may have come full circle. According to Alan Gomez, a 1961 gathering called "The Power to Change Behavior: A Symposium Presented by the U.S. Bureau of Prisons" was a key moment in "the politicization of institutionalized brainwashing, behavior modification and torture within the prison regime" that resulted in a national directive to "experiment with these techniques, originally used against American POW's in Korea, on the black Muslim prison population." With these experiments, the federal government utilized physical and psychological torture to suppress political activity and dissent and to redefine accepted notions of "cruel, inhuman and torturous treatment."[6] At a time when the Nation of Islam and Malcolm X were challenging U.S. Cold War liberalism, the FBI and law enforcement agencies monitored Black Muslims as a potential threat to the emerging orthodoxy of the Civil Rights movement, so the use of imprisoned Black Muslims in state-sanctioned torture and experimentation in the early 1960s raises profound questions, not the least of which are its possible connections to and historical precedents for the more recent tortures of Muslims in Abu Ghraib, Guantánamo, Bagram, and elsewhere.

Through the figure of the Muslim and the rise of the Muslim International has come the increasing consolidation of the two major security institutions within American imperial culture—the military and the prison—revealing the emergence of a new kind of formation of power and domination used to implement a violent global order where the law has determined that the rule of law does not apply, a logic that sanctions torture, the abrogation of habeas corpus, the birth of Guantánamo, military tribunals, the Patriot Act, preemptive war, and the legal declaration of Muslims as not "falling within the definition of 'person.'"[7] This confluence of the military and the prison regime runs deep in the current "War on Terror." According to scholar and critic Avery Gordon, Mark S. Inch, the corrections and internment branch chief at the Office of the Provost Marshal General, stated, "The synergy between the reservist's civilian employment in the corrections field and his or her duty to confine enemy combatants in Afghanistan, Cuba [Guantánamo] and Iraq . . . could not be more evident and essential to mission success."[8] According to Gordon, the 300th Military Police Brigade, the 327th Military Police Battalion, and the 800th Military Police Brigade designed Camp Delta at Guantánamo Bay, have run various detention centers throughout Afghanistan, and reorganized the prison systems in Iraq for enemy combatants and prisoners of war. In addition, prison guards and administrators at state and federal penitentiaries throughout the United States continue to contribute a great deal to America's global archipelago of imprisonment: John VanNatta, who is the superintendent of the Miami Correctional Facility in Indiana and works in Guantánamo; Captain Michael Mcintyre and Master Sergeant Don Bowen, who work at the federal penitentiary at Terre Haute, Indiana, helped to build the Iraqi prison system; and many Chicago policemen and prison guards throughout Afghanistan in prisons such as Bagram.[9]

According to journalist Leah Caldwell, in May 2003, just two months after the invasion of Iraq, Attorney General John Ashcroft gathered a group of American prison officials under the auspices of ICITAP (the International Criminal Investigative Training Program) and sent them to Iraq to prepare existing Iraqi prisons to house additional prisoners. ICITAP, which is based within the Department of Justice and funded by the State Department, has been in existence since 1986 and has been sent throughout the world to "rebuild" criminal justice systems and to support police and prison regimes in American-backed client states, including Haiti, Indonesia, and the former Soviet Union. According to Caldwell, ICITAP is a successor to a training program run by the Agency for International Development, which was stopped in the mid-1970s after it was revealed that this program was used to train police forces and prison officials abroad in murder and torture against mostly leftist insurgencies.[10]

What is especially revealing is that many of the prison officials whom Ashcroft sent to Iraq were not only employed by private prison firms around the United States but were also heads of various state departments of corrections throughout the country, including Terry Stewart (Arizona), Gary Deland (Utah), John Armstrong (Connecticut), and

Lane McCotter (Texas, Mexico, and Utah). In fact, all of those listed here have been involved in legal cases and accused of a range of human rights abuses by inmates in the United States, including denial of medical treatment, harsh conditions, sexual harassment, torture, and even death. McCotter, who was forced to resign as head of Utah's State Board of Corrections as a result of the death of an inmate shackled naked to a chair, was, according to Gordon, later chosen by then attorney general John Ashcroft to head the reopening of Iraqi jails under American rule and also to train Iraqi prison guards, just one month after the Justice Department had released a report following the death of a prisoner due to the lack of medical and mental health treatment at one of the Management and Training Corporation's jails, a private firm in which McCotter was an executive.[11] To add insult to irony, McCotter and Deland were at the ribbon-cutting ceremony at Abu Ghraib when it first opened, and McCotter described Abu Ghraib as "the only place that we agreed as a team was truly closest to an American prison.'"[12]

Just as the administrative and institutional framework for U.S. colonial imprisonment in Iraq, Afghanistan, and Guantánamo has deep ties to the domestic prison establishment, state corrections, and even private prison corporations, so too did some of the guards involved in the Abu Ghraib tortures have careers within U.S. prisons. According to Anne-Marie Cusac, Ivan L. (Chip) Frederick II, and Charles Graner had worked in the United States as corrections officers. Frederick was a guard in Virginia while Graner, who was described as one of the "most feared and loathed of American guards" at Abu Ghraib and who is infamously known for his sinister glasses and wicked "thumbs up" signs in the released photos of torture, was an officer at the Greene County Prison in Pennsylvania.[13]

According to Cusac, the Taguba Report investigating torture at Abu Ghraib found that U.S. military personnel placed Iraqi detainees in sexually explicit positions, engaged in forced sodomy on them with chemical lights and possibly even a broom handle, beat them, and wrote vulgar epithets on their bodies. Cusac goes on to reveal that in 1998, Greene County guards with whom Graner had worked were charged with sodomy with a nightstick, unlawful nude searches, and using prisoners' blood to write "KKK" on the floor of the prison.[14] In fact, according to Gordon, Graner was repeatedly "implicated in violence against prisoners at the Pennsylvania super-maximum security State Correctional Institute at Greene . . . and given supervisory roles at Abu Ghraib because of his *guard experience*."[15]

Ironically, part of the Bush administration's reconstruction plans for Iraq included the building of a "Supermax" prison where Abu Ghraib now stands as a way of erasing the stain and stigma of the tortures that went on there. The "Supermax" prison has proliferated throughout the United States, becoming the penal blueprint for imprisonment, and is widely seen as the most repressive kind of carceral power available. According to Gordon, "The Abu Ghraib photographs did not expose a few bad apples or an exceptional instance of brutality or perversity. They exposed the modus operandi of the lawful, modern, state-of-the-art prison. Nowhere is this clearer than in the growth over the past 25 years of what is called super-maximum imprisonment, the cutting edge in technology and the prototype for re-tooling the military prison for the war on terror." In fact, Supermax prisons emphasize the state's desire for ultimate control, as the "language of security has authorized Supermax imprisonment by treating it not as punishment but as a set of administrative procedures for managing high-security populations." More specifically, the policies and procedures used in Supermax facilities in the United States, "now legally sanctioned as ordinary and acceptable norms of prison life, were once considered violations of the U.S. Constitution's Eighth Amendment prohibiting cruel and unusual punishment. The Supreme Court's Eighth Amendment cases are the legal and linguistic basis for the 'detainee interrogation' memos prepared for the War on Terror."[16]

In addition, the formation of Control Management Units (CMUs) within U.S. prisons is also indicative of the larger pattern of institutional violence and surveillance of Muslim prisoners. Having emerged in two prisons in Indiana and Illinois, these CMUs—known as "Guantánamo North"—are essentially "behavior modification units" that seek to mimic Supermax conditions within federal prisons as they target inmates who are considered "politicized," while also drastically limiting their contact with the outside world, including severe limitations on family visits, receiving phone calls and letters, and also preventing inmates from participating in services that other prisoners participate in. While 6 percent of the federal prison population is Muslim, these CMUs are over

70 percent Muslim, mostly from the Muslim Third World. According to the Center for Constitutional Rights, "in the last several years, subsequent to media scrutiny of defendants' targeting of Muslims, more non-Muslims have been moved to the CMU. Guards on the units have referred to these non-Muslim prisoners as "balancers," so as to present the perception that Muslims are not being solely targeted.[17]

The violent application of U.S. state power against the Muslim International is also revealed in the institutional matrices that the U.S. prison system is exporting to the Muslim Third World as sites within the American empire. Predicated upon the subjection of Black bodies, these new forms of carceral power are rooted in the post–Civil Rights era of mass incarceration, as the lines between the domestic and the foreign spaces of empire continue to get blurred. The "War on Terror," with the establishment of Abu Ghraib, Guantánamo, and other structures of imperial imprisonment, is being combined with the "War on Crime," which has its own carceral logic around "Black criminality," to violently assault and make legible Black Islam as a threat to U.S. state interests.

Home Is Where the Hatred Is

Mass incarceration in the United States, along with its exploding prison structure, was created to address "Black criminality" in the post–Civil Rights era, a direct response to national fears of Black rebellion, with mass incarceration disproportionately targeting Black communities under various guises since Nixon, be it "law and order" or the "War on Crime." Scholars such as Michelle Alexander have referred to the existence and persistence of a "new Jim Crow" in the United States, which has authorized legal forms of discrimination in housing, employment, education, and the stripping away of voting rights, as Black bodies are an overwhelmingly disproportionate part of the overall prison population.[18]

By serving as proxies in the post–Civil Rights repression of Black communities, local law enforcement agencies in major metropolitan areas have developed an institutional logic geared toward the targeting and policing of Blackness. The post-9/11 climate and the ruling paradigm of the "Muslim terrorist" have been conflated with fears of "Black criminality" as a means to not only further police and incarcerate Black bodies but also to police, silence, and destroy the presence of Black Islam within the United States. As U.S. tentacles of incarceration have expanded outward in the creation of Abu Ghraib, Guantánamo, Bagram, and other prisons, the resurgence of the fear of Black Islam in the United States in the post-9/11 era has revealed an emerging connection between local policing and the U.S. military.

Former LAPD chief William Bratton had been advocating and lobbying that Los Angeles become the national nerve center for an official agency collaboration between Homeland Security and local law enforcement throughout the country, having made tremendous institutional strides. Known for his part in the draconian implementation of the Manhattan Institute's "Broken Windows" policy in New York in the early 1990s under Rudolph Giuliani, which led to police abuse cases such as Abner Louima and Amadou Diallo, Bratton declared a "War on Gangs" in Los Angeles, referring to gang activity as "homeland terrorism" and lamenting that the federal government "needs to get preoccupied with the internal war on terrorism as well."[19] For Bratton and for the intensified repression by the U.S. security state in the post-9/11 era, the linking of local policing to global war has a somewhat historical basis. As we've seen, Malcolm X, the Black Panther Party, and other activists in the past drew connections between colonialism in the Third World and the policing of urban centers in the United States. While Malcolm compared colonial war elsewhere in the world to the repression of Black peoples in the United States as a means to reveal the global dimensions of white supremacy, Bratton and the U.S. security state use the language of "terrorism" to justify and sanction continued white domination in the present. And in doing so, Bratton provides the ideological cover and generates the political capital and will not only for a broader assault on Black and Brown communities in the United States but also for the policing and crackdown on Black Islam.

But Bratton takes the ideological and material links between domestic policing and colonial war much further. According to him, about seventy LAPD officers have trained in Iraq with the U.S. military at any one time, and LAPD officers have also trained marines on how to gather evidence at a bomb scene and give their guidance on urban policing to the U.S. military abroad.[20] In addition, the military is helping the

LAPD prepare for the "eventuality" of suicide bombers and improvised explosive devices (IEDs) in Los Angeles. In fact, according to Bratton, a team of soldiers from the U.S. military in Baghdad visited Los Angeles to share with the LAPD their knowledge about "IED's and suicide bombers and the tactics employed by death squads and insurgents in Iraq." Bratton continues, "We're always wondering why we don't have suicide bombers and IED's here. We're trying to learn from each other. It's only a matter of time before we are experiencing the issue here. We have no idea why it hasn't occurred. What they're dealing with is what we may face." For Bratton, there are "many similarities between what is going on in Baghdad and here. The similarities to gang warfare are strong."[21]

The racial and ideological calculus behind such comparisons helps generate the necessary fear and political will needed for increased domestic repression, and Bratton reveals the ways in which the logic of the "War on Terror" is being mapped domestically and combined with existing narratives of Black criminality through the "War on Crime" discourse to create an alchemy of repression that links Muslims, Blackness, prisons, and gang culture.[22] Bratton mentions the "growing influence of converted Muslim radicals in the U.S. prison system," who upon release will spread their new ideas to their companions, such that gangs will conspire with "terrorist" organizations to carry out attacks on U.S. cities. As Bratton says, "There is a potential of some gangs who are disaffected to latch on to the Islam movement. We've seen movement in that direction."[23]

Bratton's rhetoric echoes a larger concerted chorus of voices that are constructing Black Islam as an "indigenous" component to the global "threat" posed by Muslims. This combination of domestic and global racial anxieties has come to define the post-9/11 era, with the concentration of state power around the "Muslim terrorist" and the "Black criminal" authorizing a reinvigorated domestic repression of Black Islam. Not surprisingly, high-level officials, numerous think tanks, policy institutes, non-governmental organizations, and official state agencies have published reports and presented to several congressional committees and other law enforcement agencies their fears about Black Islam, within and outside prisons, and its potential for "radicalization," revealing an enduring anxiety about Black Islam and its historical role within Black political culture. This kind of institutional power bearing down upon what is being constructed as an emerging frontline in America's "War on Terror" is an extension of a broader assault on the Muslim International and also a continuation of the most pernicious forms of racial profiling that have impacted Black communities dating all the way back to slavery—what Loic Waquant argues is the historical continuity between the slave plantation and the mass incarceration of Black peoples within the United States.[24]

A 2004 Department of Justice report issued a series of warnings about the possibilities of Black Muslim "radicalization" within prisons, the emergence of "Prison Islam," and the lack of monitoring of and by Muslim chaplains, which could lead to "extremist" ideologies circulating within prisons.[25] In 2005, FBI director Robert Mueller told the Senate Intelligence Committee, "Prisons continue to be fertile ground for extremists who exploit both a prisoner's conversion to Islam while still in prison, as well as their socio-economic status and placement in the community upon their release,"[26] and the Republican senator Susan Collins, from Maine, has said that "radical Islam" within U.S. prisons is "an emerging threat to our national security."[27] In April 2006, Attorney General Alberto Gonzalez also weighed in on the topic of Muslims in prison and the "challenges to detection" that this population poses to authorities.[28] A 2006 study by the Homeland Security Policy Institute, at the George Washington Institute in conjunction with the University of Virginia, was released at a Senate Homeland Security and Governmental Affairs Committee hearing on "homegrown terrorists." It argues that because of limited funds there is little supervision of Muslims within prisons. Consequently, "radical Islam is spreading and raising a new generation of potential terrorists." And it warns that "Jailhouse Islam," which is "based upon cut-and-paste versions of the Qu'ran and incorporates violent prison culture into religious practice,"[29] is a threat to prison security. In addition, Charles Colson, who was special counsel to Richard Nixon during Watergate, in 1974, and who ran the Prison Fellowship Ministries, says that al-Qaeda training manuals "specifically identify America's prisoners as candidates for conversion because they may be disenchanted with their country's policies." Colson asserts, "Terrorism experts fear these angry young recruits will become the next wave of terrorists. As U.S. citizens, they will combine a desire for 'payback' with an ability to blend easily into American culture."[30] In addition, Roy Innis, the national chair and executive director of the Council of Racial Equality (CORE), has also met with federal officials and has been vocal about the threat he perceives coming from Black Muslims, who are not properly monitored either within or outside prisons.

As a "U.S. citizen" who can "blend easily into American culture" and who according to Attorney General Gonzalez poses "challenges to detection," Black Islam has become the site upon which the projection of racial anxiety from the foreign Muslim—who is deemed more recognizable by his "foreign-ness"—is branded. But because of the historical relationship of Blackness within the United States and the contempt that this familiarity bred, Black Muslims in the United States are potentially more threatening because they are not racially legible in the same ways that the foreign Muslim is. By being U.S. citizens who can blend easily into American culture, Black Muslims can engage in a strange form of national/racial passing, in which Blackness is perceived as "American" only insofar as it can identify whether one is a Muslim or not, a logic that is then used to call into question any Black body and his potential relationship to Islam. Clearly, the history and legacy of Black Islam, through figures such as Malcolm X, continue to inform ideas about the relationships among Blackness, Islam, and U.S. empire, as history and legacy have resisted incorporation into a domestic narrative predicated on imperial expansion.

Rap DNA

Imprisoned in 2000 and sentenced in 2002 to life in the Georgia state prison at Reidsville, Jamil Al-Amin was transferred in 2007 to the federal Supermax prison in Colorado, a prison where the federal government houses its most "dangerous inmates" and where Al-Amin is now in a "behavior modification program." The October 2007 *60 Minutes* piece on the Colorado Supermax focused on the security of the prison and the secrecy surrounding its operations, and it talked almost completely about the immigrant Muslims who were inside: the "Shoe Bomber," Richard Reid, the "twentieth 9/11 hijacker," Zacarias Moussaoui, the convicted "mastermind" of the 1993 World Trade Center bombing, Ramzi Yousef, and others. While Al-Amin's transfer to this prison is no doubt indicative of the state's desires to violently continue the narrative of Black captivity that sits at the heart of the empire, it is also part of a broader assault on the legacy and possibilities of Black Islam in a post-9/11 climate. Even in the State of Georgia prison system, Al-Amin was deemed a "high security" captive and was subjected to around-the-clock surveillance and solitary confinement, even though the proceedings of his trial and subsequent conviction were called into question by several prominent legal experts and international human rights organizations. Al-Amin's history, within the Civil Rights movement (as a member of SNCC), as a Black Power activist, and as a Muslim leader to thirty-four different urban communities in the United States over several decades, embodies the multiple histories and identities that have consistently challenged American militarism, racism, and economic injustice nationally and internationally. During his trial he was constructed by the state as the embodiment of the "homegrown terrorist." But his is not the case of the captive who becomes "radicalized" in prison but the case of the revolutionary who is imprisoned by the state. His captivity can in many ways be seen to represent the continued attempts by the state to silence and destroy the legacy of Black Islam and to rewrite the history of Black radicalism and Third World internationalism over the last fifty years, as well as the sustained attack on Black community-based leadership, the suppression of political dissent in the United States, and the broader repression of and war on the Muslim International taking place within American imperial political culture.

While in prison, Al-Amin has completed a manuscript titled "Rap DNA," which extends the legacy of powerful Black political prison writings that narrate a resistance to captivity and transcend the boundary between the free and the unfree—that vicious structuring logic of America that is centered on Black captivity and containment. Like his first book— the vastly overlooked Black Power manifesto *Die Nigger Die!* (1969), which is a brilliant political autobiography and narrative of rebellion— "Rap DNA" is also a stunning act of what Michael Eric Dyson has called "Afrecriture,"[31] the poignant act of writing Black presence into history. Written in rhyme form and the embodiment of the talking book, "Rap DNA" is a powerful glimpse into a revolutionary aesthetic that invokes and challenges a range of Black thought within the violent crucible of American slavery. The opening lines state: "I am the seed of the survivors of the Middle Passage, the harvest from those who could not be broken, would not be broken, never a slave."[32] With this as the opening salvo, "Rap DNA" also explores Fanon, Langston Hughes, Rakim, the murder of Amadou Diallo, critical race theory, Al-Amin's experiences in exile, the Patriot Act, American militarism, the "War on Terror," and an incredible range of ideas through lyricism and irony, insight and wit.

But it is Al-Amin's reclamation of the moniker "Rap" that is most compelling, because this becomes in many ways the voice through which he narrates. This is striking because it suggests an embrace of his multiple identities and histories, which so often get overlooked within narratives of conversion. Though not an embrace of Hubert Brown (his former name), the reclamation of "Rap" works on multiple levels: as an embrace of his persona as the fiery Black Power orator of the past and also an embrace of the *act* of speaking. To "rap" then is a radical act that is a scream against the silence imposed by the captive power of the prison. And as the title of his writings, "Rap DNA" not only suggests that this radical act of speech as "rap" continues beyond conversion and is imprinted upon his very being, but also that these writings and his history are the ideological blueprint and lifeline for rap music as well. In fact, throughout the writings, he brilliantly challenges contemporary hip-hop artists in rhyme style, battling them on page to use hip-hop as a forum for transcendence, redemption, and rebellion, while also laying claim to being the father of hip-hop. He says, "If Christian music is alive / It's the only music named after someone besides Rap that survives." And then later, where he politicizes the gangster figure, he says, "No gangster rap music / Rap was the gangster of his time." In a piece called "Conflict or Conciliation" contained in the manuscript, he writes:

> Your kind of hatin ain't new
> in '68 Congress was hating too
> Passed a law named after me
> Trying to stop the flow of the R-A-P
> For the first time in history of their ten most wanted list
> The FBI changed it to eleven
> And before the manhunt could even start
> They moved Rap to the top of the chart
> And Rap became public enemy number one
> And I ain't talking about Billboard son.

By invoking his history with the American political and legal establishment, Al-Amin uses his past not only to inform contemporary generations about Black history but also to impress upon the hip-hop generation that material excess and record sales are tied not to Black uplift and transformation but to Black repression and degradation. In his view, rap music should aspire to be at the top of the FBI's charts as a barometer of its Fanonian possibilities, not the music industry's attempts to promote a commodified rebellion in the form of hip-hop.

"Rap DNA" also gives eloquent testimony to his life of struggle and his persistent attempts to connect Black radical thought and praxis, not within the confines of a collective bourgeois racial identity or a narrow nationalism, but within the broader tradition of Black internationalism, which has linked Black struggle in the United States with those in Africa, Asia, and Latin America. His poem titled "Seconds," also within the manuscript, is a battle cry from behind enemy lines that highlights the painfully enduring question about the role of Blackness within the American imperial project. He writes:

> Always talking that we, us, our, my country
> our war our team our dream
> USA USA how many kids you kill today?
> Negroes greatest dream? Take one for the team
> Black by popular demand
> Demand to be 21st century buffalo soldiers
> More than willing to kill in a foreign land
> Women, children, another man
> Buffalo soldiers like their fathers of old
> Put the sin of empire on their soul
> Give their sons and daughters to spread tyranny and slaughter
> In the name of empire's new world order.

In "Seconds," Al-Amin critically explores the historical role of Black peoples as potential imperial citizens who have supported the expansionist project of the United States not only in the distant past but more recently in the current "War on Terror." In providing a historical context for current Black complicity with U.S. imperial designs, Al-Amin links the founding myth of Manifest Destiny to current U.S. expansionism in the Muslim Third World, suggesting that the enduring power of white supremacy is intimately linked with the complicity of those who are its victims.

Like Rakim, Chuck D, Mos Def, Ice Cube, and numerous other Muslim rappers who have used Black Islam as a platform to challenge and imagine through words different worlds of possibility, Al-Amin uses the crucible of the prison to meditate and reflect upon the larger place of Black Islam within the current political climate. More than a critique of an imperial Blackness, "Seconds" reads like a call to arms about the prophetic and political destiny of Black Islam and the Muslim International as the site for and source of radical possibility. Despite the new "compass of suffering" and geographies of violence being inaugurated in the post-9/11 era through the site of the prison, Jamil Al-Amin's poetic imagination keeps alive the enduring spirit of Malcolm X, Black Islam, and the Muslim International.

Epilogue

WAR, REPRESSION, AND THE LEGACY OF MALCOLM

> The small man builds cages for everyone he knows,
> While the sage, who has to duck his head when the
> moon is low,
> Keeps dropping keys all night long for the beautiful
> rowdy prisoners.
>
> —Hafiz, "Dropping Keys"

GUANTÁNAMO IS STILL OPEN. Drones keep flying, and more threats loom. Though there was a tremendous euphoria around the election of Barack Obama and a utopian belief that this was, in fact, a transformative moment, his presidency has meant very little to the "War on Terror" and next to nothing for racial injustice—except more of the same. Obama tried to capitalize on the euphoria early in his presidency, in June 2009, in his highly publicized address given in Cairo, Egypt, to Muslims around the world. Calling it "A New Beginning," Obama went to Cairo as an envoy of empire as he sought to make the case that American power is a benevolent one in its "War on Terror." But the vision he laid out differed sharply from that of Malcolm X, who forty-five years earlier also went to Cairo, to address the Organization of African Unity, which was holding its African Summit there. Egypt had become a symbolic site within the post–World War II Black radical imagination, for it hosted the follow-up to the historic Bandung Conference and, through Gamal Abdel Nasser, embodied a defiant anti-imperialism that was the inspiration for Black radicals, Black Muslims, the larger Muslim Third World, and the rest of Africa, Asia, and the Americas.

Malcolm's visit to Cairo was a prehistory, or prequel if you will, to Obama's visit over four decades later, and he went there as part of his own Organization of Afro-American Unity in seeking support from Nasser and other African leaders to internationalize the plight of Black peoples in the United States, making a moral and ethical plea: just as apartheid South Africa was internationalized, so too should the circumstances of Black peoples in the United States be. In making his case, Malcolm warned the delegates not to be fooled by the "imperialist wolf" of the United States or its State Department's attempts to use propaganda to convince African nations that the United States was making serious progress toward racial equality. As Malcolm said, "This propaganda maneuver is part of her deceit and trickery to keep African nations from condemning her racist practices before the United Nations."[1] While Malcolm went there to *internationalize* the plight of Black peoples in the United States, Obama went there to *universalize* American power. Whereas Obama went to Egypt to reclaim and co-opt this sacred land under U.S. empire and to put a benevolent face on American power, Malcolm had been there seeking to strip away the veneer of benevolence and reveal the naked truth about U.S. racial injustice and imperial ambition.

This short history of Egypt and the Muslim Third World as the site of converging histories and competing interests between the African diaspora, U.S. empire, and the Muslim International is emblematic of the broader panoramic lens through which I have tried to situate the current era in *Black Star, Crescent Moon*. With Obama as president and Blackness and empire more directly linked in the post-9/11 era of war against the Muslim Third World, I have sought to show the relatively recent histories linking Blackness, Islam, and the Muslim Third World through politics and art. Revealed as a constant and ongoing battle between Euro-American power and the Muslim International, in *Black Star, Crescent Moon* I hope to provide a historical lens through which to better understand the current moment of U.S. empire and to reveal the ideological parallels between the Cold War and the post-9/11 era, as questions around race, U.S. empire, and internationalism continue to be the recurrent concerns and unresolved dilemmas of the U.S. state.

Although in *Black Star, Crescent Moon* I explore a broad historical sweep and a diverse group of political actors, artists, writers, and filmmakers, it is Malcolm X who emerges in this narrative as having arguably the most defining influence on the politics and art of the nexus of Black radicalism and the Muslim Third World. For Malcolm was arguably the most visible Black activist who refused to capitulate to the Cold War liberalism of the time, and he became the most prominent and vocal critic who not only challenged Black political orthodoxy during the Cold War, but he also challenged the very deeply rooted assumptions in the United States around race, Blackness, and empire that had forced Black political orthodoxy to assume its positions in the first place. Malcolm's racial internationalism was far-reaching, as it had a profound impact on Black political culture during decolonization, the Cold War, and the emergence of Black Power in the late 1960s and again in the 1980s and 1990s through hip-hop culture.

As the post-9/11 climate has intensified its war on Black communities and has more directly placed the Muslim Third World and Muslim communities within its sight lines, it would be important to consider Malcolm's Muslim Internationalism and his challenges to Black political orthodoxy during the Cold War as a lens toward understanding the current political landscape in which the Muslim Third World, Islam, and Blackness define U.S. domestic and foreign policy. The current hypernationalism of U.S. political culture and the massive repression of the warfare state has severely undermined and challenged the possibilities of internationalism that are vitally urgent in this neoliberal moment. But though the tactics of repression may have changed to suit the times, the strategy of containing and erasing Black freedom struggles and people's movements in the Third World is not new. For in many ways, as I have argued, the Cold War was a coded race war against Black and Third World liberation movements, as the United States and its allies sought to undermine the challenges to European and American dominion over the globe.

As Black activists in the post–World War II era tied their demands for equality to the national liberation struggles of the Third World, the Truman Doctrine declared "communism" the biggest threat to the security of the United States and to democracy and freedom around the world. The "Red Scare" sought to contain and destroy not only Black freedom movements in the United States but also the national liberation movements around the world that Black freedom movements were connected to. As a result, the Cold War fractured this groundswell of

Black internationalist thought in the United States as some Black organizations and activists who were struggling for equality and freedom took the position that "Negroes are Americans" as a response to a Cold War climate that deemed dissenters as "communist" and therefore subject to state-sanctioned persecution. In embracing "Americanness," these activists and organizations that became the Civil Rights movement sought to tie the idea of Civil Rights to U.S. foreign policy goals and objectives. As a result, they abandoned their support of Third World peoples and any critiques of American foreign policy in favor of the argument that Jim Crow, segregation, and racial violence were America's Achilles's heel that would undermine America's global ambitions in the war for the hearts and minds of a Third World that was already deeply skeptical of white supremacy after centuries of European colonialism. In doing so, these mainstream Black activists and organizations rooted themselves in American traditions, as they sought to leverage constitutional protections, legal frameworks, and political institutions to pass legislation that sought to end persecution and racial violence throughout the country. Though they received some measure of legislative redress, including the passage of the 1964 Civil Rights Act, among others, they ultimately failed to obtain the initiatives not only that they were seeking but that they had been promised, as they ultimately only ended de jure forms of discrimination and did not bring about systemic changes in Black inequality.

But their embrace of "Americanness" also meant the support of an anticommunist U.S. foreign policy that viewed communism as a bigger threat to the Third World than colonialism. This left little to no room of commonality between Black peoples in the United States and the people of Africa, Asia, and Latin America, for the United States used the broad rubric of anticommunism as a proxy to intervene, usurp, and destabilize popular people's struggles and anticolonial movements in the Third World. In lending their support to U.S foreign policy and its liberal internationalism, these mainstream Black organizations provided a stamp of approval to U.S. foreign policy and the seeming fulfillment of the Jeffersonian ideal of the United States as an "empire of liberty." While this framed the United States as benevolent and "race-free" to a deeply skeptical Third World, it also meant only tepid and tame critiques by the mainstream Civil Rights organizations of U.S. wars and intervention in the Third World, with almost no critique at all of the fundamental premises and posture of U.S. foreign policy as an extension of European colonialism.

Similarly in the post-9/11 era, "terrorism" is being framed as the biggest threat to the security of the United States, the larger Western world, and to their interests in the Third World, a logic that only justifies U.S. hegemony throughout the Global South. As a result, just as during the Cold War with the label "communist," there has been a tremendous chilling effect on critiques of U.S. foreign and domestic policies for fear of being labeled a "terrorist" or an "al-Qaeda sympathizer." Because of the immense assault on Muslim communities in the form of violence, deportations and disappearances, and a broader rhetorical and ideological attack on Islam and on Muslims as "anti-American," Muslim organizations and many activists have rooted themselves in American traditions and claimed that "Muslims are Americans" in an effort to assuage fears, to leverage legal frameworks and constitutional "freedoms" and "protections" in an attempt to halt the assault on Muslims in the United States. On the international front, just as in the Cold War, this claim that "Muslims are Americans" has contained critiques of U.S. foreign policy around strategy and tactics rather than more systemic critiques of the imperial foundations of the United States and its violent expansionism.

Malcolm's significance today for both Black and Muslim activists and organizations is profound. While many activists, artists, scholars, and organizations are infusing the ideas of Malcolm within their work, we must continue to draw the deep connections that Malcolm did between domestic struggles for racial justice and our fundamental challenges to U.S. militarism and imperial power. For Malcolm did not separate these; instead, he saw them as deeply intertwined, a move that Dr. King also embraced in the latter stages of his life. Malcolm's Muslim Internationalism and his Pan-Africanism was rooted in his resounding critiques of the matrix of racism, imperialism, and militarism, a political vision that was forged out of the crucible of the hypernationalism of the Cold War and Third World decolonization. And with the United States at war with the Muslim Third World and the hypernationalism of the post-9/11 era, Malcolm's ideas and his Muslim Internationalism can help to challenge the imperial consensus that has characterized the Obama era. As *Black Star, Crescent Moon* has shown, there has historically been a deep sense of solidarity among Black activists and artists in the United States with the anti-imperialism of the Muslim Third World, so in addition to challenging the current Black political establishment's tepid critiques of Obama's domestic politics, Malcolm's ideas can challenge mainstream Black political orthodoxy's embrace of the rhetoric of "terrorism" and its alignment with U.S. nationalism, empire, and its violent expansion. For as Malcolm argued in Cairo (and Detroit and beyond), American propaganda has sought to use Black identification with the United States as a sign of racial equality, whether domestically through what he saw as Civil Rights tokenism and "reform" or internationally through strategies that try to present U.S. global power with a benevolent face to the Third World (what Malcolm called that "veil of global diplomatic art"). In either case, Malcolm challenged these strategies of the state by redefining Black peoples not as national minorities but as part of a global majority.

For Muslims in the United States, Malcolm's political vision has challenged all immigrants—especially those from the Muslim Third World—to resist the seductions of the label American and the domestication of their politics within a national framework. For just as the embrace of "Negroes as Americans" and Civil Rights failed the ideal of Black equality, the embrace of a "Muslim-American" identity and the desire to be a "good citizen" and achieve "honorary whiteness" ultimately conforms to a dangerous and dubious model of liberal multiculturalism, "diversity" and anti-Blackness. For to be "Muslim-American" is to embrace an identity and a politics that is nationally bounded and that seeks acceptance and inclusion instead of addressing the very forces that excluded Muslims in the first place and that led to racial profiling, deportations, surveillance, and war: namely, white supremacy, militarism, and capitalism. On the international front, the embrace of "Muslim-American" has led to a tacit, if not an explicit, support of the Bush Doctrine, U.S. foreign policy, and "antiterrorism"—a position that accepts the racist Orientalist logic of the "bad Muslim" and fails to give dignity to challenges to U.S. state power around the world. By domesticating and containing a critical internationalism, the embrace of "Muslim-American" fractures Muslims in the United States not only from the anti-imperialism of the Muslim Third World but also from the broader struggles of the peoples of Africa, Asia, and Latin America. For instead of offering a fundamental critique of U.S. power, its aims, and objectives, "Muslim-American" offers tacit support and tepid criticism of U.S. empire. This is the central logic of the political calculus that drives the anti-Muslim and Islamophobic sentiment in the United States, whether it takes the form of congressional hearings on "radicalization," protests against the Ground Zero mosque, fears of Sharia law, or omnipresent warnings of sleeper cells and "terrorists." For it is the policing of Muslim politics and identities that is at stake, a policing that seeks to ensure Muslim fealty to "Americanness" and Muslim loyalty to a larger project of imperial multiculturalism, an allegiance that gives a stamp of approval and an air of benevolence to U.S. policy in the Muslim Third World.

By embracing Malcolm's ideas in a post-9/11 world, Muslims will not capitulate to the racial logic of the United States and its problematic framing of "moderate" and "radical" Muslims. We should not shun and fear the idea of "radicalization"; instead, we need to reclaim it in the spirit of Malcolm, a radicalism predicated on racial justice, economic equality, and a sustained engagement to end U.S. militarism throughout the world. By embracing radicalism instead of Americanism, Muslims will not only resist the temptations of "diversity" and multiculturalism that is the immigrant ideal, but we can also reject the American narrative that seeks to domesticate our struggles within a nationalist framework and that ultimately folds us into that mythic idea of American universalism that claims to be an "empire of liberty." By embracing radicalism and forging a Muslim Left, we can deepen our understanding of power and link our struggles not only here domestically but also globally, giving our politics a more critical edge and shaping and sharpening the possibilities of the Muslim International.

As I've argued in *Black Star, Crescent Moon*, the Muslim International is where overlapping diasporas and shared struggles can exist, and it is "measured by the compass of suffering" that connects a geography of violence and a shared struggle against racial terror, global capital, patriarchy, and war.[2] This compass of suffering links the Muslim Third World to Europe and the Americas, Mogadishu to Marseilles, Palestine to L.A., Jakarta to Algiers, Baghdad to Brooklyn, Caracas to Cairo, Dakar to Peshawar, and every place in between. Bringing together the politics of Black radicalism, the Muslim Third World, and internationalist struggles in Africa, Asia, and the Americas, *Black Star, Crescent Moon* reveals the Muslim International to exist in a broad range of political and artistic spaces: it was Malcolm X on podiums in Cairo and soapboxes in Harlem, Muhammad Ali's fistic fury against opponents in the ring and against the Vietnam War. It's the tension between the screen and the streets, and the artistic and aesthetic resistance offered by Third Cinema and the Black Arts Movement. It's between Ali La Pointe and Dan Freeman, and in Fanon's pen and the poetry of hip-hop.

And just as Malcolm brought into the Muslim International the future and destinies of non-Muslim Africans throughout the diaspora—including non-Muslim Black peoples in the United States—numerous activists, scholars, artists, and organizations today are exploring the politics of the Muslim Third World as a site and source of political and artistic possibility. Organizations such as Critical Resistance and the Malcolm X Grassroots Movement as well as Cynthia McKinney and media outlets such as the Black Agenda Report link U.S. wars abroad with racial and economic justice movements in the United States, while artists such as Mos Def, Dead Prez, Nas, Lupe Fiasco, Immortal Technique, M.I.A., and One Day as a Lion use the anti-imperialist politics of the Muslim Third World within their lyrical and artistic imaginations to challenge the dominant paradigms and the prevailing consensus around U.S. power, linking struggles here in the United States with those in the Muslim Third World. In reinvigorating and reshaping the already vibrant space of the Muslim International, these artists and activists force and compel the Muslim International to be a broad and inclusive space that understands the overlapping histories and interconnected struggles that not only have shaped the modern world, but also shape the conscience of the Muslim International as a site for radical justice and equality.

In connecting refugee camps to rebel activity, prisons to political movements, and concert stages to book pages, the struggles revealed in this book constantly confronted a more fateful dilemma: that with jails, torture chambers, refugee camps, repressive nation-states, and a violent global order, what does it mean when the world itself becomes a prison? For Malcolm X and the artists and activists in *Black Star, Crescent Moon*, their radical activity and their rhetorical rebellion bore witness to the defiant histories of those who came before, while providing eloquent testimony and an enduring memory for those who will come after.

ACKNOWLEDGMENTS

I must first thank my fantastic editor, Richard Morrison, and everyone at the University of Minnesota Press. Thanks so much, Richard—we were on the same page from day one, and I couldn't have asked for more from you. You are great to work with and brilliant, too! To all the reviewers of this manuscript who helped to make it better: thanks for the time and insights.

I thank the Humanities Center and the School of Humanities at the University of California, Irvine, for the enduring support that helped me finish this project. My appreciation for support goes to Ngugi Wa Thiongo and the International Center for Writing and Translation as well. Thanks to Sheila O'Rourke, Kimberly Adkinson, and the committee for the University of California President's Postdoctoral Fellowship. Thanks also to the Schomburg Center for Black Culture in New York, in particular Diana Lachatanere, Andre Elizee, and Alice Adamczyk, for all their support.

I would like to shout out to all the people at the places where I was able to share my work. To the UCLA Law School and the Critical Studies faculty there for inviting me several times, including at the Inaugural Critical Race Studies Symposium, especially Cheryl Harris, Kimberle Crenshaw, Devon Carbado, and Saul Sarabia: to sit at your collective feet and learn was, and continues to be, memorable. Thanks for sharing. To Amina Yaqin and Peter Morey at the School of Oriental and African Studies (SOAS) in London: thanks for allowing me to share my work at the Framing Muslims series with such a vibrant and engaged group. Thanks also go out to the organizers of the Hip-Hop Film Festival and Conference at UCLA and also to the organizers of the UC Davis Black History Month lecture series Prisons, Politics, and Film. To Rosemary

Hicks, Zareena Grewal, and Juliane Hammer for inviting me to the Islam in/and the United States workshop at Columbia University: incredible work, sisters! Keep doing you! To the faculty and staff in Africana studies at the Claremont Colleges, especially Dipa Basu and Sid Lemelle: thanks for the invite and the space. To George Lipsitz, Avery Gordon, and Cedric Robinson for inviting me to the Radical Imaginaries Symposia at the University of California, Santa Barbara: I am still inspired by what was said and in awe of all you do. To Alex Lubin and the Center for American Studies and Reseach (CASAR) at the American University in Beirut—thanks for the invite and for the beautiful hospitality. To Dominic Pettman, Ken Wark, and the Culture and Media Department at the New School: thoughtful, eclectic, and fresh—and I wouldn't have wanted it any other way. To the people at Project 2050 and the New World Theater: thanks for opening up your incredible work to me. To Imam Zaid Shakir and the Eras of Change organizers at the University of Southern California: so insightful and so much science being dropped. I was humbled to have been a part of it.

I thank my colleagues at the University of California, Irvine, and those around the country for their support. First and foremost, to the late great Lindon Barrett: thanks for everything, and I do mean everything. Rest in Power, my man, Rest in Power! You are missed. To the faculty and staff, including Karen Lawrence, Vicky Ruiz, Linda Vo, Doug Haynes, Winston James, Bridget Cooks, Victoria Johnson (aka Dr. J), Glen Mimura, Bliss Lim, Fatimah Tobing-Rony, Ulysses Jenkins, Ed Dimendberg, Donna Iliescu, Peter Chang, Vikki Duncan, Beth Pace, Caroline McGuire, Eve Yonas, and Matt McCabe: thanks for everything! To all those who provided guidance, advice, and friendship along the way: George Lipsitz, Todd Boyd, Tara McPhereson, Aamir Mufti, Mark Anthony Neal, Ali Behdad, George Sanchez, Clyde Woods (Rest in Power), Howard Winant, Sara Gualtieri, Vijay Prashad, Inderpal Grewal, Herman Gray, Dorinne Kondo, James Braxton Peterson, and Nayan Shah—thanks.

To all the students who continue to inspire and remind me, especially Danielle Vignieaux, Teishan Latner, Mark Villegas, Dan McClure, Saira Fazli, Rebecca Cho, Stefka Hristova, Mary Schmitt, Graham Eng-Wilmot (thanks for the heads-up on Jihad Records), Shea Mirzai, Erendira Espinoza-Taboada, Mishana Garschi, Anita Subrahmanyam,

Russell Curry, Nida Chowdhry, Yasser Ahmed, Osama Shabaik, Nasir Malim, Omar Kurdi, Sobia Saleem, and Soham Patel. Keep makin' it happen!

To all the writers, artists, musicians, rebels, hustlers, and saboteurs who keep me inspired: keep not giving a fuck! And remember: they want it to be one way, but it's the other way.

Big shout out also goes to Robin D. G. Kelley for your support, bredda—you've blazed a trail, and I'm grateful. To Michael Eric Dyson and Marcia Dyson: thanks for the love and support. You two are blessed, and so am I for having been around you. One love. To Sam Greenlee for the laughs, the stories, and the insight: you're a gem, my man! To Emory Douglas, your brilliance and insight are incredible. Thanks for sharing with me! Thanks to Christine Acham for so much: I am so glad that we're still at it. Thanks to Asad and Renee Sotelo, looking forward to more! Big shout out goes to Cognito, Jewel, and Willa—Fro-mates forever! Thanks to Yasiin Bey and Umi for the support and especially for the brilliant work you do—keep shinin'! To Kevin Durst, Zaphira Yacef, and Saadi Yacef: thanks for sharing so much with us—and over such great food, too! To Arshad Ali, Ali Mir, Yousef K. Baker, Eli Martinez, Arash Davari, and Shirin Vossoughi, thanks for the sharp minds, the critical thought, oh, and the good times, too! To Emil Herscher (aka Center): thanks for sharing conversation, music, and grub. See you at the top! To Junaid Rana and Maryam Kashani, thank you two for the laughs, the wisdom, and the space to unload. To Vivek Bald, Kym Ragusa, and Maya: you are all so lucky to have each other, and the world is even luckier—we can't wait to see you again! To Ponnie Javidan and Giv Parvaneh (and Dahlia): thanks for being there for us, and now that you're closer—look out! Viva the Clash! To Oscar Michel, Zack de la Rocha, and Adilifu Nama: thanks for the love, the laughs, and the support, bredren! I learn so much from you all. Domino!

To the fam worldwide who face the unspeakable: stand strong and remember neither their walls nor their world can hold us. To the Daulatzai and Amani families, I'm truly blessed to have you all—your love and support are what carry me. And finally, to the other half of the sky, who watches over me and kept reminding me that it mattered. One love.

NOTES

Introduction

1. Dianne Feinstein, "Opening Welcome Remarks at the 2009 Presidential Inauguration," speech given in Washington, D.C., January 20, 2009.

2. Malcolm X, "The Ballot or the Bullet," speech given in Detroit, April 14, 1964.

3. See Michael Eric Dyson, *I May Not Get There with You: The True Martin Luther King, Jr.* (New York: Free Press, 2000).

4. See Robin D. G. Kelley, *Yo' Mama's Disfunktional! Fighting the Culture Wars in Urban America* (Boston: Beacon Press, 1997); and George Lipsitz, *The Possessive Investment in Whiteness: How White People Profit from Identity Politics* (Philadelphia: Temple University Press, 1998).

5. See Penny M. Von Eschen, *Race against Empire: Black Americans and Anti-colonialism, 1937–1957* (Ithaca, N.Y.: Cornell University Press, 1997); Brenda Gayle Plummer, *Rising Wind: Black Americans and U.S. Foreign Affairs, 1935–1960* (Chapel Hill: University of North Carolina Press, 1996); Mary L. Dudziak, *Cold War Civil Rights: Race and the Image of American Democracy* (Princeton, N.J.: Princeton University Press, 2000); and Thomas Borstelmann, *The Cold War and the Color Line: American Race Relations in the Global Arena* (Cambridge, Mass.: Harvard University Press, 2003).

6. See Roderick D. Bush, *The End of White World Supremacy: Black Internationalism and the Problem of the Color Line* (Philadelphia: Temple University Press, 2009); William Appleman Williams, *Empire as a Way of Life* (New York: Oxford University Press, 1980).

7. Manning Marable's recent biography of Malcolm X is a stunning work of archival history through which he weaves his narrative of Malcolm X. But despite Marable's research and the breadth of his historical imagination and framing of Malcolm, his reading of Malcolm in his post–Nation of Islam and post-Mecca period seems to suggest that Malcolm was oriented more toward a Civil Rights framework, an assertion rooted in the assumption that Malcolm

was choosing between integration and separation and that, once he left the Nation, he moved toward integration and Civil Rights frameworks. As my project suggests, Malcolm's choice was not between integration and separation but rather between integration and internationalism, and in his post-Mecca period, Malcolm continued to center race and the intractable forms of white supremacy squarely within his political vision, even strongly suggesting that the legal frameworks and political institutions in the United States were incapable of providing Black freedom and equality. As my project suggests, Malcolm was deeply opposed to the Cold War liberal assumptions of Civil Rights and, as a result, continued to cultivate a terrain of anti-imperialism and antiracism. In addition, Marable's reading of Malcolm in the post-9/11 era seems to want to "rescue" Malcolm from the throes of "Islamic radicalism." In doing so, Marable fails to grasp the complexities of Muslim identities and overlooks the multiple and various forms of resistance that can be and are embodied by Muslims who do not conform to what Mahmood Mamdani refers to as the "good Muslim" or the "bad Muslim"(see Mahmood Mamdani, *Good Muslim, Bad Muslim: America, the Cold War, and the Roots of Terror* [New York: Pantheon Books, 2004]). In addition, by framing Malcolm in this way, Marable undermines the range of political positions, ideological orientations, and critical postures that Muslims in general can embody, and he unwittingly replicates the very containment of Black Islam that is the legacy and redemptive force of Malcolm X. See Manning Marable, *Malcolm X: A Life of Reinvention* (New York: Viking, 2011).

8. Because of the initial concern that the label *Black Muslim* suggested they were somehow un-Islamic and distinct from the global community of Islam, many in the Nation of Islam rejected the label, which had originated in C. Eric Lincoln's 1961 book *The Black Muslims in America* (Boston: Beacon Press). Informed by the belief that the Nation of Islam was seen as a heterodox interpretation of Islam, some have rejected the term with the assumption that the qualifier *Black* challenges the universality of Islam and continues to espouse a supposed racial separatism. While recognizing that Black Islam is not monolithic and is incredibly diverse, however, I use *Black Islam* or *Black Muslim* throughout this book to refer to anyone who identifies as Muslim and is African-descended. I do not mean to collapse or undermine the brilliant diversity of Black Islam (including Sunni, Shia, Five-Percenter, Nation of Islam, etc.), but instead I use the qualifier *Black* to underscore the highly racialized and even anti-Black context in which Black Muslims exist and out of which Black religious discourse emerges. In addition, I also use *Black Muslim* to underscore the critique of the nation-state that some Black Islamic traditions emerge from, in particular that of Malcolm X in both his pre- and post-Mecca moments. While I do know that some Black Muslim communities identify in personal and political ways with the

project of U.S. nationalism, I am utilizing the term *Black* in order to reference the diasporic and political dimensions that this word has come to signify (i.e., Black Power, Black Marxism, Black radicalism, etc.) and the political histories and empowered identities that it mobilizes, in particular within and against U.S. state formation. In addition, although I may sometimes use *African American Muslim*, I do so not to highlight a U.S.-centered identity but rather, like Malcolm X's Organization of Afro-American Unity (OAAU), to highlight a hemispheric identity that constitutes Blackness within the Americas more broadly, from Canada, through the Caribbean, to Brazil. In either case, I am keenly aware of the ways in which U.S. nationalist projects sought and continue to seek to contain Black internationalist impulses, and as a result, with this project, I hope to highlight those who have contested that containment and reframed race within a global context to challenge U.S. empire.

9. See Michael Angelo Gomez, *Black Crescent: The Experience and Legacy of African Muslims in the Americas* (Cambridge: Cambridge University Press, 2005); Sylviane A. Diouf, *Servants of Allah: African Muslims Enslaved in the Americas* (New York: New York University Press, 1998); Aminah Beverly McCloud, *African American Islam* (New York: Routledge, 1995); Richard Brent Turner, *Islam in the African-American Experience* (Bloomington: Indiana University Press, 1997); Edward E. Curtis, *Black Muslim Religion in the Nation of Islam, 1960–1975* (Chapel Hill: University of North Carolina Press, 2006).

10. "Growing Number of Americans Say Obama Is a Muslim: Religion, Politics and the President," Pew Research Center Publications, August 19, 2010, accessed on July 11, 2011, http://pewresearch.org/pubs/1701/poll-obama-muslim-christian-church-out-of-politics-political-leaders-religious.

11. Malcolm X, *Malcolm X Speaks: Selected Speeches and Statements*, edited by George Breitman (New York: Grove Weidenfeld, 1990), 11.

12. Louis A. DeCaro, *On the Side of My People: A Religious Life of Malcolm X* (New York: New York University Press, 1996), 124.

13. Henry Luce, "The American Century," *Life*, February 17, 1941.

14. See Von Eschen, *Race against Empire;* Plummer, *Rising Wind;* Dudziak, *Cold War Civil Rights;* Borstelmann, *The Cold War and the Color Line;* James L. Roark, "American Black Leaders: The Response to Colonialism and the Cold War, 1943–1953," *African Historical Studies* 4, no. 2 (1971): 253–70.

15. Anouar Majid, *We Are All Moors: Ending Centuries of Crusades against Muslims and Other Minorities* (Minneapolis: University of Minnesota Press, 2009), 5. See also Gil Anidjar, *Semites: Race, Religion, Literature* (Stanford, Calif.: Stanford University Press, 2008); Talal Asad, *Formations of the Secular: Christianity, Islam, Modernity* (Stanford, Calif.: Stanford University Press, 2003); Mamdani, *Good Muslim, Bad Muslim;* and Junaid Akram Rana, *Terrifying Muslims:*

Race and Labor in the South Asian Diaspora (Durham, N.C.: Duke University Press, 2011).

16. While Edward Said's *Orientalism* (New York: Random House, 1978) is a seminal text in understanding Europe's relationship and creation of the Muslim Other, it by no means should be seen as totalizing, nor should we assume that all Orientalisms (British, French, U.S., etc.) are the same. In addition, it is important to recognize the limitations of Orientalism in relationship to Black Islam in the United States. In my project I seek to decenter Said's *Orientalism* as the master narrative for understanding the politics of Islam and Muslims in the United States, because traditional Orientalism must contend not only with the ways in which the United States sought to distance itself from European empires in the post–World War II era but also with how U.S.-based Orientalism had to redefine itself and emerge in relation to the history of U.S. racialization and empire building. This is not to say that European Orientalism and U.S.-based Orientalism are discrete and radically divergent. Instead, what I'm suggesting is that the history of Black Islam challenges Saidian Orientalism in its Eurocentrism and forces U.S.-based Orientalism to contend with the domestic politics of anti-Blackness and the institution of slavery, which are central to the emergence and the enduring legacy of Black Islam.

17. Frantz Fanon, *The Wretched of the Earth*, edited by Richard Philcox (New York: Grove Press, 2004), 102.

18. See Alex Lubin, "Locating Palestine in Pre-1948: Black Internationalism," in *Black Routes to Islam*, ed. Manning Marable and Hishaam D. Aidi (New York: Palgrave Macmillan, 2009), 17–32; Bill V. Mullen, *Afro-Orientalism* (Minneapolis: University of Minnesota Press, 2004); and Sherman A. Jackson, *Islam and the Blackamerican: Looking toward the Third Resurrection* (Oxford: Oxford University Press, 2005). In fact, as Sherman Jackson has noted, Black Orientalism has also served to undermine and question the legitimacy of Islam to African America, seeing African American Muslims as less Black. For Jackson, Black Orientalism employs a historical narrative that places U.S. racial slavery and subjugation as the primary paradigm for understanding various forms of subjugation across time and geography, excluding, according to Jackson, ancient Egypt's own slavery.

19. See Nikhil Pal Singh, *Black Is a Country: Race and the Unfinished Struggle for Democracy* (Cambridge, Mass.: Harvard University Press, 2004); Vijay Prashad, *Everybody Was Kung Fu Fighting: Afro-Asian Connections and the Myth of Cultural Purity* (Boston: Beacon Press, 2001); Robin D. G. Kelley, *Freedom Dreams: The Black Radical Imagination* (Boston: Beacon Press, 2002); Mullen, *Afro-Orientalism*; Gerald Horne, *Black and Brown: African Americans and the Mexican Revolution, 1910–1920* (New York: New York University Press, 2005);

and Gerald Horne, *The End of Empires: African Americans and India* (Philadelphia: Temple University Press, 2008). See also Von Eschen, *Race against Empire*; Sudarshan Kapur, *Raising Up a Prophet: The African-American Encounter with Gandhi* (Dehli: Oxford University Press, 1993); Winston James, *Holding Aloft the Banner of Ethiopia: Caribbean Radicalism in Early Twentieth-Century America* (London: Verso, 1999); and Cynthia Ann Young, *Soul Power: Culture, Radicalism, and the Making of a U.S. Third World Left* (Durham, N.C.: Duke University Press, 2006).

20. Singh, *Black Is a Country*, 53.

21. Aimé Césaire, *Notebook of a Return to the Native Land*, edited by Annette Smith, translated by Clayton Eshleman (Middletown, Conn.: Wesleyan University Press, 2001), 43.

22. See Melani McAlister, *Epic Encounters: Culture, Media, and US Interests in the Middle East, 1945–2000* (Berkeley: University of California Press, 2001).

23. See Earl Lewis, "To Turn as on a Pivot: Writing African Americans into a History of Overlapping Diasporas," *American Historical Review* 100, no. 3 (1995): 765.

24. Robin D. G. Kelley, *Race Rebels: Culture, Politics, and the Black Working Class* (New York: Free Press, 1996); Asef Bayat, *Life as Politics: How Ordinary People Change the Middle East* (Stanford, Calif.: Stanford University Press, 2010). See also James C. Scott, *Domination and the Arts of Resistance: Hidden Transcripts* (New Haven, Conn.: Yale University Press, 1992).

25. See Imamu Amiri Baraka, *Black Music* (New York: William Morrow, 1967), 180–211.

26. Samuel P. Huntington, *The Clash of Civilizations and the Remaking of World Order* (New York: Touchstone, 1996).

1. "You Remember Dien Bien Phu!"

The opening epigraph is from James Baldwin, "The International War Crimes Tribunal," *The Cross of Redemption: Uncollected Writings*, edited by Randall Kenan (New York: Pantheon, 2010), 201–2.

1. See Elijah Muhammad, *Message to the Blackman in America* (Chicago: Muhammad Mosque of Islam no. 2, 1965).

2. See Aimé Césaire, *Discourse on Colonialism*, ed. Joan Pinkham (New York: Monthly Review Press, 1972).

3. Malcolm X, *February 1965: The Final Speeches* (New York: Pathfinder, 1992), 165.

4. Quoted in DeCaro, *On the Side of My People*, 239.

5. Ibid., 239.

6. Plummer, *Rising Wind,* 277.

7. Roark, "American Black Leaders," 253.

8. Quoted ibid., 255.

9. See ibid.

10. Ibid.

11. Quoted ibid., 255–56.

12. Ibid., 255–56.

13. Ibid., 258. See also Von Eschen, *Race against Empire.*

14. Von Eschen, *Race against Empire,* 40.

15. "X" [George F. Kennan], "The Sources of Soviet Conduct," *Foreign Affairs* (July 1947), accessed on July 11, 2011, www.foreignaffairs.com/articles/23331/x/the-sources-of-soviet-conduct.

16. Roark, "American Black Leaders," 253.

17. See Paul Gordon Lauren, "Seen from the Outside: The International Perspective of America's Dilemma," in *Window on Freedom: Race, Civil Rights, and Foreign Affairs, 1945–1988,* ed. Brenda Gayle Plummer (Chapel Hill: University of North Carolina Press, 2003).

18. Quoted in Roark, "American Black Leaders," 268.

19. See Von Eschen, *Race against Empire.*

20. Quoted in Roark, "American Black Leaders," 263.

21. Von Eschen, *Race against Empire,* 3.

22. Ibid., 40.

23. Quoted in Michael L. Krenn, *Black Diplomacy: African Americans and the State Department, 1945–1969* (Armonk, N.Y.: M. E. Sharpe, 1998), 16.

24. The President's Committee on Civil Rights, "Chapter IV: A Program of Action: The Committee's Recommendations," *To Secure These Rights: The Report of the President's Committee on Civil Rights,* December 1947, 149, accessed on July 11, 2011, www.trumanlibrary.org/civilrights/srights4.htm.

25. See Paul Gordon Lauren, "Seen from the Outside: The International Perspective of America's Dilemma," *Window on Freedom: Race, Civil Rights, and Foreign Affairs, 1945–1988,* ed. Brenda Gayle Plummer (Chapel Hill: University of North Carolina Press, 2003).

26. Quoted in Von Eschen, *Race against Empire,* 148.

27. Quoted in Singh, *Black Is a Country,* 141.

28. Quoted in Lauren, "Seen from the Outside," 32.

29. Penny M. Von Eschen, "Challenging Cold War Habits: African Americans, Race, and Foreign Policy," *Diplomatic History* 20, no. 4 (1996): 635–36.

30. See Penny M. Von Eschen, *Satchmo Blows Up the World: Jazz Ambassadors Play the Cold War* (Cambridge, Mass.: Harvard University Press, 2004).

31. Quoted in Bush, *The End of White World Supremacy,* 195.

32. Von Eschen, *Race against Empire*, 97.

33. See Horne, *Black and Brown*; Horne, *The End of Empires*; Kelley, *Freedom Dreams*; Young, *Soul Power*; Prashad, *Everybody Was Kung Fu Fighting*; Mullen, *Afro-Orientalism*; and Peniel E. Joseph, *Waiting 'til the Midnight Hour: A Narrative History of Black Power in America* (New York: Henry Holt and Co., 2006).

34. Young, *Soul Power*, 50.

35. McAlister, *Epic Encounters*, 87.

36. See ibid.

37. James Baldwin, *The Fire Next Time* (New York: Dell Press, 1963), 46.

38. McAlister, *Epic Encounters*, 93.

39. Malcolm X, upon his return to the United States after his pilgrimage to Mecca and after having left the Nation of Islam, was asked about his "new" name, Malik El-Shabazz. Malcolm replied that he had had that name when he first joined the Nation of Islam several years before but that, after leaving the organization and after his pilgrimage to Mecca, he would continue to use the "X," that symbol of the unknown that signifies the lost past that was violently stripped from Black peoples. When probed why, he replied, "I'll probably continue to use Malcolm X as long as the situation that produced it exists"—a constant reminder to himself, Black peoples, America, and the world (including Sunni Muslim universalists) that white supremacy and vicious forms of anti-Blackness were still at large. (Malcolm X quoted in the 1972 documentary *Malcolm X: His Own Story as It Really Happened*, directed by Arnold Perl.)

40. See Marvin X and Faruk X, "Islam and Black Art: An Interview with Leroi Jones," in *Dictionary of Literary Biography: Black Arts Movement*, ed. Jeff Decker (Detroit: Gale, 1984).

41. Turner, *Islam in the African-American Experience*, 159.

42. Muhammad, *Message to the Blackman in America*, 31.

43. McAlister, *Epic Encounters*, 93.

44. Quoted in DeCaro, *On the Side of My People*, 124.

45. Quoted in Plummer, *Rising Wind*, 258.

46. See ibid.

47. Quoted in Lincoln, *The Black Muslims in America*, 225.

48. Malcolm X, *Malcolm X Speaks*, 123.

49. Quoted in DeCaro, *On the Side of My People*, 124.

50. Capturing the zeitgeist of decolonization and the anticolonial struggle, Bandung occurred within years of several monumental moments, including the partition and independence of India from Britain, the U.S. overthrow of Mossadegh in Iran, the U.S.-backed assassination of Arbenz in Guatemala, Gamal Abdel Nasser's rise to power and the Suez Crisis, the overthrow of the

Anglo-American-backed monarchy in Iraq, the Vietnamese victory over the French at Dien Bien Phu, the Algerian struggle against the French, the overthrow of Bautista by Fidel Castro and Che Guevara in Cuba, and Kwame Nkrumah's ascension in Ghana, just to name a few.

51. Manning Marable and Vanessa Agard-Jones, eds., *Transnational Blackness: Navigating the Global Color Line* (New York: Palgrave Macmillan, 2008), 153.

52. Quoted in Cary Fraser, "An American Dilemma: Race and Realpolitik in the American Response to the Bandung Conference, 1955," *Window on Freedom: Race, Civil Rights, and Foreign Affairs, 1945–1988*, ed. Brenda Gayle Plummer (Chapel Hill: University of North Carolina Press, 2003), 120.

53. Ibid., 134.

54. Richard Wright, *The Color Curtain: A Report on the Bandung Conference* (Jackson: University Press of Mississippi, 1994), 12.

55. With Malcolm X's fiery insights, Harold Cruse's sharp pen, and Robert Williams's defiant globe-trotting, a global stage was set for a new generation of Black radicals to emerge throughout the 1960s and into the 1970s. Deeply inspired by Cruse, Malcolm, and Williams, Max Stanford and others formed the RAM in the mid-1960s, and they, too, saw Black peoples in the United States as part of the Bandung world of Africa, Asia, and Latin America. Stanford (who converted to Islam in the early 1970s and became Muhammad Ahmad) was profoundly influenced by both Robert Williams's and Malcolm's ideas on Black self-determination and internationalism, and he ultimately formed a close relationship with Malcolm, during which Malcolm became an officer in RAM. For Stanford and his comrades, worldwide inequality existed not simply between capital and labor but also between Western imperial interests and the people of the Bandung world of Asia, Africa, and Latin America, and they clearly saw Black peoples in the United States as part of that Bandung world. In fact, in a 1964 position paper titled "Projects and Problems of the Revolutionary Movement," Stanford wrote, "RAM's position is that the Afro-American is not a citizen of the U.S.A., denied his rights, but rather he is a colonial subject enslaved. . . . black people in the U.S.A. are a captive nation suppressed and . . . their fight is not for integration into the white community but one of national liberation." RAM also organized the Second Conference of the Afro-American Student Movement in Nashville in 1964, for which the theme was "The Black Revolution's Relationship to the Bandung World," and an article in the 1965 issue of the RAM journal *Black America* was titled "The Relationship of Revolutionary Afro-American Movement to the Bandung Revolution." For RAM and its early history, "Bandung Humanism" became the rubric and central theme for defining Black politics and solidarities, as RAM saw Black peoples in the United States in alliance with national liberation struggles taking place in

Cuba, Algeria, Vietnam, China, and elsewhere. See Robin D. G. Kelley and Betsy Esch, "Black Like Mao: Red China and Black Revolution," *Souls: A Critical Journal of Black Politics, Culture and Society* 1, no. 4 (Fall 1999): 6–41.

56. See Malcolm X, "The Message to the Grassroots," in *Malcolm X Speaks: Selected Speeches and Statements*, edited by George Breitman (New York: Grove Weidenfeld, 1990).

57. Ibid., 6.

58. Ibid., 6.

59. Ibid., 7.

60. Ibid., 7.

61. Ibid., 8.

62. Malcolm X, *Malcolm X Speaks*, 50.

63. Malcolm X, "The Message to the Grassroots," 10.

64. Ibid., 11.

65. Ibid., 12.

66. Quoted in Bush, *The End of White World Supremacy*, 196.

67. Malcolm X, *February 1965*, 125–26.

68. Ibid., 126.

69. Malcolm X, "The Ballot or the Bullet" speech.

70. Malcolm X, *Malcolm X Speaks*, 34.

71. Malcolm X, "The Ballot or the Bullet" speech.

72. Malcolm X, *February 1965*, 175–76.

73. Malcolm X, *Malcolm X Speaks*, 73.

74. Ibid., 76.

75. Ibid., 76, 77.

76. Ibid., 84.

77. Quoted in Malcolm X, *By Any Means Necessary*, edited by George Breitman (New York: Pathfinder, 1992), 110; italics his.

78. Malcolm X, *Malcolm X Speaks*, 78.

79. Quoted in John Henrik Clarke, A. Peter Bailey, and Earl Grant, *Malcolm X: The Man and His Times* (New York: Macmillan, 1969), 257.

80. Quoted ibid., 258. The State Department's systematic attempts, through the USIA and other organs and agencies, was a well-thought-out and cleverly designed plan to project the image of America abroad so as not to impact American foreign policy negatively in Africa and Asia. Rather than addressing Black claims to racial justice and economic equality, the United States shifted its efforts to projecting an image of racial democracy, regardless of the reality. But Malcolm was one of the few who challenged this perceived authority and the monopoly that the United States had on this idea, calling it that "veil of global diplomatic art." Throughout his travels and even in the United States, Malcolm

continued to highlight the abject racism of the United States, giving a detailed view of the underbelly of Jim Crow in America by explaining that the Civil Rights Act was a façade to "misguide states in Africa in accepting an angelic image of [American] dollarism"—a euphemism Malcolm often invoked to explain American neocolonialism in the post–World War II moment. (See Malcolm X, *Malcolm X Speaks*, 152). Malcolm also said, "At the international level in 1964, they used the device of sending well-chosen black representatives to the African continent, whose mission it was to make the people on that continent think all our problems had been solved. They went over there as apologists. . . . they go primarily to represent the United States government. And when they go, they gloss things over, they tell you how well we are doing here, how the civil rights bill has settled everything, and how the Nobel Prize was handed down. . . . they actually succeed in widening the gap between Afro-Americans and Africans" (Malcolm X, *February 1965*, 44).

81. Malcolm X, "Zionist Logic," *Egyptian Gazette*, September 17, 1964.

82. Malcolm X, *Malcolm X Speaks*, 66.

83. Malcolm X, "One Big Force under One Banner: An Interview with Gordon Parks," in *Malcolm X: The Final Speeches* (New York: Pathfinder Press, 1992), 241.

84. Huey Percy Newton, *The Huey P. Newton Reader*, ed. David Hilliard and Dagmar Weise (New York: Seven Stories Press, 2002), 51–52.

2. To the East, Blackwards

The opening epigraph is from "Carmichael Urges a 'Vietnam' in U.S.," *New York Times*, July 28, 1967, 10.

1. Robert F. Williams, *Negroes with Guns* (New York: Marzani and Munsell, 1962), 82.

2. Harold Cruse, "Revolutionary Nationalism and the Afro-American," in *Black Fire: An Anthology of African-Americans Writing*, ed. Leroi Jones and Larry Neal (New York: William Morrow, 1968), 40.

3. Stokely Carmichael, "Black Power and the Third World," in *New Revolutionaries: Left Opposition*, ed. Tariq Ali (London: Owen, 1969), 91.

4. Kwame Ture [Stokely Carmichael] and Charles V. Hamilton, *Black Power: The Politics of Liberation in America* (New York: Vintage Books, 1992), 5.

5. Kathleen Neal Cleaver, "Back to Africa: The Evolution of the International Section of the Black Panther Party (1969–1972)," in *The Black Panther Party (Reconsidered)*, ed. Charles E. Jones (Baltimore: Black Classic Press, 1998), 216.

6. See Robert Blauner, "Internal Colonialism and Ghetto Revolt," *Social Problems* 16, no. 4 (Spring 1969): 393–408.

7. Quoted in Louis A. DeCaro, *On the Side of My People: A Religious Life of Malcolm X* (New York: New York University Press, 1996), 124.

8. Huey Percy Newton, *The Huey P. Newton Reader*, ed. David Hilliard and Dagmar Weise (New York: Seven Stories Press, 2002), 51–52.

9. See Fouzi Slisli, "Islam: The Elephant in Fanon's *The Wretched of the Earth*," *Critique: Critical Middle Eastern Studies* 17, no. 1 (March 2008): 97–108. While Fanon frames his analysis primarily through the lens of Third World Marxism, scholars such as Fouzi Slisli have noted Fanon's deafening silence on the Islamic anticolonialism that not only was central to the identity of the peasantry that Fanon so valorized but also sat at the heart of a long history of Algerian resistance to French colonialism. This "elephant in the room" (as Slisli refers to it) in *The Wretched of the Earth* suggests that the politics of Muslim anticolonialism, wherever it occurs, continues to be the silent Other within liberationist discourses that circulate in the West. Despite this, or maybe because of the looming specter that it presents, Muslim anti-imperialism carries with it a particular appeal that no doubt found traction among Black radicals who were deeply influenced by Malcolm X and his own Muslim anti-imperialism.

10. Quoted in Cleaver, "Back to Africa," 215.

11. Frantz Fanon, *The Wretched of the Earth*, edited by Richard Philcox (New York: Grove Press, 2004), 5.

12. Cleaver, "Back to Africa," 214.

13. Ibid., 215.

14. Ernesto Guevara, "At the Afro-Asian Conference in Algeria (February 24, 1965)," in *Che Guevara Reader*, edited by David Deutschmann (Havana: Centro de Estudios Che Guevara, 2003), 340.

15. See Cleaver, "Back to Africa."

16. Hoyt W. Fuller, "Algiers Journal," *Negro Digest*, October 1969, 74; Young, *Soul Power*, 39.

17. Ibid., 39.

18. William Gardner Smith, *The Stone Face: A Novel* (New York: Farrar Straus, 1963). See also Tyler Stovall, "The Fire This Time: Black American Expatriates and the Algerian War," *Yale French Studies* 98 (2000): 182–200.

19. James Baldwin, *Oxford Collected Essays*, edited by Toni Morrison (New York: Literary Classics of the United States, 1998), 377.

20. Thomas Ronan, "Ben Bella Links Two 'Injustices,'" *New York Times*, October 14, 1962, 20.

21. Martin Luther King Jr., "My Talk with Ben Bella," *New York Amsterdam News*, October 27, 1962, 12.

22. Malcolm X, *Malcolm X Speaks*, 66.

23. Francee Covington, "Are the Revolutionary Techniques Employed in the Battle of Algiers Applicable to Harlem?" in *The Black Woman: An Anthology*, ed. Toni Cade Bambara (New York: Washington Square Press, 1970), 315.

24. Paul Willemen, "The Third Cinema Question: Notes and Reflections," in *Questions of Third Cinema*, ed. Jim Pines and Paul Willemen (London: British Film Institute, 1989), 6.

25. Glauber Rocha, "An Esthetic of Hunger," in *New Latin American Cinema*, vol. 1, *Theory, Practices, and Transcontinental Articulations*, ed. Michael T. Martin (Detroit: Wayne State University Press, 1997), 60.

26. Quoted in Fernando Solanas and Octavio Getino, "Towards a Third Cinema: Notes and Experiences for the Development of a Cinema of Liberation in the Third World," in *New Latin American Cinema*, vol. 1, *Theory, Practices, and Transcontinental Articulations*, 33.

27. Ed Guerrero, *Framing Blackness: The African American Image in Film* (Philadelphia: Temple University Press, 1993), 72.

28. Quoted ibid., 73.

29. Quoted ibid., 73.

30. Guerrero, *Framing Blackness*, 76.

31. Ibid., 97.

32. Ntongela Masilela, "The Los Angeles School of Black Film Makers," in *Black American Cinema*, ed. Manthia Diawara (New York: Routledge, 1993), 107–17.

33. Quoted in Young, *Soul Power*, 224.

34. Ibid., 234.

35. Lerone Bennett Jr., "The Emancipation Orgasm: Sweetback in Wonderland," *Ebony*, no. 26, September 1971, 108.

36. Ibid., 108–9, 110.

37. Ibid., 109.

38. Ibid., 110.

39. Ibid.

40. Ibid., 118.

41. Ibid., 112, 114.

42. Ibid., 114.

43. Ibid.

44. Sam Greenlee, interview with the author, June 2004.

45. Ibid.

46. "Edutainment: HHW Speaks with Sam Greenlee: Author of 'The Spook Who Sat by the Door,'" Hip-Hop Wired, accessed July 11, 2011, http://hiphopwired.com/2009/12/10/spook/.

47. Sam Greenlee, interview with the author, June 2004.

48. See Christine Acham, "Subverting the System: The Politics and Production of *The Spook Who Sat by the Door*," *Screening Noir* 1, no. 1 (Fall/Winter 2005): 113–25. See also the documentary film *Infiltrating Hollywood: The Rise and Fall of "The Spook Who Sat by the Door,"* directed by Christine Acham and Clifford Ward (independent, 2010).

49. See *Infiltrating Hollywood*.

50. Ibid.

51. Ibid.

52. Acham, "Subverting the System."

53. Sam Greenlee, interview with the author, June 2004.

54. Malcolm X, "The Message to the Grassroots," 5.

55. Ibid., 6.

56. Sam Greenlee, interview with the author, June 2004.

57. Sam Greenlee, *Baghdad Blues* (New York: Bantam Books, 1976), 34.

58. Ibid., 70.

59. Ibid., 48.

60. Ibid., 57.

61. Ibid., 82.

62. Ibid., 21.

63. See Amy Kaplan, *The Anarchy of Empire in the Making of U.S. Culture* (Cambridge, Mass.: Harvard University Press, 2002). As Kaplan writes in this compelling work, "International struggles for domination abroad profoundly shape representations of American national identity at home, and cultural phenomena we think of as domestic or particularly national are forged in a crucible of foreign relations."

64. Greenlee, *Baghdad Blues*, 134.

65. Ibid., 152.

66. Ibid., 160.

67. Sam Greenlee, interview with the author, June 2004.

68. Greenlee, *Baghdad Blues*, 120.

69. Said, *Orientalism*.

70. Greenlee, *Baghdad Blues*, 134.

71. Ibid., 178–79.

72. Sam Greenlee, interview with the author, June 2004.

73. Greenlee, *Baghdad Blues*, 179.

3. Return of the Mecca

1. By "carceral imagination," I'm referring to a fundamental logic of U.S. state building, in which Black, First Nations, and Third World bodies are

contained and controlled through the larger apparatus of U.S. state power and its white supremacist and imperialist essence. While this carceral imagination has taken shape and legitimized itself in different ways in various historical moments and contexts, its emergence in the post–Civil Rights era took the form of an urban police state and the rise of the prison as a form of social control and racial domination. In this way, I'm suggesting that prisons and mass incarceration have become the operative site and even metaphor for U.S. state power, whether it be the massive prison apparatus in the United States, which has replicated previous forms of racial domination dating back to slavery and Jim Crow, or the emergence of imperial incarceration evinced by Abu Ghraib, Guantánamo, Bagram, and other so-called Black sites in the perpetual "War on Terror." In addition, the carceral imagination is revealed through U.S. empire and its Eurocentric inheritance, which has constructed the "nation as prison," in which the Third World, through neoliberal economic policies, support, and installation of proxy rulers, along with the creation of a security-state through heightened militarism, has become the operative model of global rule.

2. Baraka, *Black Music*, 180–211.

3. See Sohail Daulatzai, "A Rebel to America: 'N.Y. State of Mind' after the Towers Fell," in *Born to Use Mics: Reading Nas's Illmatic*, ed. Michael Eric Dyson and Sohail Daulatzai (New York: Basic Books, 2009), 33–60. Also see Clarence Lusane and Dennis Desmond, *Pipe Dream Blues: Racism and the War on Drugs* (Boston: South End Press, 1991).

4. See Herman Gray, *Watching Race: Television and the Struggle for "Blackness"* (Minneapolis: University of Minnesota Press, 1995). Also see Michael Paul Rogin, *Ronald Reagan, the Movie: And Other Episodes in Political Demonology* (Berkeley: University of California Press, 1987).

5. See Daulatzai, "A Rebel to America." Also see Gray, *Watching Race*.

6. Ibid.

7. See the publication by the Center on Juvenile and Criminal Justice: Lisa Feldman, Vincent Schiraldi, and Jason Ziedenberg, "Too Little Too Late: President Clinton's Prison Legacy" (Washington, D.C.: Justice Policy Institute, February 2001), accessed on July 11, 2011, www.cjcj.org/files/too_little.pdf.

8. See Eric Schlosser, "The Prison Industrial Complex," *Atlantic Monthly* (December 1998): 51–79. The State of California has the biggest prison system in the industrialized world, housing more prisoners than France, Britain, Germany, Japan, Singapore, and the Netherlands combined, and the State of New York, under liberal governor Mario Cuomo's reign (1982–95), added more prison beds than all previous governors in the state's history combined.

9. Michelle Alexander, *The New Jim Crow: Mass Incarceration in the Age of Colorblindness* (New York: New Press, 2010), 2. In her brilliant book, Alexander

reveals that in the post–Civil Rights era and through "War on Crime" rhetoric and policies, Black incarceration has been stunning. Despite Blacks being only 12 percent of the general population, Black inmates make up 50 percent of the prison population, and overall, over 80 percent of Black incarcerations are for nonviolent drug offenses. According to Alexander, mass incarceration has become a more contemporary form of racial control that replicates previous mechanisms of racial exclusion. Despite the removal of de jure forms of racial discrimination through Civil Rights legislation, racial discrimination is now legal through mass incarceration, because convicted felons who have completed their sentences can be discriminated against in housing, employment, and education, as well as stripped of the right to vote.

10. See Ian Haney-López, *White by Law: The Legal Construction of Race* (New York: New York University Press, 1996). Also see Alexander, *The New Jim Crow.*

11. See Edward W. Said, *Covering Islam: How the Media and the Experts Determine How We See the Rest of the World* (New York: Pantheon Books, 1981).

12. See David Ansen, "The Battle for Malcolm X," *Newsweek*, August 26, 1991, accessed on July 11, 2011, www.newsweek.com/1991/08/25/the-battle-for-malcolm-x.html.

13. See "The Two Faces of Farrakhan," *Newsweek*, October 30, 1995.

14. Huey Percy Newton, *The Huey P. Newton Reader*, edited by David Hilliard and Dagmar Weise (New York: Seven Stories Press, 2002), 52.

15. McAlister, *Epic Encounters*, 87.

16. Muhammad, *Message to the Blackman in America*, 31.

17. McAlister, *Epic Encounters*, 93.

18. Quoted in DeCaro, *On the Side of My People*, 124.

19. Quoted in Lisa Gail Collins and Margo Natalie Crawford, introduction to *New Thoughts on the Black Arts Movement*, ed. Lisa Gail Collins and Margo Natalie Crawford (New Brunswick, N.J.: Rutgers University Press, 2006), 5.

20. Ibid., 5–6.

21. Malcolm X, *By Any Means Necessary*, 54–55.

22. Fanon, *The Wretched of the Earth*, 159.

23. Ameer (Amiri) Baraka, "The Black Aesthetic," *Black World/Negro Digest* 18, no. 11 (September 1969): 5.

24. Fanon, *The Wretched of the Earth*, 167.

25. Malcolm X, *By Any Means Necessary*, 54.

26. Fanon, *The Wretched of the Earth*, 236–37.

27. Quoted in Cheryl Clarke, *"After Mecca": Women Poets and the Black Arts Movement* (New Brunswick, N.J.: Rutgers University Press, 2005), 51.

28. James T. Stewart, "The Development of the Black Revolutionary Artist," in *Black Fire*, ed. Jones and Neal, 10.

29. Malcolm X, "The Message to the Grassroots" speech.

30. McAlister, *Epic Encounters*, 104.

31. Marvin X and Faruk X, "Islam and Black Art: An Interview with Leroi Jones," in *Dictionary of Literary Biography: Black Arts Movement*, ed. Jeff Decker (Detroit: Gale, 1984), 128.

32. Clarke, *"After Mecca,"* 2–3.

33. See McAlister, *Epic Encounters*, 109.

34. See Baraka, "The Black Aesthetic."

35. McAlister, *Epic Encounters*, 110.

36. In fact, the relationships between the "Muslim terrorist" and the "Black criminal," or the Muslim Third World and urban America, in the 1980s and 1990s can be seen through the Iran–Contra scandal that became public in 1986. The "scandal" involved the United States secretly selling arms to Iran in exchange for both money and the hostages it held and then using that money to help fund the anticommunist Contras in Nicaragua, who in turn were using U.S. cargo planes to import cocaine into urban centers in the United States—all under the watch of the CIA. This triangle trade, so to speak, and the importation and presence of drugs in urban America were the central means on which policing, mass incarceration, and the demonization of Blackness as "criminal" focused, as the informal drug economy became the "War on Drugs," which Reagan–Bush used to legitimize the massive police state that was urban America, the ashes from which the phoenix of hip-hop emerged. As Jay-Z would say in his brilliant 2007 song "Blue Magic," in which he meditates on the politics of 1980s urban America: "Blame Reagan for making me into a monster, / Blame Oliver North and Iran–Contra / I ran contraband that they sponsored / before this rhyming stuff we was in concert." Implicating himself in the drug trade, Jay-Z spins wordplay ("I ran contraband") that suggests the elaborate CIA network through which drugs were imported from Latin America into urban areas in the United States, which intensified the "War on Drugs" hysteria that hip-hop emerged from, a form of music that Kanye West brilliantly and subversively called "Crack Music." In this way the link between the "Black criminal" and the "Muslim terrorist" is more compelling than meets the eye.

For more information, see Leslie Cockburn, *Out of Control: The Story of the Reagan Administration's Secret War in Nicaragua, the Illegal Arms Pipeline, and the Contra Drug Connection* (New York: Atlantic Monthly Press, 1987); Alexander Cockburn and Jeffrey St. Clair, *Whiteout: The CIA, Drugs and the Press* (Oakland, Calif.: AK Press, 2010); and Peter Dale Scott and Jonathan Marshall, *Cocaine Politics: Drugs, Armies, and the CIA in Central America* (Berkeley: University of California Press, 1998).

37. See Gwendolyn D. Pough, Elaine Richardson, Aisha Durham, and Rachel Raimist, eds., *Home Girls Make Some Noise: Hip-Hop Feminism Anthology*

(Mira Loma, Calif.: Parker Publishing, 2007); Joan Murray Morgan, *When Chickenheads Come Home to Roost: A Hip-Hop Feminist Breaks It Down* (New York: Simon and Schuster, 2000); Michael Eric Dyson, *Know What I Mean? Reflections on Hip-Hop* (New York: Basic Civitas Books, 2007); T. Denean Sharpley-Whiting, *Pimps Up, Ho's Down: Hip Hop's Hold on Young Black Women* (New York: New York University Press, 2008).

38. Chuck D, interview with the author, August 2006.

39. See Rogin, *Ronald Reagan, the Movie.*

40. Quoted in Robert Lipsyte, "Cassius Clay, Cassius X, Muhammad Ali," *New York Times Magazine,* October 25, 1964, 29.

41. Quoted in Mike Marqusee, *Redemption Song: Muhammad Ali and the Spirit of the Sixties* (London: Verso, 2005), 215.

42. See liner notes of Ice Cube, *Death Certificate,* album (Priority Records, 1991).

43. See Orlando Patterson, *Slavery and Social Death: A Comparative Study* (Cambridge, Mass.: Harvard University Press, 1982). Patterson, through his notion of "social death," examines slavery as a universal phenomenon and as a set of practices, ideologies, and forms of violence that perpetuate the evisceration of the slave's subjectivity.

44. See Muhammad, *Message to the Blackman in America.*

45. See Alexander, *The New Jim Crow.*

46. See Lincoln, *The Black Muslims in America*; Essien Udosen Essien-Udom, *Black Nationalism: A Search for an Identity in America* (Chicago: University of Chicago Press, 1962); and Michael Eric Dyson, *Making Malcolm: The Myth and Meaning of Malcolm X* (Oxford: Oxford University Press, 1995).

47. Malcolm X, *Malcolm X Speaks,* 8.

48. "The Greatest Story Ever Told" (Muhammad's Mosque), 1971, Muhammad Speaks, accessed July 11, 2011, www.muhammadspeaks.com/GreatestStory.html.

4. "Ghost in the House"

1. bell hooks, "Eating the Other," in *Black Looks: Race and Representation* (Boston: South End Press, 1992), 31.

2. Dyson, *Making Malcolm,* 148.

3. Herman Gray, "Remembering Civil Rights: Television, Memory and the 1960's," in *The Revolution Wasn't Televised: Sixties Television and Social Conflict,* ed. Lynn Spigel and Michael Curtin (New York: Routledge, 1997), 350–56.

4. Quoted in Marqusee, *Redemption Song,* 9.

5. Quoted ibid, 9.

6. Quoted ibid, 9.

7. Grant Farred, *What's My Name? Black Vernacular Intellectuals* (Minneapolis: University of Minnesota Press, 2003), 35.

8. Carmichael, "Black Power and the Third World," 91.

9. Quoted in Farred, *What's My Name?* 53.

10. Quoted in Thomas Hauser, *Muhammad Ali: His Life and Times* (New York: Simon and Schuster, 1991), 82.

11. Quoted in Marqusee, *Redemption Song*, 175.

12. Quoted in Farred, *What's My Name?* 33.

13. Quoted ibid., 215.

14. See George Herring, "America and Vietnam: The Unending War," *Foreign Affairs*, Winter 1991/92, accessed on July 11, 2011, www.foreignaffairs.com/articles/47440/george-c-herring/america-and-vietnam-the-unending-war.

15. Quoted in McAlister, *Epic Encounters*, 245.

16. See Richard Dyer, *White* (London: Routledge, 1997).

17. See David A. Hollinger, *Postethnic America: Beyond Multiculturalism* (New York: Basic Books, 2000); Todd Gitlin, *The Twilight of Common Dreams: Why America Is Wracked by Culture Wars* (New York: Henry Holt and Co., 1996).

18. Charles Krauthammer, "The Unipolar Moment," *Foreign Affairs: America and the World*, 1990–91, accessed on July 11, 2011, www.foreignaffairs.com/articles/46271/charles-krauthammer/the-unipolar-moment.

19. Bernard Lewis, *Islam and the West* (New York: Oxford University Press, 1993), 60.

20. Quoted in Leon T. Hadar, "The 'Green Peril': Creating the Islamic Fundamentalist Threat," *Cato Policy Analysis* 177 (August 27, 1992), accessed on July 11, 2011, www.cato.org/pubs/pas/pa-177.html.

21. Quoted ibid.

22. "X" [George F. Kennan], "The Sources of Soviet Conduct."

23. Huntington, *The Clash of Civilizations and the Remaking of World Order*, 217.

24. Quoted in Robert Kaplan, "Looking the World in the Eye," *Atlantic* (December 2001), accessed on July 11, 2011, www.theatlantic.com/past/docs/issues/2001/12/kaplan.htm.

25. Edward W. Said, "The Clash of Ignorance," *Nation* (October 22, 2001), accessed on July 11, 2011, www.thenation.com/article/clash-ignorance.

26. Huntington, *The Clash of Civilizations and the Remaking of World Order*, 307.

27. Quoted in Von Eschen, *Race against Empire*, 148.

28. Quoted in Kegan Doyle, "Muhammad Goes to Hollywood: Michael Mann's Ali as Biopic," *Journal of Popular Culture* 39, no. 3 (June 2006): 398.

29. Quoted in Ludo de Witte, *The Assassination of Lumumba* (London: Verso, 2001), 185.

30. Malcolm X, *By Any Means Necessary*, 64.

31. Doyle, "Muhammad Goes to Hollywood," 398.

32. See ibid., 383–406.

33. Farred, *What's My Name?* 245.

34. Ibid., 246.

35. In fact, *When We Were Kings* embodies this through a narrative device, telling the fight in flashback primarily through the experiences of two white men—Norman Mailer (of "the White Negro" fame) and George Plimpton—for they become the frame and lens through which we "remember" Ali and the tumultuous period of the 1960s and early 1970s.

5. Protect Ya Neck

1. Kaplan, *The Anarchy of Empire in the Making of U.S. Culture*, 1.

2. See Turner, *Islam in the African-American Experience*.

3. Chuck D, interview with the author, August 2006.

4. Marvin X and Faruk X, "Islam and Black Art," 128.

5. Michel Foucault, *Discipline and Punish: The Birth of the Prison* (New York: Vintage Books, 1995), 14.

6. Alan Gomez, "Resisting Living Death at Marion Federal Penitentiary, 1972," *Radical History Review*, no. 96 (Fall 2006): 60.

7. See "Judges Dismiss Suit Seeking Damages for Guantanamo Torture," Center for Constitutional Rights, accessed on July 11, 2011, www.ccrjustice.org /newsroom/press-releases/judges-dismiss-suit-seeking-damages-guantanamo-torture.

8. Avery Gordon, "Supermax Lockdown," Middle-East Online, November 18, 2006, accessed on July 11, 2011, www.middle-east-online.com/english/ ?id=18365.

9. Ibid.

10. See Leah Caldwell, "The Masterminds of Torture, Humiliation and Abuse: From Supermax to Abu Ghraib," *Counterpunch*, October 15, 2004, accessed on July 11, 2011, www.counterpunch.org/caldwell10152004.html.

11. See Gordon, "Supermax Lockdown."

12. Caldwell, "The Masterminds of Torture, Humiliation and Abuse."

13. The quoted phrase is from Anne-Marie Cusac, "Abu Ghraib, USA," *The Progressive*, August 6, 2004, accessed on July 11, 2011, www.alternet.org/ story/19479/.

14. See ibid.

15. Gordon, "Supermax Lockdown."

16. Ibid.

17. See www.abs-cbnnews.com/global-filipino/world/03/06/11/special-us-prison-units-fill-muslims.

18. See Alexander, *The New Jim Crow*.

19. Quoted in Megan Garvey and Richard Winton, "City Declares War on Gangs," *Los Angeles Times*, December 4, 2002, A1.

20. See Pamela Hess, "Analysis: Police Take Military Counsel," UPI Security and Terrorism, August 24, 2006.

21. Quoted ibid.

22. These alarmist rhetorical strategies have a history that dates back to the rise of the Nation of Islam, particularly in the 1950s and 1960s as well as during the uprisings in Los Angeles in 1992, when the gang truce was brokered with the help of the Nation of Islam. Jeff Fort and the El Rukns in the 1980s, an offshoot of the Blackstone Rangers in Chicago, is another prominent case in point.

23. Hess, "Analysis: Police Take Military Counsel."

24. See Loic Waquant, "From Slavery to Mass Incarceration," *New Left Review* 13 (January–February 2002).

25. See U.S. Department of Justice, "A Review of the Federal Bureau of Prisons' Selection of Muslim Religious Services Providers," Office of the Inspector General, April 2004, accessed on July 11, 2011, www.justice.gov/oig/special/0404/final.pdf.

26. Quoted in Hess, "Analysis: Police Take Military Counsel."

27. Quoted in "US: Prisons Are Breeding Grounds for Muslim Terrorists," Western Resistance, September 21, 2006, www.westernresistance.com/blog/archives/002992.html.

28. See Testimony before the World Affair Council of Pittsburgh, "Stopping Terrorists before They Strike: The Justice Departments Power of Prevention," April 16, 2006.

29. "Out of the Shadows: Getting Ahead of Prisoner Radicalization," Special Report by the George Washington University Homeland Security Policy Institute, 2006, iv.

30. Quoted in Bill Berkowitz, "African American Muslims," *Z Magazine*, June 2003, accessed on July 11, 2011, www.zcommunications.org/african-american-muslims-by-bill-berkowitz.

31. See Michael Eric Dyson, *Open Mike: Reflections on Philosophy, Race, Sex, Culture and Religion* (New York: Basic Civitas Books, 2003).

32. Jamil Al-Amin, "Rap DNA," unpublished.

Epilogue

1. Malcolm X, *Malcolm X Speaks*, 76.

2. The quoted phrase is from Césaire, *Notebook of a Return to the Native Land*, 43.

PERMISSIONS

An earlier version of chapter 2 was published as "To the East, Blackwards: Bandung Hopes, Diasporic Dreams, and Black/Muslim Encounters in Sam Greenlee's Baghdad Blues," *Souls* 8, no. 3 (Fall 2006): 59–74.

An earlier version of chapter 3 was published as "War at 33 1/3: Hip-Hop, the Language of the Unheard, and the Afro-Asian Atlantic," in *The Vinyl Ain't Final: Hip Hop and the Globalization of Black Popular Culture*, ed. Dipannita Basu and Sid Lemelle (London: Pluto Press, 2006), 100–116.

Earlier versions of chapter 5 were published as "Protect Ya Neck: Muslims and the Carceral Imagination in the Age of Guantánamo," *Souls* 9, no. 2 (Spring 2007): 132–47; and "Protect Ya Neck: Muslims and the Carceral Imagination in the Age of Guantánamo (Remix)," in *Black Routes to Islam*, ed. Manning Marable and Hishaam Aidi (New York: Palgrave Macmillan, 2009), 207–26.

The book's epigraph, "A Prison Evening," by Faiz Ahmed Faiz, was originally published in *The Rebel's Silhouette: Selected Poems*, translated by Agha Shahid Ali (Salt Lake City: Peregrine Smith Books, 1991); reprinted by University of Massachusetts Press, 1995. Copyright 1991 by Agha Shahid Ali.

Lyrics from "Tribes at War" reprinted in chapter 3 were written and performed by Nas and Damian Marley, featuring K'naan. From the album *Distant Relatives*, copyright 2010 Universal Republic Records.

INDEX

"Above the Clouds" (song), 117

Abu Ghraib, 171, 172, 175, 180, 214n1; American corrections officers working as guards in, 178; Taguba Report investigating torture at, 178–79

Acham, Christine, 71, 73, 213n48

"Aesthetics of Hunger, The" (Rocha), 57, 58

Afghanistan: proxy war against Soviet Union in, 97

"Afrecriture," 185

Africa: as promised land of redemption for diaspora, hopes for, xxi; reconnecting with, Black Islam and, xiv–xv

African American Muslim: use of term, 203n8

African Blood Brotherhood, xxi, 78

African Summit (Cairo, 1964), 39–41

Afro-American Student Movement, Second Conference (Nashville, 1964), 208n55

Afro-Asian Conference (Algeria, 1965), 52

Afro-Asian People's Solidarity Conference (Cairo, 1957), 23, 24

Afro-beat, 133–34

Afrocentricity, 98, 115

Afro-diasporic imagination: history of, xxii–xxiii

"After Mecca": Women Poets and the Black Arts Movement (Clarke), 107

Agard-Jones, Vanessa, 208n51

Agency for International Development, 177

Ahmad, Muhammad (Max Stanford), 16, 47, 208n55

Ahmadi Muslims, 111

Al-Amin, Jamil Abdullah (H. Rap Brown), 123, 220n32; constructed by state as "homegrown terrorist," 169–70, 185; conversion to Islam, in prison, 174, 175; conviction of murder, 169–70; history as Black Power activist and Muslim leader, 185; prison writings of, 172, 185–88; as symbol and icon of Black Islam, 170; transfer to Supermax prison in Colorado, 170, 184–85

Alexander, Michelle, 95, 123, 180, 214n9

Algeria, xxvii, 50–56, 145; as anticolonial epicenter for Black radicals, 43, 46, 49; Fanon's analysis of revolution in, influence of, 49, 50–52; interactions and encounters of U.S.-based Black

SOHAIL DAULATZAI is associate professor of film and media studies and African American studies at the University of California, Irvine. He is coeditor (with Michael Eric Dyson) of *Born to Use Mics: Reading Nas's "Illmatic."*